Participatory Democracy in Brazil

RECENT TITLES FROM THE HELEN KELLOGG INSTITUTE FOR
INTERNATIONAL STUDIES

Scott Mainwaring, *series editor*

*The University of Notre Dame Press gratefully thanks Helen Kellogg Institute for
International Studies for its support in the publication of titles in this series.*

Gabriela Ippolito-O'Donnell
The Right to the City: Popular Contention in Contemporary Buenos Aires (2012)

Susan Fitzpatrick-Behrens
*The Maryknoll Catholic Mission in Peru, 1943–1989: Transnational Faith and
Transformation* (2012)

Barry S. Levitt
Power in the Balance: Presidents, Parties, and Legislatures in Peru and Beyond (2012)

Sérgio Buarque de Holanda
Roots of Brazil (2012)

José Murilo de Carvalho
The Formation of Souls: Imagery of the Republic in Brazil (2012)

Douglas Chalmers and Scott Mainwaring, eds.
Problems Confronting Contemporary Democracies: Essays in Honor of Alfred Stepan
(2012)

Peter K. Spink, Peter M. Ward, and Robert H. Wilson, eds.
*Metropolitan Governance in the Federalist Americas: Strategies for Equitable and
Integrated Development* (2012)

Natasha Borges Sugiyama
Diffusion of Good Government: Social Sector Reforms in Brazil (2012)

Ignacio Walker
Democracy in Latin America: Between Hope and Despair (2013)

Laura Gómez-Mera
Power and Regionalism in Latin America: The Politics of MERCOSUR (2013)

Rosario Queirolo
*The Success of the Left in Latin America: Untainted Parties, Market Reforms, and
Voting Behavior* (2013)

Erik Ching
*Authoritarian El Salvador: Politics and the Origins of the Military Regimes, 1880–
1940* (2013)

Brian Wampler
*Activating Democracy in Brazil: Popular Participation, Social Justice, and
Interlocking Institutions* (2015)

For a complete list of titles from the Helen Kellogg Institute for International Studies,
see http://www.undpress.nd.edu

PARTICIPATORY DEMOCRACY IN BRAZIL

Socioeconomic and Political Origins

J. RICARDO TRANJAN

University of Notre Dame Press
Notre Dame, Indiana

Library of Congress Cataloging-in-Publication Data

Names: Tranjan, J. Ricardo, author.
Title: Participatory democracy in Brazil : socioeconomic and political
origins / J. Ricardo Tranjan.
Description: Notre Dame, Indiana : University of Notre Dame Press, 2015. |
Includes bibliographical references and index.
Identifiers: LCCN 2015031820 | ISBN 9780268042400 (pbk. : alk. paper) |
ISBN 0268042403 (pbk. : alk. paper)
Subjects: LCSH: Political participation—Latin America. | Local government—
Latin America—Citizen participation. | Democracy—Latin America. |
Political culture—Latin America. | Latin America—Politics
and government.
Classification: LCC JL966 .T7 2015 | DDC 320.981—dc23
LC record available at http://lccn.loc.gov/2015031820

CONTENTS

ABBREVIATIONS

ANC   National Constituent Assembly (Assembléia Nacional Constituinte)

ARENA   National Renewal Alliance (Aliança Nacional Renovadora)

CEB   ecclesial base community (*comunidade eclesiail de base*)

CEBRAP   Brazilian Centre of Analysis and Planning (Centro Brasileiro de Análise e Planejamento)

CELAM   Latin American Episcopal Council (Consejo Episcopal Latino-americano)

CDP   popular democratic committee (*comitê democrático popular*)

CLT   Consolidate Labor Laws (Consolidação das Leis do Trabalho)

CNBB   National Conference of Brazilian Bishops (Conferência Nacional dos Bispos do Brasil)

IEPES   Institute for Political, Economic and Social Studies (Instituto de Estudos Políticos, Econômicos e Sociais)

IDS   Institute for Development Studies

ISI   Import Substitution Industrialization

MDB   Brazilian Democratic Movement (Movimento Democrático Brasileiro)

MST   Landless Workers' Movement (Movimento dos Trabalhadores Sem Terra)

PB   participatory budgeting (*orçamento participativo*)

PCB   Brazilian Communist Party (Partido Comunista Brasileiro)

PCdoB   Communist Party of Brazil (Partido Comunista do Brasil)

PMDB   Brazilian Democratic Movement Party (Partido do Movimento Democrático Brasileiro)

PRC   Santa Catarina Republican Party (Partido Republicano Catarinense)

PRO   Revolutionary Labor Party (Partido Revolucionário Operário)

PRP   Popular Representation Party (Partido de Representação Popular)

PSD   Social Democratic Party (Partido Social Democrata)

PSDB   Brazilian Social Democratic Party (Partido da Social Democracia Brasileira)

PSP   Progressive Social Party (Partido Social Progressista)

PT   Workers' Party (Partido dos Trabalhadores)

PTB   Brazilian Labor Party (Partido Trabalhista Brasileiro)

SAB   association of the friends of the neighborhood (*sociedade de amigos do bairro*)

UDN   National Democratic Union (União Democrática Nacional)

GLOSSARY OF FOREIGN TERMS

---

autêntico (pl. *autênticos*): the more radical members of the Brazilian Democratic Movement

bandeirante (pl. *bandeirantes*): colonial scout

cabo eleitoral (pl. *cabos eleitorais*): political canvassers

caboclo (pl. *caboclos*): Brazilians of mixed European and indigenous backgrounds

celebração (pl. *celebrações*): the socializing part of religious gatherings

conscientização: consciousness raising

coronel (pl. *coronéis*): local strongmen

diretório and *sub-diretório* (pl. *diretórios*): party city chapters and party neighborhood chapters

mutirão (pl. *mutirões*): self-construction projects, most often the building of popular houses

paulista (pl. *paulistas*): of, from, or pertaining to the state of São Paulo

politicagem: politicking

pelego (pl. *pelegos*): co-opted union leader

reinvidicação (pl. *reinvidicações*): a demand to public officials grounded on moral or legal rights

tenentismo: political movement of rebelling lieutenants in the first half of the twentieth century

vendeiro (pl. *vendeiros*): owner of the local supply store and middleman of coffee trade

ACKNOWLEDGMENTS

This book is based on a doctoral thesis completed at the Balsillie School of International Affairs, University of Waterloo, under the supervision of Frederick Bird and Kathryn Hochstetler. Fred provided unremitting support for this project since I began to conceptualize it. Notably, he supported my decision to pursue a qualitative historical approach in a time when political science graduate students are pressured to adopt quantitative methods. Kathy shared her comprehensive and in-depth knowledge of Brazil, and continually pushed me to hone my arguments; she provided decisive encouragement in the book proposal and manuscript revision phases, which included the extensive rewriting of the original text.

William Nylen, Brian Wampler, and Philip Oxhorn provided invaluable advice on how to turn a promising doctoral thesis into a publishable book. They epitomized the best of academia by offering thoughtful, trenchant, and constructive criticism to a younger scholar while showing respect and admiration for my work. The content of their comments were instrumental in improving the quality of this book, and the manner in which they were delivered made the review process an extremely rewarding experience. The latter can also be said about the editors of the University of Notre Dame Press, with whom it has been a great pleasure to work.

Others at the Balsillie School have my most sincere gratitude. I had the privilege to have Rhoda Howard-Hassmann on my doctoral supervisory committee. She offered valuable guidance on how to make this research project accessible and relevant to non-Brazilianists. Eric Helleiner has been for many years a mentor and a model. He has taught me that academic research is not a zero-sum game. Andrew Thompson's assistance was also instrumental in the completion of my thesis. And though spread across the globe, my cohort was always supportive. During my field research, I was hosted by the Núcleo de Pesquisas de Políticas Públicas da Universidade de São Paulo (NUPPs), where I partook in many stimulating academic events. I would like to thank José Álvaro Moisés for providing me with this opportunity and offering valuable comments on my research project. Charmain Levy and Paulo J. Krischke also took the time to read drafts of parts of this project and provided helpful comments. I am greatly indebted to my interviewees in Lages, Boa Esperança, and Diadema, including former mayors Dirceu Carneiro, Amaro Covre, and Gilson Menezes. The Centro de Documentação e Pesquisa Vergueiro, headed by Luiza Peixoto, had a vital role in my field research. I also found valuable documents in the Centro de Memória de Diadema, the archive of the Instituto Brasileiro de Administração Municipal, and the personal archive of historian-activist Valdo Ruviaro.

Back in Canada, the John P. Robarts Library provided me with working space next to the stacks on Brazilian history, which made my thesis writing time much more productive. I revised the manuscript while teaching as a sessional lecturer at the Départment de science politique de l'Université du Québec à Montréal, where I had rich exchanges about participatory democracy and Brazilian politics with Caroline Patsias and Julián Durazo-Herrmann. My doctoral research was funded by the Balsillie School of International Affairs' Balsillie Fellowship, and the Social Science and Humanities Research Council of Canada's Vanier Graduate Scholarship. I would like to thank these institutions for the financial support that made this project possible.

My dearest friends Jayna Mitchell, Bruno Dobrusin, and Chris Allen have pondered with me for hours on end on the why and how of this endeavor. My partner Yamie came into my life in what is considered the most dreadful period of a doctoral program: the comprehensive exams. She made my life more joyful then, and thereafter, and shared me with this thesis/manuscript/book for five years—*merci mon amour.*

Introduction

Brazil's political trajectory resembles that of other Latin American countries whose current democratic systems were established after the mid-1970s in what became known as the Third Wave of Democratization (Huntington 1991). What distinguishes the Brazilian case is the emergence of various local-level participatory initiatives concomitantly with the establishing of representative democracy. In addition to access to long-denied political rights, such as the right to freely elect presidents, citizens were allowed to participate in decision-making processes in municipal governments and specialized government agencies, either directly or through civil society representatives. The best-known initiative is participatory budgeting (PB). First implemented in its current form in the city of Porto Alegre in the early 1990s, participatory budgeting allows citizens to decide how to spend the portion of the municipal budget allocated to new investments. Another widespread participatory mechanism is the public policy council, which brings together civil society groups, service providers, and state representatives in bodies responsible for overseeing the management of public services. National public policy conferences, city master plans with public audiences, and water basin management committees also permit citizens to participate in public administration. Brazil is now considered a "benchmark for participatory policies in the rest of Latin America, as well as Europe, and parts of Southeast Asia" (Avritzer 2009, 2). As of 2010, participatory budgeting had been replicated in fifty-three countries (Sintomer, Herzberg, Allegretti, and Röcke 2010, 76).

The historical origin of participatory democracy in Brazil has received little specific attention from scholars. There is a large and rich body of

1

research on democratization in Brazil (1974–1989) that examines the various actors, aspects, and particular moments of this long and encompassing process. There are also meta-analyses of the period, which include widely cited arguments about transformations in the size and character of the country's civil society (Doimo 1995; Avritzer 2002; Hochstetler 2000; Dagnino 2003; Holston 2008). Studies on participatory democracy draw on this body of knowledge to identify the enabling conditions for participatory initiatives. The four most frequently identified variables are the creation of the Workers' Party (Partido dos Trabalhadores, PT), which had close links with popular and progressive sectors (Meneguello 1989; Keck 1992); the 1988 constitution, which increased municipal autonomy and included various articles encouraging citizen participation in public administration (Michiles et al. 1989; Souza 1997); rapid urbanization, which created growing needs for public infrastructure and social services (Thery 2009; Singer 2009); and an active civil society that arose in reaction to the military regime and as a consequence of fast urbanization (Avrtizer 2000; Wampler and Avritzer 2004; Holston 2008). These processes have been studied individually, and there is a broad consensus that together they spurred participatory innovation in Brazil.

This book tells the story of the creation of participatory democracy in Brazil, how it came about and how it assumed its current shape. The largely successful trajectory of participatory democracy in the post-1988 period is well documented, but much less is known about its beginnings in the 1970s and 1980s. Few will know, for example, that the city of Lages had an initiative called participatory budgeting as early as 1980. Some authors make brief references to short-lived and less successful experiences in the 1980s (Baiocchi 2003, 7–8; Wampler 2007, 154; Borba and Lüchmann 2007, 17; Gret and Sintomer 2005, 17; Baiocchi, Heller, and Silva 2011, 43–44). Goldfrank (2011, 150) showed evidence that PT officials in Porto Alegre discussed earlier participatory initiatives when designing the city's PB.[1] What were these experiences and where did they take place? How is it possible that these took place before the creation of the PT, before the 1988 constitution, and in rural areas where civil society was unorganized and urban infrastructure unnecessary? Why were they short-lived? What lessons did party officials draw from them?

To answer these questions, this book places the famous Porto Alegre PB at the end of three interrelated and partially overlapping processes: (1)

a series of incremental steps toward broader political participation taking place throughout the twentieth century, (2) short-lived and only partially successful attempts to promote citizen participation in municipal administration in the 1970s, and (3) setbacks restricting direct citizen participation in the 1980s. Chapters 1 and 2 examine the incremental steps toward participation with particular focus on the 1930–1980 period. Chapters 3 to 5 describe the best-known short-lived initiatives of the 1970s. And chapter 6 discusses the tempering of participatory democracy in the 1980s. The first part of the analysis shines light on the mutually influencing relationship between structural and institutional variables, which are often examined separately in studies of democratization. The case studies illustrate this intertwined relationship and call attention to how socioeconomic factors affect it. The third part of the analysis places developments in participatory discourses and practices in the 1980s within the context of national-level political-institutional changes; in doing so, it helps to bridge the gap between the local-level participatory democracy and the democratization literatures.

SOCIOECONOMIC AND POLITICAL ORIGINS

In Brazil, decades of state-led industrialization efforts profoundly altered the social and economic configuration of cities throughout the country, large and small, urban and rural. These changes weakened political arrangements rooted in previous socioeconomic formations, leading to the emergence of new political actors who forged contending political coalitions, seized local government, and pushed participatory reforms that extended political participation to previously excluded segments of the population. This trajectory is in accordance with the key postulates of structuralist theories of democratization. Moore (1966) argues that the weakening of the landed class, the strengthening of cities, the transition toward commercial agriculture, and some level of upheaval preventing the formation of an alliance between the emerging bourgeoisie and the old aristocracy are the enabling conditions for the establishment of parliamentary democracy. According to Rueschemeyer, Stephens, and Stephens (1992), industrialization helps to weaken the strongest opponents of democracy, the landlord class, and strengthen its major supporter, the working class. Two classics in the Brazilian literature make similar if less developed arguments. Buarque de Holanda (1936, 122) posits that democracy in Brazil is a "lamentable misunderstanding" since a rural and semifeudal aristocracy "tried to accommodate it, as much as they could, to their rights and privileges." Nunes Leal (1949, 257) concludes his seminal work arguing that putting an end to the patrimonialist system corrupting democratic institutions in Brazil requires "a profound alteration of the agrarian structure"—in other words, an agrarian reform that weakens the power basis of the landlord class.

This theoretical approach helps explain the local-level democratization processes examined in this book, but it misses an important aspect of the story. Structuralist scholars pay insufficient attention to political variables that account for when and how subaltern social groups mobilize to take advantage of the political opportunities brought about by structural changes. In 1970s Brazil, it is impossible to ignore the role of the grassroots arm of the Catholic Church, the birth of the new unionism movement, and the way in which the military regime–imposed two-party system created a heterogeneous opposition party that devoted much energy to municipal politics, since this was the only level of government with direct elections. These were the main proponents of participatory democracy in the period and, in all three cases, calls for bottom-up participation emerged as responses to institutional histories of exclusion and controlled inclusion. Progressive clergymen advocated for a less hierarchical church, attentive to the poor and their economic and political exclusion. The new unionism movement rose against a tradition of state-regulated unionism and co-opted union leaders. And progressive elements of the official opposition party mobilized in reaction to the regime's façade representative system. Chapter 1 discusses these patterns of exclusion and controlled inclusion, and chapter 2 examines in detail the three participatory movements of the 1970s.

The core argument of this book is that two interrelated processes spurred the first participatory municipal administrations in Brazil. Industrialization efforts weakened local elites and provided new opportunities for contending political coalitions. As the case studies show, the impact of industrialization varied according to socioeconomic conditions from city to city and from urban to rural regions. At the same time, the long history of institutional exclusion of some segments of the population, and the controlled inclusion of others, fuelled nationwide movements calling for citizen participation. In some cities, both processes coalesced leading to the first participatory municipal administrations in the country's history. Despite numerous challenges and shortcomings, these early initiatives helped to promote participatory discourses and practices. In the 1980s, however, these practices adapted to the political institutional context of a functioning representative system in Brazil.

The present analysis brings together concepts from structuralist and institutional theories to explain the social, economic, and political factors driving participatory innovation in the 1970s. The analytical framework draws on historical institutionalism to explain the gradual weakening of elite coalitions and the subsequent partial and controlled inclusion of subaltern groups. Patterns of inclusion/exclusion help us to understand who promotes direct citizen participation, who is satisfied with the façade electoral arrangements of the 1970s, and how the political-institutional context of the 1980s influences participatory discourses and practices. However, the institutionalist approach fails to take into account material processes fueling social processes that compel elites to make more inclusive arrangements. Socioeconomic variables are also helpful in understanding what groups are included first and what excluded groups demand once they have access to government. To capture these aspects of the processes at hand, the analytical framework borrows concepts and insights from the structuralist school, which offers tools to better understand the formation of political coalitions following industrialization and urbanization. These two perspectives together are necessary to present social change as a gradual and comprehensive process over an extended period.

THE FIRST PARTICIPATORY MUNICIPAL ADMINISTRATIONS

Participatory democracy theorists are concerned with the question, can "the successful experiences in Brazilian cities be reproduced in places where the conditions may be very different" (Avritzer 2009, 3). To tackle this question, it is crucial not to overlook the structural processes sustaining the Brazilian experience. Canel (2011) has shown that local economic contexts have considerable impacts on participation. His study of

three districts in Montevideo, Uruguay, found that the success of participatory reforms was directly related to each district's socioeconomic
history. Heller (2009) argued that economic policies help to explain the
inability of representative democracies in southern countries to include
subaltern groups in local government. In India and South Africa, liberalization further strengthened middle-class sectors that favored government access through privileged intermediaries over broad-based
participation.

The literature on participatory democracy in Brazil has focused
almost exclusively on the post-1988 period and has paid considerably
more attention to urban contexts.[2] This focus has limited the scope of
the socioeconomic analysis. Researchers have studied the socioeconomic
position of citizens who partake in participatory budgeting and found
that, overall, they are below average income brackets but do not come
from the poorest segment of society (Fedozzi 2007; Marquetti 2008;
World Bank 2008). Studies have also looked at the economic impact of
participation, with analyses of PB showing positive results in terms of
increased public investment in areas prioritized by the poor (Marquetti
2008; World Bank 2008; Touchton and Wampler, 2014). The fact that poor
segments of society are taking effective advantage of participatory channels is an encouraging finding, and more studies should examine conditions that allow for pro-poor investments. Nevertheless, this remains a
fairly narrow focus. It tells us about the potential outcomes of initiatives
in contexts similar to post-1988 urban Brazil but little about the forces
spurring or inhibiting such initiatives.

Brazil's most dramatic structural changes took place in the 1940–1980
period, when the percentage of people living in urban areas increased
from 31 to 68 percent of the total population. By the early 1990s, 76 percent of Brazilians lived in urban milieus (IBGE 1987, 1996, 1997). These
figures describe the breeding grounds of social movements that emerged
in the 1970s and early 1980s, urban agglomerations without appropriate
public infrastructure and social services. A progressive approach was to
allow people to decide how to use public resources to meet their pressing
needs. The PT opted for this approach, while more conservative parties
preferred to retain the monopoly over public expenditure and satisfy the
interests of the middle classes. While this common interpretation of the
period is generally accurate, this book shows that socioeconomic factors

played a more complex role in local-level democratization and participatory innovation in Brazil.

Chapters 3 to 5 present case studies of participatory municipal administrations in the late 1970s and early 1980s: Lages, in the state of Santa Catarina, from 1978 to 1982; Boa Esperança, in the state of Espírito Santo, from 1978 to 1982; and Diadema, in the state of São Paulo, from 1982 to 1988. Lages was a rural regional center, slowly industrializing, and divided between agriculture and a new industrial impetus. In the early 1980s, it was the showcase participatory administration of *autênticos*, the progressive group within the official opposition party. Boa Esperança was home mainly to small farmers, threatened by the encroachment of large cattle and eucalyptus farms. Many of these farmers chose to sell out and migrate to booming urban centers. The city's participatory administration was based on the preexisting organizational structure of the grassroots arm of the Catholic Church as well as on its leaders. Diadema was one of the booming urban centers that attracted people from places like Boa Esperança, but could not offer jobs, infrastructure, and social services for all of them. It was at the heart of the new unionism movement and the first PT administration in the country.

The objective of these three chapters is fivefold. (1) To examine how and to what extent structural changes undermining the power of local elites helped to spur participatory innovation. (2) To examine how participatory discourses translated into participatory practices. (3) To analyze to what extent the formats of participatory initiatives were influenced by local socioeconomic contexts. (4) To offer a contrast with participatory models that emerged in the early 1990s. (5) To document valuable experiences with local-level participatory democracy that have received little attention in the literature but that can be useful examples of how participation works in contexts different from post-1988 Brazil.

There were numerous other participatory initiatives in the examined period.[3] The three selected cases allow for a comparison of initiatives spurred by different participatory movements and demonstrate the distinct impacts of state-promoted industrialization and urbanization policies. By examining experiences spurred by different participatory movements, this book portrays the country's participatory ideals, which later became entangled in the PT's political program and the eclectic repertoires of social movements. The purpose of choosing different

socioeconomic contexts is to broaden the geographic focus of the literature. Studies of democratization in Brazil usually examine the effects of
rapid urbanization on cities, with less attention paid to what happens in
the countryside. Since this book aims to offer a comprehensive account, it
is important to examine both sides of the radical socioeconomic changes
the country witnessed between 1940 and 1980. In this sense, tiny Boa
Esperança is as significant as bourgeoning Diadema, and Lages is a rich
example of the median.

The case selection also takes into account notoriety and the level
of development of the examined initiatives. It is difficult to unequivo-
cally assert that these three cases were the most developed and best-
known experiences in the country during the examined period. Archival
research and consultations with experienced scholars have convinced me
that my case studies were well chosen. The exception is the city of Piracicaba, in the state of São Paulo, where a variety of participatory initiatives
were created in the late 1970s.[4] The reason for not including Piracicaba
here is that it resembled the case of Lages. Preference was given to Lages
to expand the geographical scope of the study, given that Diadema is also
in the state of São Paulo.

The case selection approach used here is "selecting on the dependent
variable," that is, intentionally choosing the most successful initiatives.
However, the main objective of this study is not to evaluate the success
of these initiatives but to describe how participation was implemented.
Although scholars that favor large-N studies frown on studies that select
on the dependent variable, proponents of qualitative research have
argued for the usefulness of this method. Small-N qualitative research
that selects on the dependent variable is more likely to generate novel
interpretations of historical processes, which is precisely the objective of
this research (George and Bennett 2005).

THE TEMPERING OF PARTICIPATORY DEMOCRACY

The emergence of participatory democracy in Brazil is usually pin-
pointed as the late 1980s, when progressive forces created initiatives that
would profoundly challenge the patterns of state–civil society relations.
In contrast with this view, chapter 6 shows that the 1980s witnessed the

tempering of participatory ideals and practices. Former champions of participatory democracy adapted their discourses and practices to the new political-institutional context of a competitive party system. The 1986–1988 Constituent Assembly approved moderate amendments endorsing citizen participation in public administration, but vetoed more radical amendment proposals on the issue. Civil society became recognized for its diversity of needs, goals, and strategies. And the Catholic Church, which played an active political role during the military regime, retreated to its more traditional social role.

The origin of the PT's commitment to participation is well known, as is the fact that the PT of Porto Alegre designed a successful participatory model. The process of learning how to put that commitment into practice has received less attention. The PT did not get it right the first time. The party's first participatory administrations in Diadema, Fortaleza, São Paulo, and Santos, among others, were marked by internal struggles, electoral defeats, and difficulties in combining civil society participation and political imperatives. Some mayors left the PT, others abandoned the idea of participatory democracy, and still others found ingenious, if less ambitious, ways of including citizens' voices in government.

According to Nylen (1997), these initial experiences constituted a necessary institutional learning process: "a heterodox PT political project emerged rooted in the practice and experience of PT municipal governance throughout Brazil" (439). Nylen shows that PT members put aside the "doctrinal purity" of the initial years without "abandoning the basic principles" in which the party had been founded. The outcome was a pragmatic approach to municipal administration, one in which citizen participation was still highly valued but did not come at the cost of good government. Moreover, Nylen argues that this was not an isolated or accidental process. The PT put in place institutions with the goal of facilitating this nationwide party-building process. If Porto Alegre's civil society was exceptionally well organized in the early 1990s (Avritzer 2006), the PT was by then more seasoned than in previous administrations. This fact is not sufficiently emphasized in the literature. In what concerns institutional learning within the PT, this book builds empirically on Nylen's arguments by taking into consideration the entire 1982–1989 period, with detailed attention paid to the Diadema case. It also builds analytically by situating the party's institutional learning process within the historical process of the emergence of participatory democracy.

This study also examines the often-neglected role of the Movimento Democrático Brasileiro (MDB), the single legal opposition party during the military regime that became the Partido do Movimento Democrático Brasileiro (PMDB) at the end of the imposed bi-party system in 1979. A large number of MDB's most progressive militants and intellectuals joined the PT, as did some elected PMBD officials (Meneguello 1989; Keck 1992; Kinzo 1988). It is inaccurate, however, to credit the PT for all efforts to promote participatory democracy. In the 1970s, a faction of the MDB called *autênticos* (authentics) was committed with promoting participatory democracy and tried to create channels for direct citizen participation in several municipal administrations. In the early 1980s, when PMDB politicians continued to try and create participatory channels, heated debates ensued regarding differences between the models the PMDB and the PT espoused. The progressive members of the PMDB eventually found a new party that did not actively promote participation, and in the 1990s they implemented conservative economic reforms at the national level. Notwithstanding the fate of *autênticos*, two political groups were implementing participatory channels in the 1980s. The role of *autênticos* was a key aspect of the history of participatory democracy in Brazil.

The PB literature rarely examines the government side of participation initiatives; it is more often focused on the effects on civil society. Wampler (2007, 2008) tried to address this imbalance by arguing that the level of "mayoral support" for PB has a direct impact on its success. He argues that an administration's willingness to delegate authority to civil society is determined by whether it sees PB as a way to reward party affiliates, reach out to potential constituents, or develop a participatory brand for the party. Wampler also lists ideological commitment to participation as a fourth important aspect. This approach is more nuanced than that proposed by Avritzer (2009), in which ideological commitment or "political will" is the only aspect taken into account. Wampler's argument is based on empirical cases in the post-1988 context, which allow him to assume the existence of a functional political party system with experienced political actors. This was not the case in the Brazil of the 1970s and is not the case in many countries where PB may be considered as an alternative to weak democratic institutions. While the case studies presented in this book corroborate the argument that participatory democracy is a political strategy, they show that strategies are not always conceived in electoral terms. During a time in which the representative system was not an alternative, participatory democracy served different purposes that varied according to social, economic, and political contexts.

Studies of participatory democracy in Brazil usually mention the constitution that "began the process of building an amazing infrastructure for participatory democracy" (Avritzer 2009, 2). This legal infrastructure has two parts, decentralization measures that increase the autonomy of municipal governments and a number of articles encouraging citizen participation in public administration. The latter legally endorses the PB, the former grants it more power than in neighboring Venezuela (Goldfrank 2011). Progressive and conservative forces within the constituent assembly both promoted decentralization measures. If progressive deputies saw decentralization as a precondition for true democratization, conservative groups wished to preserve the traditional authority of local political bosses (Hagopian 1996; Souza 1997). The twofold motivation behind the increased municipal autonomy that supported participatory initiatives has been well-acknowledged (Abers 2000; Baiocchi, Heller, and Silva 2011). The articles endorsing citizen participation still require careful analysis.

The literature mentions these constitutional articles only in passing, but they are particularly relevant for this book. Widely read studies of PB include passages such as: "during the constituent assembly civil society activists made several proposals that amplified citizen participation in municipal government" (Wampler and Avritzer 2004, 98), and "the new federal constitution defined Brazil as a representative and participatory democracy, the first article of which proclaims that 'all power emanates from the people, who exercise it through their representatives or directly'" (Gret and Sintomer 2005, 13). A study of the constituent assembly proceedings reveals that several amendments proposing the expansion of citizen participation were systematically rejected with the purpose of protecting representative institutions and preserving the role of formally elected officials. For example, the article that Gret and Sintomer cite originally read "through their representatives or mechanisms of direct popular participation." The proponent of this amendment defended a mixed democratic system, as Gret and Sintomer suggested. Nevertheless, the deputy who proposed replacing "mechanism of direct popular" for just "directly" meant only referendums and citizen-initiated legislation (Assembléia Nacional Constituinte 1988, 9B, 75). Thus, with concerns to the constitution's role, this book offers a more nuanced account than that most commonly found in the literature. The final version of the 1988 constitution echoed calls for increased citizen participation while muting the most radical proposals for mechanisms that were perceived as threatening representative institutions.

Civil society is the most difficult variable to disentangle while trying to construct the history of participatory democracy. This difficulty is at the theoretical, analytical, and empirical levels. Theoretically, the term "civil society" is defined in different ways by various schools of thought (Cohen and Arato 1992). In international development studies (Howell and Pearce 2001), and Latin American politics (Dagnino, Olvera, and Panfichi 2006a), at least two different concepts are used. Analytically, citizens often have more than one affiliation, and civil society groups have a repertoire of, at times contradictory, strategies. It is therefore problematic to make casual links between citizens' affiliations and their participatory values because they participate in multiple organizations concomitantly. Their support for participatory practices is often immeasurable, since they may simultaneously engage in clientelist relations.[5] Empirically, the composition of civil society varies greatly in a country as large and diverse as Brazil, making it difficult to offer widespread claims on the topic. Piecing together all advocates of participatory democracy in Brazilian civil society is a colossal empirical task. This book has two less ambitious yet original objectives concerning the understating of civil society.

The first is to build on existent knowledge of the rise of the country's participatory civil society by enlarging the geographical focus of the debate. The most influential theories about the emergence of Brazilian civil society are based on studies of urban centers, especially São Paulo. Holston (2008) maintains that "the most significant factor in the expansion and equalization of political citizenship was the accelerated urbanization of Brazil from 1950 to 1980" (107). According to Holston, "these new and literate urban residents became new and insurgent urban citizens" (105). Concomitantly, urbanization "led to the increasing isolation and backwardness of the rural sector" and the persistence of oligarchic rule (107). In his account, the city is not an inherently democratic space that naturally grants rights to newcomers. On the contrary, cities reproduced the country's historical pattern of extending citizenship status while limiting access to rights to clearly defined groups, which Holston refers to as "differentiated citizenship." Urban centers engendered the differentiation between unionized workers and workers without legal status, as well as that of residents of publicly governed city centers and residents of unregulated urban peripheries. However, this context was more conducive to the rise of insurgent citizens who demanded equal rights than to the traditional rural context from which they were uprooted. In Holston's case studies in the city of São Paulo, access to property in the form of land and housing was the trigger for legal and political struggles wherein insurgent citizens affirmed their rights.

Urban agglomerations were also the breeding grounds of Brazil's "participatory publics." According to Avritzer (2000, 2002), the country's pattern of civic association radically changed during the country's democratization. This change was both quantitative and qualitative. From 1974 to 1985 the number of civic associations doubled in São Paulo, tripled in Belo Horizonte, and rose significantly in Rio de Janeiro (Avritzer 2000, 64). This qualitative change concerns the kinds of associations created, the kinds of demands these organizations made, and the tactics they used to advance their claims. The authoritarian "assault on democracy led social actors to reevaluate the meaning of central elements of social collective action. This reinterpretation contested the privatization of the public arena, the homogenization of collective action, and the lack of independent associations" (Avritzer 2002, 78). As a result, this large number of new associations strived for the exact opposite: politicization of the public sphere, recognition of the plurality of demands and identities, and autonomy from the state. In Avritzer's (2000) view, this process was not only about the effects of urbanization per se but how it was executed: "the trigger for this change was an authoritarian experience in which the state deeply interfered with the poor population's everyday way of life. It removed slums from the center of Brazilian cities or encouraged a huge migration from the countryside to the cities, but it did not provide adequate health care, education, or infrastructure for the poor" (65). Tired of being maneuvered, these masses reinvented themselves as participatory publics that demanded a say in decision-making.

The three case studies in this book contrast the experience of Diadema, in the industrial belt of São Paulo, with a small town of family farmers and a regional center with a rural vocation and a growing primary industrial base. The first case echoes Avritzer's and Holston's arguments. Diadema's initiative took place at what Holston would call the "fringe of the fringe." The data presented in this book shows how the city fell behind neighboring towns, where a larger portion of citizens worked in the region's factories. The case also supports Avritzer's argument regarding the rupture between new participatory and old clientelist practices. The other two cases add some nuances to our understanding of the Brazilian civil society. They show the development of civil society in Lages, a city where industrialization and urbanization was less far-reaching than in urban centers, and in Boa Esperança, a town bankrupted by these processes. Contrary to what the accounts above and much of the literature would suggest, the inhabitants of these places were not simply abandoned to the whims of the rural aristocracy. In the absence of conditions that would allow the poor to organize themselves, groups imbued with participatory values helped these populations to organize and participate in public administration. As in Diadema, participatory initiatives addressed the impacts of state-promoted industrialization and urbanization, which was felt differently, but nevertheless strongly, in these areas. As the case studies show, the challenges each group faced were also particular to the local political economic context.

The second part of the analysis of civil society looks more closely into the most prevalent civil society actor in 1970s Brazil, and the only one who can safely be said to have had a nationwide influence on the spread of participatory democracy: the Catholic Church. Studies of participatory democracy in Brazil rarely fail to mention the presence of groups associated with the Church as key civil society actors, influential forces within the PT, or both. In some cases, individual clergymen stood out as instrumental to the advancement of participatory initiatives, as with Father Estevão Hubert in the city of São José do Triunfo (Ricci 1992). Specialized literatures have examined the role of the Church in Brazilian politics. Some studies have examined the evolving political position of the Church, with particular attention devoted to its progressive period (Mainwaring 1986; Vásquez 1998; Bruneau 1974; Krischke 2010). Others have paid specific attention to the phenomenon of the ecclesial base community (*comunidades eclesiais de base*, CEBs) during its peak years (Hewitt 1986, 1991; Azevedo 1987; Krischke and Mainwaring 1986), as well as later in the 1990s, when their presence was felt mostly as an influence in other movements (Hewitt and Burdick 2000; Levy 2009; Burdick 2004; Maclean 1999).

Certain aspects of political processes contributing to the expansion of participatory democracy are more pertinent to the purpose of this book than to studies with other specific focuses. Studies of participatory initiatives do not dive into the details of the Catholic Church's reform, the specifics of the participatory ideal it promoted, or the characteristics of the community groups it organized. Most studies simply state the presence of such groups as an enabling condition for participatory innovation and point the reader to more specialized literatures. Moreover, the withdrawal of the Church from the political sphere in the 1980s is well documented in specialized literatures, but studies on participatory democracy do not discuss its implications.

Building on existing literature and complementing it with original research, this book provides readers a more in-depth and nuanced understanding of the Catholic Church's role within participatory innovations in Brazil. This is accomplished in several parts. A section of chapter 2 provides an explanation on three of the distinct levels in which the Church operated: the conceptual work of Liberation theologians, the advocacy of avant-garde clergymen, and the day-to-day organization of community groups. Chapter 2 also presents evidence of the national reach of the latter two efforts; twenty-eight original documents help to portray the work of active bishops across the country. Moreover, this chapter contains the analysis of 136 CEB booklets from eighteen states and fifty-eight cities printed between 1973 and 1993, which offer a depiction of the participatory ideals the Church promoted. Chapter 4 focuses on Boa Esperança, a rural community that relied on the CEB's organizational structure and its leaders to create a participatory municipal administration. A section of chapter 6 draws on secondary literature to describe the withdrawal of the Church from the political sphere, situating this process within the broader context of the reshaping of participatory ideals and practices.

By the early 1990s, the Church was no longer a key community organizer.[6] In urban contexts, growing social movements, neighborhood associations, and the PT absorbed the majority of the active citizenry previously formed by the Church. Though the political and grassroots branches of the Church were dismantled, the participatory ideals they promoted were carried on through other channels. The participatory democracy literature has paid little notice to the Church's political withdrawal, regarding the presence of citizens, with previous experience in progressive Catholic groups, as an enabling condition for later initiatives. In the rural context, where the conditions discussed by Holston and Avritzer were largely absent, the Church played a more pervasive role, and alternative options for political engagement were not always available after it returned to its traditional spiritual role. The literature's focus on urban contexts has prevented it from considering the impact of the Church's withdrawal for participatory democracy in the rural areas.

The creation of the PT, the 1988 constitution, and the emergence of a large and active civil society were undeniably the key drivers of participatory democracy. However, since the focus of this study is to explain the making of participatory democracy and to understand its current shape, there are certain aspects of these processes that have more relevance than when briefly presented in introductions to studies with other objectives. This book draws on existing knowledge of these aspects of Brazil's democratization processes and complements them with original archival research. It provides a more accurate account of the emergence of participatory democracy in Brazil and helps to bridge the gap between the participatory democracy and the democratization literatures.

The next section of this introduction presents an overview of participatory democracy in Brazil. It focuses on the two best-known and most widely adopted participatory mechanisms in the country, participatory budgeting and health councils. This is not an exhaustive review of the massive literature on the topic since the purpose of the book is not to engage in the numerous debates presented below but to instead examine the historical processes leading to the creation of these initiatives. It nevertheless offers an adequate introduction that renders the remainder of the book meaningful.

PARTICIPATORY BUDGETING

An introduction to participatory budgeting (PB) must inevitably begin with a summary of the history and functioning of the Porto Alegre initiative. Although not the first such initiative in the country, as it is often inaccurately presented, the Porto Alegre PB is without a doubt the most successful case. The Porto Alegre PB is based on a representative pyramid structure; local-level groups (street, quarter, or neighborhood) meet year-round and participate in annual ward assemblies where they vote on four priority investment areas out of sixteen options[7] and choose two delegates to serve as ward councilors at the municipal level. A thematic structure functions in a similar way except that citizens gather around six broad themes instead of geographical areas.[8] The Participatory Budgeting Council is the highest level forum; it is comprised of two councilors from each ward and thematic forum, a representative of an umbrella neighborhood association, a representative from the public workers' union, and two representatives from the government's executive office, who participate in the deliberations but do not have voting power. The Council's main function is to transform local demands into an investment plan that adheres to the technical criteria negotiated with the city departments.[9] The Council also monitors the implementation of the budget and reviews the program's rules (Orçamento Participativo 2008). This basic model varies considerably from city to city. In Belo Horizonte, for example, the PB cycle is biannual, decision power is concentrated at the regional assembly level, and citizens can vote online for different large infrastructure projects (Prefeitura de Belo Horizonte 2012).

Arguments in favor of PB fall in one of the following three categories. First, PB is a tool to "democratize democracy" (Fedozzi 1999; Nylen 2003; Santos and Avritzer 2002). In this view, the PB helps to break with traditional undemocratic forms of political mediation and serves as a remedy for political apathy. A second perspective argues PB allows for the political inclusion of marginalized groups and fosters citizenship learning. Abers (2000) shows that previously excluded groups joined public debates in Porto Alegre through the PB. She also calls attention to the fact that the inclusion of unorganized sectors of the population required deliberate efforts from militant public officials, just as we will see in the case studies below. Baiocchi (2005) contends that the Porto Alegre PB spurred "emerging public spheres" that he defined as an "open-ended debate about issues of collective concern and community solving" (95). According to Baiocchi, by partaking in PB, Porto Alegre militants learned new and more democratic ways of doing politics. The third set of arguments focus on PB's ability to distribute public resources more justly and prioritize investments favored by the poor (Fedozzi 2007; Marquetti 2008; World Bank 2008; Touchton and Wampler, 2014).

The widely recognized limitations of PB include its inability to mobilize the poorest segments of society and the small percentage of the budget controlled by these initiatives. In Porto Alegre, the average income of the PB participants at the ward level is below the city's average but above that of the city's poorest; participants at the council level have higher income and education than ward-level participants (Fedozzi 2007). In the PB model, only a relatively small portion of the budget designated for new investments is open for discussion. In Porto Alegre, between 2000 and 2008 this percentage ranged from 5.2 to 8.8 percent of the total municipal budget (CIDADE 2008).[10] The amount varies from city to city. In 2001–2002, Porto Alegre's investment spending per capita was US$29, while in small and wealthy Ipatinga it was US$58, and in wealthy but indebted Belo Horizonte it was US$14 (Wampler 2007, 109, 150, 219). A more disconcerting limitation of the Porto Alegre PB regards the emergence of a group of activists who managed to gain control of the process. The first comprehensive study of the initiative called attention to the fact that a group of overzealous participants felt responsible for directing the development of the PB, which became known as the "pioneer syndrome" (Fedozzi 1999). A later study mentioned "specialist militants" and the corruption of the democratic ideal that first inspired the initiative (Beras 2008). More recently, a close observer and enthusiastic proponent of the initiative admitted that "little by little, the '*cacique*' (boss/gatekeeper) culture of the presidents of neighborhood associations, which was supposed to have been buried, returned" (Baierle 2010, 57). Scholars have begun to question whether the Porto Alegre PB will last much longer (Junge 2012).

The international fame of the Porto Alegre PB began in 1996, when it was recognized as a *best practice* in urban management at the Second United Nations Human Settlement Conference in Istanbul. Thereafter the model spread rapidly. In 2004 there were 170 PB initiatives in Brazil (Avritzer 2009, 85); by 2006, 1,200 out of 16,000 Latin American municipalities had tried some form of PB (Cabannes 2006, 128); by 2008, close to 100 European local governments had implemented similar programs (Sintomer, Herzberg, and Röcke 2008, 164). In Canada, a borough of Montreal, the Toronto Community Housing Corporation, and the city of Guelph have experimented with the model (Pinnington, Lerner, and Schugurensky 2009). In the United States, a ward of Chicago has had a PB since 2010 (Lerner 2011), New York had the first round of PB in four of its 22 wards in 2012 (Sangha 2012), San Francisco's District 3 began experimenting with PB in 2013, and in the same year the nearby city of Vallejo launched the first citywide PB in the country.

This widely spread participatory model attracted much scholarly attention. Nylen (2011) has identified two generations of studies of PB. The first generation (from 1990s to mid-2000s) focused on successful cases in Brazil, mainly Porto Alegre, and found that "PB tends to uphold the Participatory Promise that participatory innovations and reforms can be efficacious" (481). The second generation of studies has a broader empirical focus that includes less successful cases of PB in Brazil as well as other countries. Whereas the first generation relied heavily on single case studies, recent research uses comparative methods to examine the variables that contribute to the success or failure of participatory initiatives. This generation tends to focus on "grey cases" that can help to "shift the focus on institutional innovation from poster-child examples to those cases that might appear less appealing, where the conditions for success are less evident, and the outcome of the innovations are less immediately clear" (Peruzzotti and Selee 2009, 7). The literature now includes numerous studies of "grey cases" (Bispo Júnior and Sampaio 2008; Cornwall, Romano, and Shankland 2008; Mesquita 2007; Pereira 2007; Sell and Wöhlke 2007); as a consequence, it is now more wary of the challenges and limitations of PB. "Most agree, for example, that PB and other participatory innovations are not instances of participatory, direct, radical, or delegative democracy, but constitute instead 'a new layer of representation'" (Nylen 2011, 482).

Second generation studies have also acknowledged that, "we continue to lack a coherent theoretical explanation to account for where and when . . . participatory experiences are likely to be successful" (Wampler 2008, 64). With this in mind, Avritzer (2009), Wampler (2007), and Borba and Lüchmann (2007) put forward frameworks that examine the necessary conditions for successful participatory institutions. Essentially, these three frameworks examine the same three variables: (1) the governing party's commitment to popular participation; (2) civil society's strength and ability to effectively participate; and (3) the institutional design of participatory channels. There are, however, noteworthy differences in the definitions of these variables.

The first variable may be referred to as *political will*, if the intention is to emphasize the ideological commitment of the governing party; according to the scholar who uses this concept, political will to include civil society organizations in municipal government is found above all in PT administrations (Avritzer 2009). Alternatively, the concept *mayoral support* calls attention to a mayor's rational calculation of incentives for delegating authority to civil society; the decision to invite the population to participate in the budget processes is a mayor's prerogative, and he or she will carefully consider whether doing so will improve his political position (Wampler 2007). The concept of *government commitment* brings both ideological and strategic aspects into account as it focuses on the importance of the participatory initiative vis-à-vis other government priorities (Borba and Lüchmann 2007).

The second variable is civil society strength. The framework put forward by Avritzer focuses on the density of the associative network demanding access to public goods. Density is measured in quantitative terms: the larger the number of civil society groups advocating for access to public goods, the better the chances of participatory initiatives. In Wampler's framework, the density of civil society is a relevant but secondary factor; the focus is on the "ability of [civil society organizations] to simultaneously engage in cooperative and contentious politics" (88). The success of a participatory mechanism depends on civil society groups' ability to take advantage of the opportunity to participate in government without losing their capacity to confront politicians when needed. Borba and Lüchmann's framework focuses on local associative traditions, which considers the density of civil society as well as the dominant types of organization in the city. In this case, it matters not only how many organizations are found in a city, but also the ways in which they are used to interacting with the government.

In all three frameworks, analyses of institutional designs (the third variable) are limited by the exclusive empirical focus on the urban post-1988 Brazilian context. Avritzer's framework examines PB and health councils, and city master plans, which allow citizens to approve or reject cities' midterm development plans. The other two frameworks are based on studies of PB. In the three cases, emphasis is on how much decision-making power is transferred to civil society and whether this power comes at the cost of civil society's autonomy. Some attention is also paid to whether initiatives include mechanisms that favor the participation of disadvantaged groups.

All three frameworks are useful in assessing the myriad of participatory initiatives put in place in Brazil since the early 1990s. It is possible to improve their comparative strength by also taking into account the processes leading to the adoption of these specific models. The PT's *political will* or *mayoral support* showcases not only its willingness to increase participation but also its commitment, in the 1980s, to create a feasible participatory model that would avoid other costly political failures (Nylen 1997). As chapter 6 shows, the institutional designs of present-day initiatives were influenced by these failures and by the 1988 constitution, which safeguarded representative institutions against more radical participatory alternatives. Thus, it should not come as a surprise that participatory initiatives transfer a limited amount of decision-making power to civil society. This was the result of conscious political and institutional choices made in the 1980s. Borba and Lüchmann's and Wampler's frameworks move away from strictly quantitative assessments of civil society's strength to focus on local associative traditions and the negotiation abilities of civil society's organizations, respectively. This is a helpful development that can be taken further by linking local traditions to national economic conditions. As Heller (2009) and Canel (2011) have shown, economic structures and policies affect the ability of local groups to profit from decentralization policies and participatory channels. A research agenda that seeks to assess whether Brazilian models can be replicated "in places where the conditions may be very different" (Avritzer 2009, 3) needs to take into account the economic context that shaped these models. A more comprehensive analysis of the learning processes of the 1970s and 1980s, in both rural and urban areas, can help us to draw more generalizable experiences from the Brazilian case.

HEALTH COUNCILS

Citizen councils are a common practice yet their formats vary greatly. In Brazil, councils began to emerge at the end of the military regime, some autonomous from political institutions, others as initiatives of politicians attempting to increase citizen participation in public administration. The councils created in the early 1980s are discussed in the case studies and in chapter 6. This section focuses on councils created after the 1988 constitution, which sanctioned the creation of policy councils at the federal, state, and municipal levels in various areas of public services. In 1996, legislation made certain fund transfers to state and municipal governments that were conditional on the existence of policy councils, which contributed to their rapid growth (Gohn 2001). As of 2009, 97 percent of Brazil's 5,472 municipalities had health councils, 91 percent had child and adolescent rights councils, 79 percent had education councils, 56 percent had environmental councils, 42 percent had housing councils, and a smaller portion of municipalities had councils for senior services, culture, urban policy, sports, women's rights, public security, disabled people's rights, public transportation, youth rights, racial equality, human rights, and gay rights (Cortes 2011, 143). At the state level, scholars point to a total of 541 councils, with all twenty-six states having councils in eight areas, namely, health, education, social assistance, environmental policies, childhood and adolescence, senior services, food security, and food services in the education system (Almeida and Tatagiba 2012, 69–70). At the national level, there are at least sixty policy councils, which served as the pillars of sixty-one national participatory conferences between 2003 and 2010 (Teixeira, Souza, and Lima 2012, 16). A vast literature examines this immense participatory infrastructure. Collective efforts of experts devoted to the subject have helped to summarize knowledge in the field (Teixeira, Souza, and Lima 2012; Pires 2011; Lavalle 2011; Pogrebinschi and Santos 2010; Avritzer 2004). This section provides a brief review of some key studies regarding policy councils.

One of the criticisms of councils is that they lack well-defined institutional formats, and mayors have too much influence over their functioning. Therefore, it is difficult to describe the exact functioning of these mechanisms. In the institutional framework set by the constitution, policy councils are directly attached to the executive arm of governments and are comprised of representatives of the state, civil society, and service providers; 50 percent of council seats are reserved for civil society and the other 50 percent are equally divided between state and service providers. Councils are intended to be an opportunity for state representatives to inform the population about their policies and receive input from civil society organizations and service providers. Council members should oversee the use of public funds and deliberate about the management of public services. In areas with well-organized and active civil societies, councils at least in part serve these purposes. However, evidence suggests that a large portion of councils are consultative bodies where members express their opinions without any commitment on the part of state representatives to follow through. In the worst cases, council members are chosen by mayors and instructed not to raise questions; their role is simply to guarantee the transfer of federal funds (Gohn 2001; Coelho 2004; Coelho and Veríssimo 2004).

The literature on councils has long been wary of the limitations of participation. In the late 1980s, Cohn (1987, 1992) used studies of health councils to challenge the assumption that decentralization alone would spur participation and lead to the strengthening of citizenship. Throughout the 1990s, numerous studies of health councils and other types of councils were published, mostly empirical works that depicted mixed results of successes and failures.[11] By the end of the decade, few theoretical advances had been made. Coelho (2004) pointed out that "the literature has attributed the success or failure of participatory mechanisms either to the degree of civil society involvement or to the level of commitment to such mechanisms on the part of the political authorities" (33). The author argued these to be necessary but not sufficient conditions for effective policy councils and posited that more attention needed to be paid to institutional factors. Her research showed that rules for selecting civil society representatives were not clearly defined in the design of councils and neither were decision-making procedures. In São Paulo, for example, the selection of representatives for health councils varied from district to district; public officials in some districts were committed to trying to include historically marginalized groups, whereas in others they simply contacted the most active groups (Coelho and Veríssimo 2004).

In recent years the literature has paid more attention to institutional design. There are two marked influences in this line of research. On the theoretical side, Fung and Wright (2003) have defended the crucial role of institutional variables in designing truly inclusive and effective participatory mechanisms. On the empirical side, Rennó (2003) argued that institutional factors, creating what Sydney Tarrow calls political opportunities, are more important in fueling civil society participation than political cultural variables. Three categories of institutional variables are examined in empirical studies. (1) The level of institutionalization of councils, measured in terms of longevity, the existence of organizational structures, and the frequency of meetings. (2) The inclusionary potential of councils, which concerns the balance of the three sectors (i.e., state, civil society, service providers) within councils, the representativeness of representatives, and the procedure to select these representatives. (3) The decision-making process of councils, which examines voting and deliberation procedures, the election of presidents, the formation of special committees, and the setting of the agenda. All these variables ultimately highlight a council's ability to serve as a democratizing tool (Faria and Ribeiro 2011).

A prolific collaboration between researchers at the Brazilian Center for Analysis and Planning (Centro Brasileiro de Análises e Planejamento, CEBRAP) and counterparts at the British Institute for Development Studies (IDS) has helped to advance knowledge on the representativeness and adeptness of civil society representatives. A provocative IDS paper argued that the assumption that individual citizens have ready access to channels of participation was largely unfounded; instead, participation is better understood as "a contingent outcome, produced as collective actors . . . negotiate relations in a pre-existing institutional terrain that constrains and facilitates particular types of action" (Acharya, Lavalle, and Houtzager 2004, 41). This approach, which the authors called the "polity perspective," focuses on trying to understand how institutional contexts encourage or hinder the participation of certain civil society groups. In 2005, the same authors pushed the argument further by suggesting that the assumption that civil society organizations autonomous from political parties and state agencies better served the interests of the groups they represent was misplaced. Research in São Paulo showed the opposite: organizations with close ties to political and state actors (especially the PT) had better information about participatory processes and more ability to influence outcomes, and as a result were also more motivated to partake in such initiatives. Most of these organizations did not have a formal membership, which made their relationship with purported beneficiaries unclear, raising concerns about the legitimacy of representation in policy councils (Lavalle, Acharya, and Houtzager 2005).

The authors then delved further into the question of the democratic legitimacy of civil society organizations. "Organized civil society is laying claim to political representation in contemporary democracies, destabilizing long-standing ideas about democratic legitimacy" (Houtzager and Lavalle 2010, 1). In a survey of 229 civil associations in São Paulo, Houtzager and Lavalle found that the vast majority of organizations do not have formal mechanisms for their constituencies to openly demonstrate their approval for the organization's work. What exists therefore is an assumed representation (*representação presuntiva*) from the part of the civil associations. Leaders of associations offered six fairly well-defined and consistent justifications for their representative status, and only one of these relied on election by the membership. The most common justification is the "mediation argument" that is based on the idea that state institutions are inaccessible to certain sectors of the population, and organizations access these institutions in the name of excluded groups. The claim of legitimacy is not grounded on the relations between the organizations and its membership but on the latter's access to the state. The standing question is whether this is an emerging form of legitimate representation or simply a distortion of the traditional forms of representation found in political parties and unions (Houtzager and Lavalle 2010).

Echoing arguments made by Lavalle and colleagues, Dagnino and Tatagiba (2010) raised questions about developments within "participatory democratic movements," which are marked by an antistate attitude characteristic of a political context that has already passed (i.e., the democratization period). Most of these movements are now involved with government agencies or political parties; in this new configuration, a movement's relationship with formal political actors becomes at times more important than its connection to the groups it defends. There is a trade-off between political efficacy and autonomy. The authors note that in the Brazilian case this relationship is even more complicated in PT administrations because of the proximity of social movements and political leaders and the former's willingness to sacrifice short-term goals in order to preserve the image of the party. Thus, the important questions are how movements negotiate their relationship with parties and state agencies and whether they manage to preserve their core democratic values despite the strategies adopted to reach the desired material goals.

In 2011, the Brazilian journal *Lua Nova* organized a special issue titled "Após Participation" (After Participation) on the relationship between participation and representation. The volume largely follows the argumentative line of CEBRAP and IDS researchers. In an insightful conceptual piece, Lüchmann (2011) called the new layer of representation discussed by Lavalle and colleagues *representação conselhista* (council representation). She argued that this form of political action is part of the repertoire of civic associations, and is combined, sometimes in a tense manner, with other political strategies. According to Lüchmann, there are two analytical gains in treating these practices as forms of political representation. First, it allows us to examine whether these alternative channels of representation are used to advance demands and interests that have been barred from the electoral representation process, in which case they would be contributing to the betterment of the democratic system. However, if represented groups are using these channels we would be witnessing an overrepresentation. Second, treating these forms of civic participation as political representation permits us to explore how they contribute to the strengthening of the representative system. Once different forms of representation are recognized, it is then possible to discuss what is expected of the representatives, what associations are qualified to play these representative roles and what accountability would entail in each context. In other words, bringing forms of participation previously seen as direct democracy to the realm of representative politics opens up a myriad of new ways of conceptualizing and empirically examining the relationship between citizens, intermediary organizations, and state agencies.

Studies of policy councils consider the same three variables as the PB frameworks discussed in the previous section, that is, political commitment, civil society involvement, and institutional designs. Coelho noted in 2004 that research had paid disproportional attention to the first two variables, but since then a lot of work has focused on institutional designs. A weakness of this literature is that much of the empirical work supporting the theoretical postulates was conducted in the post-1988 Brazilian urban context, primarily focusing on the city of São Paulo. Arguments toward the usefulness of a comprehensive analysis of the 1970s and 1980s, presented in the previous section, are also of importance here. Moreover, there is an interesting line of enquiry questioning the assumption that representation and participation can be fruitfully combined. This book supports this line of enquiry by bringing to light experiences and processes where the tension between participation and representation was tangible, while demonstrating how the country arrived at the compromise of the early 1990s.

NORMATIVE DEBATES

Since the late 1970s, participation was part of the discourse of Latin American social movements' demand for democratization. In the 1990s, international development agencies, especially the World Bank, turned to participation as a way to legitimatize and increase the efficacy of economic policies that had become unpopular. As a result, groups with distinct political projects drawing on different theoretical traditions espouse civil society participation in government (Dagnino 2007; Howell and Pearce 2001). On one side of the debate, scholars and activists focus on the emancipatory potential of citizen participation, which is assumed to be able to fundamentally transform state-society relations. In the 2000s, volumes organized by Dagnino and colleagues were the main proponents of this view in Latin America (Dagnino 2002; Dagnino, Olvera, and Panfichi 2006b; Dagnino and Tatagiba 2007). Santos (2002) edited the widely read compilation *Democratizar a Democracia* (To Democratize Democracy), which brought together case studies from different parts of the developing world and presented participatory democracy as an alternative to "(un)representative democracy." In North America, volumes organized by Roussopoulos and Benello (2003) and Fung and Wright (2003) offered case studies and critical analyses that furthered this perspective.

On the other side of the debate, international development agencies embraced what is often referred to as the neo-Tocquevillean perspective. Putnam (1993; 1995) revived the term "social capital," which soon became "the missing link" of development theory (Fine 1999). In response to empirical evidence supporting the claim of market imperfections, some economists recognized that social capital was an essential aspect of the functioning of markets and that "low stocks" of it helped to explain the inability of markets to spur development. In the early 1990s, the World Bank also adopted a "good governance" language that allowed it to become involved in political aspects previously avoided by the Bank. In the Bank's new emphasis on government efficiency and accountability, civil society plays a double role of helping to control government excesses and taking on some responsibilities previously ascribed to states (Leftwich 1993).

The waning of the neoliberal project weakened this normative debate, but the literature still offers two distinct views of the purpose of participation. In the emancipatory side, Pearce's (2010) most recent edited volume brought together studies that continue to plead for the transformative potential of citizen participation. In the introductory chapter, Pearce distinguishes between "participatory governance" and "participatory democracy." The former "encourages the formation of a category of 'participant citizen.' However, rather than autonomous and self-driven, it is made subject to a new neoliberal governance regime" (14–15). Pearce argues that participatory governance only decentralizes to local communities activities that were previously a state responsibility, while decision-making power is recentralized. Participatory democracy, on the other hand, "is based on principles of popular sovereignty and direct involvement of all citizens, including and especially the poorest, in decision making" (15). The case studies examine Latin American and British communities neglected by or unsatisfied with the first model who are now pursuing emancipation through meaningful participation.

In works published in recent years, Dagnino continues to warn readers about what she sees as muffled forms of citizen participation. "Under neo-liberalism, participation is defined instrumentally, in relation to the needs derived from the 'structural adjustment' of the economy and the transfer of the state's social responsibilities to civil society and the private sector" (Dagnino 2010, 33). Regarding the Brazilian case, the author is skeptical of the reforms advanced in the Cardoso administration (1995–2001). "The reform of the state that was implemented in Brazil in 1998 under the influence of Minister Bresser Pereira (who introduced the principles of the 'New Public Management') is very clear in relation to the different roles of the 'strategic nucleus of the State' and of social organizations. The former retains a clear monopoly over decision-making" (Dagnino 2010, 33). Thus, in line with Pearce,

Dagnino continues to hold that there are more and less democratic types of participation.

In 2012, Pateman published the article "Participatory Democracy Revisited," in which the theorist used the Porto Alegre PB as the yardstick of truly participatory innovation. "Most of the examples being called participatory budgeting fit very easily within authority structures, and citizens are not participating, as a matter of right, in decisions about their city's or town's regular budget. Most of the innovations fall far short of participatory democracy" (14). The author defined participatory democracy as initiatives that "democratize democracy" and reform "authority structures" (10), and in doing so moved us toward the "participatory society" she proscribed in her well-known 1970 volume.

In the neo-Tocquevillean side, there have been economic studies further supporting the instrumental usefulness of participation and some developments toward analyses that integrate direct citizen participation and the representative system. In 2007, the World Bank published an edited volume titled *Participatory Budgeting* (Shah 2007) with case studies from various parts of the developing world. The editor of the volume stated that "Done right, [PB] has the potential to make governments more responsive to citizens' needs and preferences and more accountable to them for performance in resource allocation and service delivery" (1). In 2008, the Bank published the most comprehensive quantitative analysis to date of the Brazilian PB.[12] The study concluded that, "participatory budgeting as a mechanism for improving pro-poor capital investments has contributed to ameliorating the living conditions of the poor in the municipalities where it has been adopted" (World Bank 2008, 91). The impact on income and poverty was found only in cities where the PB had been in place for at least ten years, but "it is worth noting that this poverty impact occurred despite a reduction in GDP per capita in these municipalities, suggesting that [PB] can contribute to a redistributive impact in the long run" (15). This is one of the most widely cited findings in support of PB.

The World Bank has become one of the main proponents of PB. According to one estimate, between 2002 and 2012 the Bank provided at least 280 million dollars in support for PB around the world (Goldfrank 2012, 3). Proponents of the emancipatory view disapprove of the Bank's involvement with PB; they see it as yet another attempt to distort the true meaning of citizen participation. According to Goldfrank (2012, 14), the normative divide described here is also found within the Bank ranks, which includes both "true believers" of PB and "and some who see PB as supporting a neoliberal agenda."

A stream within the neo-Tocquevillean view has focused attention on how participation can improve the quality of democracies in Latin America. A *quality democracy* has been defined as "one that provides its citizens a high degree of freedom, political equality, and popular control over public policies and policy makers through the legitimate and lawful functioning of stable institutions" (Diamond and Morlino 2005, xi). In the framework put forward by Diamond and Morlino, democracies vary in quality on eight dimensions, one of which is participation.[13] In this dimension, quality is high when citizens participate in the political process not only through voting but also by joining political parties and civil society organizations, partaking in the discussion of public-policy issues, communicating with and demanding accountability from elected representatives, monitoring the conduct of public office-holders, and engaging in public issues at the local community level.

As a research agenda, the democratic quality approach emphasizes the workings of the institutions of representative democracy. The book *Participatory Innovation and Representative Democracy in Latin America* (Peruzzotti and Selee 2009) presents various studies from this perspective. "The basic assumption of this volume is that any politics of the institutional betterment of representative democracy must address the question of how to productively combine participation and representation" (3). In the chapter on Brazil, Melo (2011) calls attention to overlooked shortcomings of the PB model and argues that the exaggerated focus on channels of direct participation have played down the transformative potential of formal institutions such as the Court of Account (Tribunal de Contas, TC). The PB model allows the mayor to bypass the legislative chamber, and in some cases it is implemented exactly with this objective. As a consequence, the mayor increases his authority vis-à-vis the chambers and weakens the relationship between councilors and citizens. In contrast, "TCs are constitutionally defined as ancillary bodies of the legislative branch, with the purpose of examining the accounts of the three branches of government" (32). Melo argues that more attention should be paid to channels of vertical and horizontal accountability that regulate the use of public funds as opposed to mechanisms for direct citizen participation that may weaken institutional arrangements.

The historical analysis of the emergence of participatory democracy offered in this book cautions against adamant stances regarding the purpose and format of participation. In Brazil, participatory ideals changed as a result of broad economic and institutional processes and the ways in which political actors responded to them. The purpose of participation varied from region to region according to how these broad processes were felt. The format of participatory institutions adapted to ideals, concerns with preserving a fragile representative system, and the practical experience of the PT, a political party committed with increasing citizen participation.

ORGANIZATION AND SOURCES

Chapter 1 outlines the conceptual framework used to interpret developments in the national-level political-institutional context and then uses these concepts to describe the evolution of the country's representative system from 1889 to 1985. Chapter 2 discusses the participatory movements of the 1970s, which were intrinsically related with the processes and institutions reviewed in chapter 1. A close analysis of these movements helps us to understand how direct citizen participation was conceptualized and put into practice in the late 1970s and early 1980s. Chapters 3 to 5 present the case studies of participatory municipal administrations introduced above. Chapter 6 shows how participatory discourses and practices examined in chapters 2 to 5 changed in the course of the 1980s. The political-institutional context that emerged at the end of the decade tempered these discourses and practices, making them more compatible with the representative system. The final chapter offers reflections on how the historical account laid out in this book can contribute to the study of participatory democracy.

The empirical material for this book was collected during one year of field research in Brazil, when I was a visiting researcher at the Universidade de São Paulo's Núcleo de Pesquisa de Políticas Públicas. I interviewed approximately half of the officials in charge of the Lages experience, three-quarters of the Boa Esperança team, and the mayor of Diadema. The Dirceu Carneiro Institute provided primary sources on the case of Lages, and I found at the University of Santa Catarina dissertations on the subject written by former members of the administration. In Boa Esperança, former mayor Amaro Covre kindly made available his personal archives. In Diadema, I could count on secondary literature and on material found at the archive Centro de Memória de Diadema, which included recorded interviews with several of the city's civic leaders in the 1980s. The personal archive of historian-activist Valdo Ruviaro was also helpful. Chapter 2 relies on material found at São Paulo's Centro de Documentação Vergueiro (CPV), a small activist-run archive created in 1973 by and for social movements. Chapter 6 draws on material found at the CPV and at the archive of the Instituto Brasileiro de Administração Municipal (IBAM), in Rio de Janeiro. The discussion about the 1988 con-stitution is based on a careful analysis of the official proceedings of the National Constituent Assembly, available on the Senate's website. The archives of the newspapers *Folha de São Paulo* and *Correrio Lageano* were also helpful. Finally, useful publications of limited circulation were found in the libraries Florestan Fernandes, Universidade de São Paulo, and John P. Robarts, University of Toronto. Militant-intellectuals authored a significant portion of the literature on the 1970–1980 period, and these works were clearly meant to inform the debates of the time. This limited-circulation secondary literature is particularly pertinent to the discourse analysis in chapter 6.

CHAPTER ONE

The Brazilian (Un)Representative System

The participatory ideals fuelling participatory democracy in Brazil emerged in the 1970s in response to the façade democracy of the military regime and earlier forms of political exclusion. This chapter focuses on the evolution of the Brazilian representative system, here defined as the set of institutions and processes that together permit cities, states, and the country to be governed by legislative representatives and executive leaders chosen through elections. In representative systems, the scope of suffrage, the integrity of elections, the autonomy of legislative members, and the commitment of executive leaders to the rights of citizens may vary considerably, as the Brazilian case illustrates. This chapter describes how landed oligarchies controlled the political system from the establishment of the republic in 1889 to the end of the 1920s. It then examines the slow and uneven process of political incorporation that started with the 1930 Revolution and was halted by the 1964 coup d'état. The controlled character of democratization in this period is fundamental for understanding the participatory movements that emerged in the 1970s. Before delving into this historical journey, it is necessary to discuss the concepts used here to analyze democratization processes. The first section presents a conceptual framework, and the second section applies this framework to the Brazilian case.

THE CONCEPTUAL FRAMEWORK

The framework adopted in this book is inspired by Victor Nunes Leal's seminal work, *Coronelismo: The Municipality and Representative*

Government in Brazil (1949/2009). The local-level despots of Brazilian hinterlands are known as *coronéis*. The political system that is based on their power is referred to as *coronelismo*.[1] Leal argued that *coronelismo* was not a widespread local phenomenon but a national political system based on compromises between *coronéis*, state governors, and federal representatives. This resulted from the diminishing economic power but persistent political influence of the country's landed oligarchy. In other words, local-level despotism relied on the national political-institutional context and the country's economic structure to survive. If one agrees with Leal's interpretation, the logical step is to try to understand the emergence of local-level participatory democracy as a transformation of those same conditions. This book presents the emergence of participatory democracy as a nationwide phenomenon grounded on local dynamics. To fully comprehend this emergence we must take into account the economic and institutional changes the country underwent since the 1930s as well as the ways in which local actors responded to them.

More important, the account presented in this book regards the evolution from less to more democratic state-civil society relations. Three conceptual definitions are necessary: the assumed nature of the evolution of state-society relations, the defining characteristics of democratic societies, and the key drives of changes toward a more democratic society. The framework used in this book draws elements from three theoretical approaches to understanding democracy. With concerns to state-society relations, this book sides with the political economy perspective of civil society, using as a key reference Oxhorn's (2006, 2011) work on Latin America. As part of the historical institutionalist school, North, Wallis, and Weingast (2009) defined traditional and democratic societies in a manner that is consonant with Leal's work on Brazilian *coronelismo*. However, the analytical framework to which these definitions belong does not provide adequate tools to examine democratic transitions—a charge that can also be directed at Leal's work. Structuralist analyses of democratization provide useful insights and concepts in examining democratic transitions, especially the seminal work of Rueschemeyer, Stephens, and Stephens (1992).

Oxhorn's (2006, 2011) arguments stand in juxtaposition to Marshall's (1950) classic work on citizenship. Marshall posits that different categories of citizenship rights are extended to citizens in a consecutive order, with each step of the process supporting the next. In the British context, from which the author draws his analysis, civil rights where achieved first, followed by political, and only later social rights. In this approach, all sectors of a society concomitantly go through the gradual process of citizenship inclusion. Oxhorn (2011) argues that in Latin America, urbanization, industrialization, and the adoption of distinct development models has led to the recognition, controlled inclusion, or repression of different socioeconomic groups. In his view, distinct models of state-society relations, founded on broader economic policies, spur the extension of certain types of rights to some socioeconomic groups, often to the detriment of other types of rights and other socioeconomic groups. Hence, this process varies from case to case, as opposed to the rigid model described by Marshall.

Scholars who adopt Marshall's schema tend to find the trajectory of citizenship rights in Brazil an anomaly. Carvalho (2001), for example, argues that the submissive incorporation of the masses, that is, the granting of social rights before political rights, cursed the country with a passive citizenship. Carvalho sees populism as emblematic of this passive citizenship, which was in part made possible by the subservient political culture of rural populations. Oxhorn (2011), on the other hand, argues that "populism was the hallmark of controlled inclusion" (44). In several Latin American countries, populist leaders rose to power by mobilizing the subaltern groups, but once there they "sought concessions from upper classes rather than their overthrow" (44). In the first perspective, the Brazilian trajectory is essentially derailed; whereas in England one advance led to another, in Brazil, each slip took the country farther from the right path. In the second perspective, the shortcomings of inclusion are presented as conjunctural, not congenital.

The latter perspective is more helpful in the analysis of the emergence of participatory democracy in Brazil, especially since this book contrasts different socioeconomic contexts. The economic policies adopted at the federal level had distinct impacts on state-society relations in the three examined states. As a result of the interaction of federal policies and local contexts, some groups were included, others excluded, and yet others became controlled by the state. These processes directly impacted the form of participatory innovation in different parts of the country.

In *Violence and Social Orders* (2009), North, Wallis, and Weingast propose an analytical framework to explain how societies controlled by small and powerful elites become open to the economic and political participation of all citizens. The authors call these two types of societies *limited access order* and *open access order*. In the former, elites control valuable resources and profitable activities and are capable of preventing nonelite members to access them. The means for limiting access to lucrative activities are the overt use of violence and the safeguarding of the privilege of forming social organizations. Only elites are able to form social organizations, which further strengthens them vis-à-vis others; these organizations facilitate collaboration and avoid violent struggle within the dominant elite coalition. From time to time internal or even outside contenders may successfully challenge elite arrangements, causing temporary turmoil without altering the fundamental features of this social order. In other words, elite members move up and down elite hierarchies, and new members may even replace old members, but at the end a powerful elite continues to dominate the rest of society.

In limited access orders, patronage is the main type of relationship between elite members (patrons) and nonelite members (clients). "The patrons' privileged position within the dominant coalition enables them to protect their clients from injuries caused by clients or other patrons (whether that protection is legal or physical) and their ability to distribute rewards and levy punishments among their clients" (36). Limited access societies are comprised of several patron-client networks; the larger the network and the greater the resources it controls, the higher the position of its head in the dominant elite coalition. The heads of the more powerful patron-client networks constitute the organization that governs the society; if this organization is not the state per se, it has much influence over it. In this type of society, the majority of individuals participate in political life only through subservient relations with patrons, who participate in intra-elite arrangements.

In turn, "an open access order exists only if a large number of individuals have the right to form organizations that can engage in a wide variety of economic, political and social activities" (23). Impartial institutions regulate peaceful competition for resources and political control. "The ability of political actors to use organized military or police power to coerce individuals is constrained by the ability of economic and other actors to compete for political control" (22). Whereas in a limited access order the dominant coalition includes the heads of the military forces, in an open access order the state controls the coercive apparatus, and social and economic groups are able to compete for control of the state. Moreover, constitutional arrangements deter groups in control of the state from using violence in unlawful ways.

In an open access order, state institutions treat citizens impersonally and extend to them access to the law and to at least basic levels of infrastructure, education, and social insurance. In this type of order, a market economy makes entry in the economic realm open to any citizen with the necessary resources and skills. The political system has political parties that represent diverse ideologies, and there is no restriction on the formation of civil society organizations. Whereas in limited access orders individuals' well-being depends on relationships with patrons, in open access orders citizens have alternatives for pursuing their needs and interests.

North et al.'s framework provides useful empirical categories that capture the economic, social, and political aspects of exclusion and participation, but its casual explanation of the transition from limited to open access orders neglects crucial aspects of democratization. In this approach, transition is the result of the establishment of rules and institutions that facilitate nonviolent interpersonal exchanges; at first, formal arrangements include only elite members but are gradually extended to all citizens. According to North et al., this process is controlled by the elites themselves, who come to see it as in their interest to have intra-elite relations arbitrated by formal institutions, and then slowly allow these institutions to include other groups. The authors pointed out that in England and France incorporation stemmed from the frustration of certain elites with their inability to form the corporations needed for economic undertakings, which was until then a privilege reserved to the more traditional elites. They also noted that this tension was the result of changes in the economic organization of these countries. However, this institutionalist framework does not include the economic processes fueling intra-elite conflict as a condition of the transition to an open access order. Likewise, it minimizes the influence of social and political pressures from below, emphasizing instead the calculations of elite members. Material processes spurring intra-class conflicts and empowering subordinate groups are crucial in the transitions examined in this study, and examining them requires drawing on another theoretical tradition.

Structuralist analyses of democratization processes provide useful concepts to examine the transition from a limited toward a more open access order in Brazil. In their seminal study, Rueschemeyer, Stephens, and Stephens (1992) argue that, "capitalist development affects the chances of democracy primarily because it transforms the class structure and changes the balance of power between classes" (47). According to these authors, the proponents of democracy are most likely to be the marginalized social classes that can most benefit from political opening; they are called the *subordinate classes* and include the urban working class, small farmers, and agriculture labors. The fiercest opponent of democracy has historically been the large land-owning class. Rueschemeyer et al. argue that "capitalist development enlarges the urban working class at the expense of agricultural labors and small farmers; it thus shifts the members of the subordinate classes from an environment extremely unfavorable for collective action to one much more favorable" (58). In other words, capitalist development frees a large portion of the subordinate classes from the direct control of the opponents of democracy.

Moreover, Rueschemeyer et al. posit that the role of the bourgeoisie, that is, owners of capital other than large landowners, in democratization processes varied according to the context. In some cases, the bourgeoisie rallied the subordinate classes against the large land-owning class, and in other cases it made alliances with landlords and the military in order to secure its material advantages. In South America, the latter has been the most common. Capitalist development in this continent gave origin to two types of political parties. In *clientelist parties*, middle-class groups forged broad alliances, including with traditional elites, and promoted limited political inclusion. In *mass radical parties*, middle-class groups joined the subordinate classes and pushed for full democratization. Radical parties were only successful where the urban working class was strong; otherwise elites were capable of reversing democratic advances.

Structuralist analyses offer richer accounts of democratic transitions than North et al.'s analytical framework. The limitation of Rueschemeyer et al.'s approach from the point of view of the present analysis is that it treats economic, social, and political processes separately. The focus is on how economic changes and ensuing social groups increase or not the chances of the establishment of a *real democracy*, which is defined as a stable representative system with universal suffrage and strong and autonomous legislative institutions. Although the authors discuss cases that fall in between real democracies and authoritarian regimes, the focus is on processes leading to transitions to real democracy, with less attention paid to what is referred to as *restricted democracies*. Democratization in Latin America is then presented as a series of advances and regressions between authoritarian and more or less democratic regimes. What this approach only briefly acknowledges and does not properly integrate into its overall arguments is that the gradual opening of spaces for participation in economic and social realms is an integral aspect of a democratization process broadly defined, independent of its role in the transition to a representative system with universal suffrage. Whereas the empirical categories of North et al. encompass the various facets of exclusion, its focus on elite calculation leads to a neglect of the social and political struggles fuelled by economic processes. Rueschemeyer et al.'s analysis pays close attention to the formation of social groups and political alliances in the process of capitalist development, but its conceptualization of democracy as essentially a political system delegates a secondary and instrumental role to participation in economic and social spheres.

Both frameworks can be fruitfully combined. The concepts of limited and open access orders help us to distinguish between two types of societies: one where participation is limited to personal interactions between patrons and clients and another where participation takes multiple forms. In the transition period, new social groups, political strategies, and forms of participation emerge. Populist leaders may try to rally old and new subaltern groups through broad rhetorical appeals to their constituents' needs and fears. Clientelist political parties extend patron-client networks so as to include new social groups in a more negotiated and less antagonistic manner, whereas radical mass parties bring together elite and middle-class members who try to mobilize subaltern groups in order to push for full democratization. The present study focuses on how the country's economic structure and policies hindered or spurred inclusion, controlled inclusion or exclusion of distinct groups in varied regions of the country.

THE FIRST REPUBLIC: A LIMITED ACCESS ORDER

In the colonial period (1500–1823), Brazil was divided in captaincies, which were vast portions of land the Portuguese crown trusted to noblemen and military officials deemed to have the necessary means to secure and exploit them. Captaincy generals had absolute administrative and military authority over their domains and responded only to the governor general, who was the representative of the crown in the colony. Captaincies were hereditary for most of the colonial period. During the Empire period (1823–1889), a representative system was put in place, with a relatively broad suffrage for the time, but the Emperor (the son of the King of Portugal) had the prerogative to dismiss legislatures at his discretion. The focus of this section is the period from 1889 to 1930, known as the First Republic, wherein the logic of a limited access order permeated and corrupted the representative system, leading Buarque de Holanda (1936/2002) to call democracy in Brazil a "lamentable misunderstanding."

In the 1880s, the city of Rio de Janeiro was the capital of Brazil; Minas Gerais was the most populated and politically important province; the province of São Paulo was a burgeoning coffee-based economy; the province of Rio Grande do Sul was a military force; and the province of Pernambuco was a regional leader in the Northeast. Republicanism started with a manifesto signed in 1870 by Rio de Janeiro professionals who advocated for progressive social reforms, the end of slavery, and a peaceful transition to a new political system. Republican parties in São Paulo and Minas Gerais defended the movement in the political sphere, but the actual overthrow of the Empire was carried out by militaries from Rio Grande do Sul and Rio de Janeiro (Fausto 1999).

The new republican governing elite was divided between those espousing a liberal state with great provincial autonomy and those defending the need for a strong central power capable of imposing order and promoting progress. The former group prevailed. The 1891 constitution transformed Brazil into a federative republic, and provinces, now called states, were granted fiscal autonomy and the right to organize their own military forces. Citizens elected the president directly. The legislative power was comprised of a lower house, the Chamber of Deputies, and an upper house, the Senate; in the former, seats were distributed according to demographic representation, whereas in the latter every state had an equal number of seats. Financial requirements for voter registration were removed, and any Brazilian citizen over twenty-one years of age who was not a beggar or a military man could vote as long as he was literate. That women could not vote was felt to be so obvious that it did not even deserve mention in the legislation. According to 1872 statistics, 99.9 percent of slaves and 80 percent of the free population were illiterate (Fausto 1999, 142). Votes were not secret. In the almost forty years of the First Republic, voter turnout in presidential elections varied from 1.4 to 5.7 percent of the total population (Fausto 1999, 159).

Low political participation in this period was not only the result of restricting legislation but also the outcome of a political-institutional arrangement that made votes irrelevant. The new constitution was followed by political instability. Disagreement between republicans and intrastate disputes evolved into national-level clashes, an attempted coup, the forced resignation of a president, federal intervention in states, and an armed revolt staged by federalists in Rio Grande do Sul. Debts inherited from the previous period, high military expenditure, and low coffee prices strained the country's finances, making the political scenario unstable. Campos Sales, a *paulista* (from or pertaining to São Paulo) elected president in 1898, devised a shrewd political arrangement known as "governors' policy" that balanced state autonomy and central authority. The Chamber of Deputies was responsible for verifying the legitimacy of legislative elections through its Commission for Verification of Power. The Chamber's rules determined that its eldest member served as chair of the Commission and chose four deputies to work with him. President Sales introduced a small but substantial change: the president of the chamber became the head of the Commission, as long as he was re-elected for a new mandate. In other words, the chair was a member of the legislative majority with vested interests in maintaining the political status quo (Silveira 1978).

To understand the significance of this change it is necessary to review the electoral process at this time. Municipal bodies were responsible for counting votes under their jurisprudence and issuing "diplomas" for the winning candidates. It was a remarkably corrupted electoral system. Numerous studies describe how securing votes was not as crucial as securing the diploma; a candidate could win the election but lose the vote count (Graham 1990; Kinzo 1980; Leal 1949/2009). This literature is full of quotations that depict the unabashed attitude of those involved in politics at the time. For example, a respected republican politician purportedly told a younger and disliked member of his party that he would not have his diploma recognized for three reasons, "the third is that you have not been elected" (Leal 1949/2009, 124). A myriad of terms exist to describe corrupted practices; one of the best known is a "stroke-of-a-pen election," which refers to an election in which the person responsible for vote counting bluntly falsified the proceedings.

State governors and local *coronéis* together secured election results. The former needed the coercive power that only the latter could exert, whereas *coronéis* needed financial support from governors. Intra-elite conflict existed, and contesting political groups managed to issue legitimate or fake diplomas that allowed their party members to claim a seat in the legislative chambers. The change put forward by President Sales guaranteed state governors that opposition politicians would be "beheaded" once they arrived in the capital, that is, the Commission would not recognize their diplomas; only governor-supported candidates were accepted. The governor, assisted by *coronéis*, elected the legislative deputies he wished; in return, governors instructed deputies to support the president. According to a politician and intellectual of the time, "soon elections became a mere formality. Everyone became convinced that in order to be elected for deputy, senator, or even president, it was not necessary to receive a single vote" (Assis Brasil as quoted in Kinzo 1980, 179). In this political system it was senseless to be an opposition party. Intra-elite disputes took place within the party for the nominations. Once nominations had been decided, the rest was a formality. Elections results frequently show candidates with 100 percent of the cast votes, which explains why in the three states examined in the chapters below, only one elite party existed for most of the First Republic.

Two additional characteristics of the First Republic are noteworthy. Municipal autonomy was a contentious issue among republicans. Whereas federalists thought municipal matters were under the jurisprudence of states, those espousing a stronger central government advocated for national legislation on the matter. The former view trumped the latter. As regards mayoral elections, for example, a few states decided the governor had the authority to nominate all mayors, others allowed municipal elections in all but important cities and the capital, and still others held elections in all cities. Financial autonomy was rarely granted to municipalities, as the governor's ability to approve expenditures at his discretion was the key to guaranteeing the support of *coronéis* (Leal 1949/2009).

This period is often referred to as the Coffee with Milk Republic, in allusion to the main agricultural products of São Paulo and Minas Gerais, where elites at the top of the patron-client network governed the country during the First Republic. At the time of 1891 constitution, Minas Gerais was the most populated province and was therefore guaranteed the largest number of legislative seats. São Paulo came in second in number of seats, but was first in economic power. During most of the First Republic the elites of Minas Gerais and São Paulo had a political alliance that included alternating members of their respective elites in the presidential office.

FROM VARGAS TO GOULART: TOWARD AN OPEN ACCESS ORDER

In 1928, Paulista President Washington Luis was supposed to accept the nomination of a Minas Gerais candidate, but he refused to do so and selected another Paulista. Minas Gerais and Rio Grande do Sul formed the Liberal Alliance (Aliança Liberal) and launched the candidacy of Getúlio Vargas, a politician from Rio Grande do Sul. The Alliance also included political groups excluded from the dominant elite coalition of their respective states. The president's nominee won the elections, but the Alliance organized a military insurrection that succeeded in removing the Paulista from power. This insurrection became known as the 1930 Revolution, though there were only few and isolated cases of armed struggle.

The Liberal Alliance was a coalition of five groups with distinct reasons for opposing the ruling class of the First Republic. The first was a group of young military *tenentes* (lieutenants) who had launched several short-lived revolts in the 1920s. The poorly defined goal of this group was to regenerate and modernize the nation; with a nationalist discourse and an authoritarian attitude, *tenentes* respected competent technocrats more than elected officials. The second group was comprised of liberal constitutionalist political parties supported by the emerging urban

middle classes, to whom free elections and civic liberties were imperative. The Revolution also found support among the high-ranking military
personnel disgruntled with the First Republic's handling of the armed
forces. The fourth group was coffee growers displeased by President Luis's
unwillingness to sustain monetary policies favoring their exports. Finally,
politicians and local bosses excluded from the dominant party welcomed
a crisis that could alter the political status quo (Skidmore 1967). In the
first years of government, "Vargas's Machiavellian political style encouraged each of these groups to press their claims" (Skidmore 1967, 14).
Demands were attended to in an ad hoc fashion and always with the goal
of strengthening the leader's position.

A new constitution was promulgated in 1934, the same year Vargas
was indirectly elected president for a four-year mandate. Two new political parties with concrete ideological programs emerged: on the left, a
moderate arm of the illegal Brazilian Communist Party (Partido Comunista Brasileiro, PCB) gained the support of discontented middle-class
groups and some militant labor unions; on the right, a Fascist party advocated for an authoritarian path to development. Vargas pitched these parties against each other and used a failed rebellion of the PCB to enhance
his powers. In 1937, liberal constitutionalists and *tenentes* launched candidates for the upcoming presidential election with good chances in the
dispute of the government of the country. Vargas, however, engineered a
coup d'état that further postponed democratic elections. The New State
(Estado Novo 1937–1945) "represented a hiatus in the development of
party politics organized on class or ideological lines—a form of politics
which itself had only begun to take form in Brazil in the early 1930s.
Every significant political group had been outmaneuvered and sup-
pressed" (Skidmore 1967, 32–33).

Although Vargas silenced ideological and class movements, modernization, a central objective of the revolution, was not abandoned.
Coffee remained an important export item and as such was protected
by numerous state policies, but it ceased to be the main focus of the Brazilian economy (Silva 1999). In the Vargas era, industrialization became
a state project carried out by a newly created technocratic bureaucracy.
Attempts to professionalize the public service started in the 1920s but
gained momentum with the creation of numerous sectorial ministries
after the Revolution and the formation of the Administrative Department

of Public Service (Departamento Administrativo do Serviço Público, DASP) after the 1937 coup. "The creation of DASP within the framework of the Estado Novo occurred at a moment when Brazilian authoritarianism returned with force, this time to implement a modernizing revolution in the country, to industrialize it, and to place value on technical competence" (Bresser-Pereira 2009, 151). The DASP created a number of regulatory bodies that became responsible for the state enterprises that served as the pillars of Import Substitution Industrialization (ISI) programs.

Brazil adopted the entire ISI package, namely, the nationalization of primary industries; heavy investment in infrastructure; the creation of state-owned intermediary industries, notably the National Steel Company (CNS, in 1941) and a national oil company (Petrobras, in 1953); import schemas blocking the entry of finished products and facilitating the import of capital goods; undervaluation of the currency; the creation of a development bank (BNDES, in 1952); and intensive support to select industrial sectors, for example, automobiles. In the 1930s, 12,232 industrial establishments were created, almost three times as many as in the previous decade; in the second half of the decade industrial output grew 43 percent (Bresser-Pereira 1984, 19–20).

Industrialization was accompanied by partial and controlled extension of political and social rights. The 1932 electoral code extended suffrage to women, instituted the secret vote, lowered the voting age from twenty-one to eighteen, and created a judicial body to supervise elections. The new code only took effect after the end of the dictatorial period; illiterate citizens, 51 percent of the population in 1950, were still denied the right to vote; the electoral judicial body was flawed and until 1950 contained mechanisms that allowed for corruption in the registration of voters; and electoral laws alone did not alter power relations in rural areas (Kinzo 1980, 64). Notwithstanding these limitations, these were significant steps toward the enfranchisement of the popular masses.

The Vargas government also pushed social and labor legislation. Created after the 1930 Revolution, the Ministry of Labor enacted many laws regarding working conditions and social welfare that culminated in the 1943 Consolidated Labor Laws (Consolidação das Leis do Trabalho, CLT), a decree that governed labor relations. Legislation applied only to urban sectors, and rural workers were overtly neglected. At the same time, the government kept a strong grip on organized labor. The Brazil of Vargas has been characterized as "the most full-blown system of corporatism in Latin America" (Collier and Collier 1991, 186). From 1930 to 1935, the government repressed and demobilized incipient labor movements, often accusing them of representing a communist threat. The government imposed a rigid framework on the functioning of labor unions: only one union was allowed per jurisdiction, all workers were obligated to pay a syndical tax that was channeled to the unions through the state, and the state monitored union activity and intervened whenever deemed necessary. Unions were not meant to represent class interests. Instead, they "were conceived primarily as social service organizations that would distribute benefits to workers and generally contribute to a collaborative social order" (Collier and Collier 1991, 187). Union leaders were subordinated to the Ministry of Labor and typically acted in the interest of the government in order to secure the personal benefits associated with their position (Collier and Collier 1991).

Vargas's corporatist state represented a transition from a patrimonial to a state-organized bureaucratic form of political engagement, which has been interpreted both as an advance and a lasting hindrance in the development of autonomous forms of political participation. According to O'Donnell (1973), Vargas's manipulation of the working class thwarted the emergence of more spontaneous forms of workers' organizations, "but it also had the effect of giving urban workers an organizational basis that, with all its weakness considered, was incomparably stronger than anything they had before. . . . Even in this subordinate position, the urban popular sector was given its first chances to have some effective weight in national politics" (59). Schmitter (1971) advanced the thesis that the controlled incorporation of workers gained roots and outlived the Vargas era; the right to strike, the author noted, was not granted until 1966 and only with considerable restrictions.

The case study of Diadema illustrates the significance of the corporatist state in the move toward an open access order. Tightly controlled at first, the urban working class became one of the best-organized social groups in the country. The new unionism movement, which reacted against the persistence of the corporatist system, was a key exponent of participatory ideals in the 1970s. The co-opted labor leaders, known as *pelegos*, were one of the main targets of groups promoting participatory democracy. The new unionism movement was also the main pillar of the PT, the party that has most actively promoted participation since the 1990s. Diadema was the PT's first experience with participatory democracy. The impacts of these partial and incomplete reforms are made more visible through the analysis of local cases.

Toward the end of the dictatorial regime, between 1943 and 1945, Vargas coordinated the creation of two political parties, the Social Democratic Party (Partido Social Democrata, PSD), which represented traditional rural elites, and the Brazilian Labor Party (Partido Trabalhista Brasileiro, PTB), which organized urban workers in state-controlled unions. Vargas also reinvented himself as "the father of the poor," and welfare benefits were associated with the leader's benevolent protector image. The support of these two distinct social groups and the skillful use of populist rhetoric allowed a pro-Vargas coalition to dominate national politics for the following fifteen years, while increasingly more autonomous unions, social movements, and ideology-based parties formed at the local level.

In 1945, political parties faced a larger than ever and fast-changing electorate. Almost six million citizens voted in the 1945 presidential election; five years later, the electorate had grown to 7.9 million, or 42.5 percent of the adult population, and almost twelve million Brazilians voted in 1960 (Kinzo 1980, 65; Skidmore 1967, 192). This electorate was also increasingly more urban: the percentage of the total population living in urban areas increased from 31 percent in 1940 to 45 percent in 1960 (Thery 2009, 8–9). This urbanization process was geographically uneven, with Southeast capitals receiving migrants from the Northeast as people were "attracted by the prospects of employment on coffee plantations or in the factories of São Paulo or seduced by the mirage of the 'big city'" (Thery 2009, 10). In 1960, 57 percent of the southeastern population was already urban. Urbanization and continuing industrialization brought changes to the structure of occupations. More than 5.6 million jobs were created in the 1950s; 36 percent of these were in the primary sector, and the remaining were in manufacturing, commerce, public administration, and services (Faria 1989, 151). The question, then, is how this large number of new voters was included in political life.

A pro-Vargas coalition formed by the PSD and the PTB was politically successful at the national level and managed to isolate the liberal constitutionalists of the National Democratic Union (União Democrática Nacional, UDN). The PSD candidate elected in 1945 had Vargas's support. Vargas returned to power in 1951, but then committed suicide in 1954.[2] Juscelino Kubitschek, the last president of the period to finish a mandate (1956–1961), was also elected by the PSD-PTB coalition. The decaying agrarian sector and the growing unemployed urban masses made the need to industrialize a national priority. Industrial elites were not strong enough to head the process, traditional rural elites were still capable of stalling development, and urban labor unions were already a significant political force. Vargas and Kubitschek led a "developmentalist alliance" that brought these groups together. Peasants and rural workers were deliberately excluded—the price paid for the support of rural elites. The unionization of agriculture workers was not legally endorsed until the early 1960s, and the literacy requirement for voter registration excluded a disproportionately large portion of rural dwellers. Urban labor movements outside the official corporatist channels were fiercely repressed, and the agro-export sector was also largely excluded (Cardoso and Faletto 1979).

The absence of a dominant elite coalition and the only incipiently organized popular sector was a fertile ground for populism. In this context, populism refers to a phenomenon in which a charismatic politician presents himself as the representative of voiceless social groups. Although from another social class, this political leader mingles in a fraternal, often paternal manner with the lower classes, which are regarded as a homogenous group usually referred to as "the people," "the community," or simply "the poor." In the absence of a dominant political elite, a populist leader claiming to represent "the people" and to be above class interests portrays himself as an arbitrator committed to the country's general welfare. Notwithstanding variances in style and local contexts, this was the general strategy used by Vargas, Kubitschek, and other populist politicians of the period (Weffort 1980).

In the Brazilian context, populism is often described as the urban, less patrimonial version of *coronelismo*. Populist leaders targeted the urban mass of factory workers and underemployed citizens living in peripheral neighborhoods. Some authors suggested that rural migrants with a subservient political culture become easy targets of populist politicians. This interpretation is found, for example, in Carvalho's (2001) analysis of the period: "[Vargas's] emphasis on social rights found fertile grounds on the population's political culture, especially the poor population of the urban centers. The latter grew rapidly due to migration from rural areas and from northeastern to southern cities" (26).

Weffort (1980, 55) also considered the transition from rural areas to urban centers an essential first step in the "dissolution of traditional patterns of submission." However, Weffort argued the adherence to populism was more than simply a political culture factor; new urban groups experienced a significant material ascension that was not accompanied by social and political inclusion. Populist politicians offered this emerging class an opportunity to enter the political realm and further advance their acquired benefits in a reformist rather than radical manner. According to Weffort, a social class with explicit demands was behind the populist phenomenon.

As with corporatism, scholars consider populism a partial and incomplete rupture from the previous patron-client political system. Bresser-Pereira (1984) put it succinctly: "at least now it is necessary to try to convince the electorate" (79). Carvalho (2001) admitted that this period witnessed advances in citizenship rights but argued that this submissive incorporation of the masses had the negative effect of generating a passive citizenship. Weffort (1980) thought that populism opened a channel for the political participation of a new economic class that would eventually impose a serious challenge to the political system: "to make economic development compatible with democratic development" (164). When consolidated democracies succumb to the inflammatory rhetoric of politicians disposed to exploit times of crisis, populism is rightly regarded as a digression. In the case of Brazil, in this period populism helped to move the country toward an open access order, for it included new sectors of the population into the political life of the country, even if at times in a deceitful manner.

As with the case of state corporatism, the role of populism and clientelism, in the move toward an open access order, are more visible in lower-level politics. At the national level, populism was the tactic of the pro-Vargas coalition and represented a continuation of the previous era. In subnational disputes, populism was often the strategy of politicians not included in the dominant elite coalition. Aside from the two aforementioned presidents, Jânio Quadros was the most successful populist politician of the period. A schoolteacher from a modest family, Quadros became the mayor of São Paulo in 1953 with 70 percent of the vote. He became the governor of the state two years later and the president of the country in 1960. Quadros refused to join the main parties and promoted an image of an outsider committed to moralizing politics.[3] Quadros's main opponent was Adhemar de Barros, another populist politician and head of a small personalistic party (Weffort 1980). Diadema, located in the outskirts of São Paulo, was dominated by this style of politics, which was a key target of participatory discourse in the area, together with corporatism. Rural regions were also touched by this phenomenon. In Espírito Santo, the first governor from outside the political elites was Francisco Lacerda de Aguiar (1955–1960), a populist leader known by the affectionate nickname Chiquinho. In 1972, populist Juarez Furtado became the first mayor of Lages to win an election without being directly nominated by the powerful Ramos family. These populist politicians represent a partial but marked break with patrimonial politics, and, as the case studies show, they help to incorporate new segments of the population into political life.

The inflamed discourses of populist leaders were accompanied by agreements and compromises that guaranteed electoral victories. At the national level, the PSD-PTB coalition secured the support of the key players. At the local level, politicians had to build clientelist networks. Clientelism can be defined as a scenario "where the game of politics is centered around individual politician's distribution of patronage and 'favors' . . . and candidates' promises of such, in exchange for political/financial support and votes" (Nylen 2003, 15). Canvassers, pejoratively known as *cabos eleitorais*, served as intermediaries between the people of a particular neighborhood and populist politicians; they diligently campaigned for a candidate in return for priority treatment by the elected administration. Clientelist networks were organized around *sub-diretórios* (party neighborhood chapters), as Furtado did in Lages or in neighborhood associations, as the societies of the friends of the neighborhood (*sociedades de amigos do bairro*, SABs) common in São Paulo and Diadema.

Clientelist practices inhibited broad and autonomous popular political engagement since only appointed subdirectory leaders could negotiate "favors" (Moisés 1978). Nevertheless, clientelism was also a significant step toward a more open social order because it brought new social groups to the negotiation table. Andrade (1996b) argued that in the more traditional patron-client relations the level of dependence and devotion of a client was much higher than in clientelism based on party machines: "If, on the one hand, [the new clientelism] bonds (through political favors) many community leaders to the government's party, making them dependent on the political party machine, on the other hand, it makes the support of these leaders contingent." Hilgers (2012) and colleagues challenged the idea that clientelism is always detrimental to democracy, positing that it may accompany, or even supplement, democratic practices. In Lages, clientelism emerged as a new form of participation that included more social groups than the previous political arrangement. However, a group pushing participatory reforms soon challenged it. The 1982 elections marked the main conflict between the two strategies, and clientelism proved stronger. In Diadema, clientelism practices persisted for three decades, but once the PT was elected, clientelist politicians never regained the city. This difference in outcomes can be partially explained by the socioeconomic conditions of each city.

Autonomous social movements and ideology-based political parties significantly increased in this period. After the end of the Estado Novo, unions launched an unprecedented series of illegal strikes and gained important concessions from the PSD-PTB administration. In the following decade, gradual steps toward autonomy included the creation of confederations that in the 1960s demanded profound institutional reforms (Collier and Collier 1991). Authentic union leaders began to emerge and replace co-opted *pelegos* (Bresser-Pereira 1984). Peasants and rural workers organized and started to press for land distribution and political inclusion, and the Peasant Leagues (Ligas Camponesas) became a considerable disturbance to northwestern political elites (Morais 2002). The Catholic Church, under the influence of the Conciliar Vatican II, began to support numerous grassroots movements (Krischke 2010). At least some SABs were independent organizations and played an important role in the movement for the municipal autonomy of the peripheral districts of São Paulo (Moisés 1978).

Moreover, smaller parties with more clearly defined constituencies began gaining space in federal and state legislative chambers. The PCB had significant positive results in the two years following the end of the Estado Novo but was made illegal in 1947. The number of seats held by small parties in the Chamber of Deputies tripled between 1945 and 1962 from 5.6 to 16.2 percent. The growth of small parties forced the more traditional coalitions to seek a closer relationship with the electorate, leading to ruptures within these groups (Souza 1976). Souza (1976) has argued that the fragmentation of the political party system did not cause the 1964 breakdown, a common thesis at the time. On the contrary, the emergence of new political parties signaled the renewal of the Brazilian representative system and the inclusion of new social groups.

The 1964 coup d'état is generally associated with the breakdown of the PSD-PTB coalition and more broadly with the radicalization of politics. In 1961, the eccentric Jânio Quadros renounced the presidency six months after being inaugurated. He claimed to face a political deadlock and his renunciation was probably a bluff aimed at gaining extraordinary executive powers. Congress, however, accepted his request. The vice president, at the time elected separately, was the leader of an ever-more-radical PTB and was visiting communist China when Quadros stepped down. In the following three years, Cold War dynamics fuelled political polarization in Brazil. The successful 1959 Cuban Revolution inspired leftists across Latin America, including groups inside and closely associated with the president's PTB. In the perspective of conservative forces, the communist threat was stronger than ever and needed to be neutralized. When the president finally took the side of leftist groups and began to endorse land reform, the military stepped in.

THE MILITARY REGIME: STALLING DEMOCRATIZATION

The direct presidential election of 1960 was not repeated until 1989. Gubernatorial elections took place in 1965; defeated in five states including the capital district, the military abolished the multiparty system and established a façade two-party system. Direct legislative elections were maintained at the federal, state, and municipal levels. Legislative chambers indirectly elected presidents and governors. Mayors were the only executive post with direct elections, except for state capitals and cities with hydro and mineral resources. The National Renewal Alliance (Aliança Nacional Renovadora, ARENA) was the majority party for the entire period, and its task was to sanction and legitimize decisions of the military junta running the country. The Brazilian Democratic Movement (Movimento Democrático Brasileiro, MDB) was the controlled legal opposition. The rules of the game altered whenever electoral support for the MDB increased; legislative chambers were closed, elections postponed, the number of senators altered, and deputies lost their political rights. Between 1964 and 1965 alone, 513 senators and state and municipal deputies had their mandates revoked (Carvalho 2001, 164).

Labor unions and other social organizations were either dismantled or repressed, and "in a very short period, virtually all the radical and militant union leadership was replaced by passive pro-government appointees" (Mericle 1977, 309). According to one estimate, there were 536 state interventions in unions between 1964 and 1970 (Carvalho 2001, 164). Interventions were selective and random, instituting generalized fear and self-censorship. The corporatist mechanisms created in the 1930s were used to control union activities and co-opt the leadership. Moreover, laws passed in the beginning of the regime decreased job security and made almost all types of strike illegal. During two illegal strikes in 1968, the regime made patently clear its willingness to violently suppress protest (Mericle 1977). The leaders of the Peasant Leagues were arrested and the movement subdued (Page 2002).

In 1968, in response to mounting opposition, the military passed a decree known as the AI-5, which temporarily closed the national legislative chambers, abolished habeas corpus, and instituted the death penalty by firing squad. The AI-5 marked the raise of the hard-liners, a faction of military who, contrary to its moderate counterpart, did not see the role of the military as that of a provisional government managing a short-lived crisis; instead, hard-liners believed a military government to be the only alternative to develop Brazil and subdue the communist threat. As totalitarian regimes usually do, the Brazilian military portrayed itself as the guardian of the national interest, and as a result, those who challenged the regime were regarded as national enemies. In the following years the persecution, torture, and killing of opponents of the regime became an institutionalized practice.

The military regime also closely controlled the economy. In the 1960s, Brazil began to face some of the shortcomings of the ISI policies that affected most Latin American countries, namely, regional concentration of industry, the industrial sector's inability to absorb the rapidly growing urban population, and growing income inequality (Baer 1972). Income inequality was the consequence of the creation of proportionally few, relatively high-skills jobs in one region, but was also related to the way the government financed industrialization. Beginning in the mid-1950s, industrialization was increasingly funded through inflation generated by the government's printing of money. In this case, inflation was a way of taxing wage workers and small farmers, because their real income decreased disproportionally more than that of the business class, who passed increases in the prices of inputs on to consumers (Singer 1976). Rising prices were made easier by the oligopolistic character of ISI markets, while wage increases were difficult to achieve in the context of outlawed strikes. Real minimum wages dropped 38 percent between 1958 and 1966 (Bresser-Pereira 1984, 96).

In the first years of the military regime, an orthodox economic team adopted policies aimed at ending inflation, and its policies included forced wage decreases, increases in the mandatory contribution to the state's pension plan, price freezes, and increased tariffs on public services (Baer 1977). In the late 1960s, savings from the forced pension plan and international loans allowed the government to fuel another economic expansion. Numerous incentives also attracted foreign companies to install factories in the country. The 1968–1974 period became known as the years of the "economic miracle," when industrial growth averaged 12.2 percent per year (Baer 1977, 11). In 1974, growth began to slow. The government borrowed heavily abroad and allowed inflation to rise in an unsuccessful attempt to avoid a recession. In 1980, international banks refused to roll over the country's debt, and a set of contractionary fiscal policies were implemented (Bresser-Pereira 1984). Two defaults on international debt, high levels of inflation, and economic stagnation marked the 1980s.

From an economic perspective, this period witnessed significant advances in the overall process of the nation's industrialization. Nevertheless, only a small middle and upper class benefited from these advances at the time. Capital-intensive domestic industries and foreign companies employed and supplied a small portion of the population. Wage earners, small farmers, and in some cases small business owners had to finance the industrial expansion that benefited them disproportionally less than the wealthier segments of Brazilian society. The percentage of the national income in the hands of the poorest 50 percent dropped from 17.4 in 1960 to 12.6 in 1980, whereas the percentage in the hands of the richest 10 percent rose from 39.6 percent to 50.9 percent (Bresser-Pereira 1984, 184). The repressive character of the regime made it difficult for the poor segments of society to try to influence or resist this economic development approach that ignored their needs.

AS THE CASE STUDIES will illustrate in detail, the Vargas era was not a definite blow to the traditional elites of the country. Vargas's power rested on agreements with local elites across the country. However, industrialization and urbanization were accelerated in this period and spurred the emergence of new social groups not subjected to patron-client networks. New social groups were incorporated into the political life of the country through the controlling hands of the corporatist state. The state institutions created in the Vargas years were not meant to facilitate the interaction of competing social groups as much as to control them, but at least rules began to become codified as rights and extended to groups other than the elites. Urban groups were incorporated first. The rural population continued under the authority of local elites, who remained politically significant though no longer able to restrain access to economic and political activities. In the 1950s, emerging social groups began to demand autonomy from the state and form social organizations detached from the government bureaucracy. This decade also witnessed the rise of populist politicians who used their personal appeal to the masses to compensate for their lack of support from established patron-client networks. Traditional elite parties were forced to reach out to the emerging classes; this was done through the creation of clientelist parties that exchanged political support for favors in a less hierarchal manner than in patron-client relationships.

Overall, this period was marked by the partial and controlled inclusion of new popular sectors. In its essence, the corporatist state, populist politicians, and clientelist parties were new channels for the participation of previously excluded and new social groups, who were now in a position to demand political inclusion. Albeit far from normative ideals of democracy, these were noteworthy democratic advances. Counterfactually, it is possible to imagine a scenario in which representative political

parties, independent unions, autonomous social movements, and combative neighborhood associations would slowly gain strength and form a
democratic society. However, in a time of tremendous social inequalities
and extreme political polarization, some of the new social groups pressured for major economic reforms. When the state signaled it was willing
to push these reforms, traditional elites and the emerging middle class,
benefiting from recent economic development, called on the coercive
apparatus to protect their interests.

The military regime closed the political system and pushed economic programs that largely disregarded the living conditions of the poor
majority. This was an immense setback in the slow and uneven process
toward an open access order that started with the 1930 Revolution. The
party system became a façade, new social movements and organizations
were dismantled, and unions were brought back under the control of the
state. It was in this context of a partially open social order with closed
political institutional channels that new participatory movements, based
on new participatory ideals and rooted in different economic contexts
emerged. Participatory movements in the 1970s condemned patronage,
corporatism, populism, and clientelism; these movements carried a deep-
rooted mistrust of the formal political institutions that had been permeated and corrupted by these practices, including political parties. Direct
citizen involvement in political processes was considered the only truly
democratic option. Citizen participation became exalted as an end in and
of itself.

CHAPTER TWO

Participatory Movements under Authoritarian Government

The authoritarian period (1964–1985) witnessed the emergence of participatory movements that began to form in the mid- to late 1960s and gained force in the mid-1970s, spurring various types of participatory initiatives in the late 1970s and early 1980s. These movements were not only a reaction against the military regime, they were efforts to fundamentally reform institutions that had previously barred the meaningful participation of ordinary members. The core demand of these movements was not just the reestablishment of a legitimate representative system but also the construction of alternative democratic institutions, which in their conceptualizations required the direct participation of ordinary citizens. The educational material these movements produced show that they rejected all forms of partial and controlled incorporation; patronage, corporatism, populism, and clientelism were bundled together as undemocratic and unjust practices, and direct citizen participation was presented as the alternative. As the political opening began in the late 1970s, these movements coalesced into a broad participatory movement that supported numerous social and political organizations, campaigns, and protests, as well as participatory municipal administrations. Together these participatory ideals and practices constituted the first phase of the participatory system that in the 1990s included hallmarks of participatory budgeting and policy councils. The objective of this chapter is not to reduce the struggles of the period to direct participation in municipal government; rather, the goal is to

57

situate the precursory participatory municipal governments in their political context.

This chapter examines the most influential participatory movements of the period. The first section discusses what is here referred to as disenchanted Marxism. While Marxist groups were not always proponents of citizen participation, it is important to examine the character of Marxism in the period and the influence it had over other social movements. The second section examines the *autênticos* (authentics) of the Brazilian Democratic Movement (MDB), a group within the legal opposition party that tried to organize a true political resistance to the military regime; *autênticos* maintained that MDB mayors had to govern with the direct participation of community organizations. The third section turns to the ecclesial base communities (CEBs), the grassroots arm of the Catholic Church. Members of these groups were strongly encouraged to be actively involved in the political life of their communities. The fourth section focuses on the new unionism, a labor movement that refused to accept the limits on union activities imposed by the corporatist framework established in the 1940s. This movement became the backbone of the Workers' Party (PT), an internally democratic party committed to promoting citizen participation.

Each section begins with a brief review of the sphere of action of these movements and then describes their genesis, main tenets, and key proponents. For analytical purposes it is useful to treat each movement separately. The conclusion of the chapter considers how the movements overlapped. Chapter 3 examines the *autênticos* administration of the city of Lages. Chapter 4 describes how the mayor of Boa Esperança relied on CEBs' organizational structure and leaders to create a participatory administration. Chapter 5 analyzes the experience of Diadema, a PT participatory administration headed by new unionism members and Marxists groups.

DISENCHANTED MARXISTS

In the twentieth century the Latin American left was comprised of groups with varied interpretations of Marxist theories inspired by socialist experiments in the Soviet Union, El Salvador, China, and Cuba. If the character of the revolution was a contested topic among these groups, the final goal was clear: the construction of a socialist state (Löwy 1999). In the 1970s, however, Marxist groups in Brazil were fragmented and lacked a project capable of galvanizing the support of popular classes. Moreover, most of these groups had embraced democratization and the mobilization of civil society as meaningful struggles, which represented a break with doctrines that disdained democratic goals. In this context, Marxists either assisted participatory movements or were unable to substantially oppose them. In one case, Diadema, Marxists groups played an ambivalent role of supporting participation while trying to limit it to certain sectors of society. It is, therefore, worth briefly reviewing how Brazilian Marxists became fragmented and democratic.

In the mid-1930s, the Brazilian Communist Party (PCB) adopted the Stalinist doctrine promoted by the Communist International. According to this view, the region was semicolonial and, as such, its first step toward socialism was the struggle against feudalism and American imperialism. In this national democratic strategy, the expansion of capitalism and the strengthening of a national bourgeoisie must precede a socialist revolution. Thus, in this period the PCB supported democracy. Garcia, however, noted that in this phase the PCB "thinks of democracy fundamentally as a means"; according to him, the adjective "bourgeois" disfigured the concept and prevented substantial reflections on it (Garcia 1996, 121). This doctrine led the PCB to seek alliances with the corporatist apparatus, even if that meant a loss for the workers in the short term.

Beginning in 1959, the Cuban Revolution and the writings of Fidel Castro and Che Guevara inspired a new wave of revolutionary movements throughout Latin America. The PCB leadership rejected the Castroist current, leading some of its members to leave the party and form new organizations. In 1962, the Maoist faction of the PCB founded the Communist Party of Brazil (Partido Comunista do Brazil, PCdoB), which in the early 1970s backed one of the few rural guerrillas in the country (Araguaia). The army annihilated insurgents (Löwy 1999). One of the survivor rebels, José Genoíno, became the president of PT in 2002. Other PCB dissidents formed the National Liberation Alliance (Aliança Libertadora Nacional) and the October Eighth Revolutionary Movement (Movimento Revolutionário Oito de Outubro). The former counted on the support of workers associated with the PCB, and the latter was an offshoot of student movements (Garcia 1996). Another noteworthy organization is the

Palmares Revolutionary Armed Vanguard (Vanguarda Armada Revolu-cionária Palmares), which brought together smaller groups that included people such as legendary army captain Carlos Lamarca, killed in action (1971); Carlos Minc, later active member of the PT and of the Green Party (Partido Verde), and Minister of Environment (2008–2010); and the current president of Brazil, Dilma Rouseff (2011–).

Overall, Brazilian guerrillas were highly unsuccessful in their dis-organized actions against the large oppressive apparatus of the military regime (Garcia 1996). Alves (2005) explained this was due in part to the adoption of focalism as the main fighting strategy. Focalism was used in the 1959 Cuban Revolution and relied on the idea that the uncoordinated actions of autonomous guerrilla cells eventually lead to a nationwide insurrection. Cuba is much smaller than Brazil. In a country of conti-nental proportions, isolated guerrilla attacks did not mount to anything other than more repression. The fiasco of the armed struggle spurred the left's search for a new paradigm (Burgos 2002).

A new alternative emerged as a new Marxist doctrine spread through-out the continent. In orthodox Marxist thought, civil society belongs to the greedy economic sphere, an interpretation grounded in a materialistic reading of Hegel's examination of the concept. Antonio Gramsci offered an alternative conceptualization of civil society that allowed Marxists to come to terms with the idea of civil society (Cohen and Arato 1992). In his *Prison Notebooks*, Gramsci argued that a dominant group must exert control of both political and civil society in order to become a hegemonic force. The political society is the sphere of legal and overt control, while civil society is the arena of cultural dominance where subaltern classes "spontaneously" give consent to the hegemonic group. Civil society is also the arena where a counterhegemonic bloc is able to challenge the established order (Hoare and Nowell-Smith 1971, 263).

According to Burgos (2002), Gramsci began to play a major role in Latin American academia at the end of the 1960s. During this period, many countries in the continent were under rightist authoritarian regimes, and a number of intellectuals were writing from underground or from exile. The left had failed to seize control of the state using tactics learned from Lenin and the Cuban Revolution; the need to deliberate on new ways of constructing a socialist society and the desire to respond to oppressive regimes required bridging the gap between theoretical analysis and political actions. At the same time, democracy had become the demand around which resistance was organized, and therefore new strategies had to endorse democracy in order to gain popular support. Gramsci allowed Latin scholars to put forward the idea that revolution is not a single explosive act but a process in which political democracy is a necessary terrain where revolutionary forces gain strength.

Sader (1988) argues that in the 1970s Marxist groups were fragmented, without a clear doctrine, and more receptive to democratic ideals. Marxists participated in various social movements without heading any of them. The influence of Marxism was felt in religious groups, unions, and parties but never very markedly. In terms of practical political activities within the limits of the regime, Marxists became particularly involved in popular education projects and adult literacy campaigns inspired by Paulo Freire's methods. Sader explained that Marxists tended to deliberatively overlook the humanism and Christian values intrinsic to Freire's method and focus instead on the more instrumental aspects of "consciousness raising" (*conscientização*). The weak links between these activities and Gramsci's postulates was the closest Marxists had come in terms of revolutionary work.

This disenchanted Marxism played an indirect role in the participatory movements discussed below. Insights from historical materialism fuelled theological debates within the arm of the Catholic Church responsible for spurring community mobilization. It is possible to find moderate Marxist and socialist groups within the MDB, especially in youth groups. The new unionism movement had an uneasy relationship with the PCB but was more open to support from other Marxist groups. By the end of the decade, Marxists of various shades converged into the PT. However, at its foundation, the party clearly stated that it did not embrace specific Marxist doctrines. Marxist groups became simply factions within the party. In some cases, the doctrine of Marxist groups clashed with the more participatory ideals that sprouted in the 1970s. Diadema was one these cases.

MDB *AUTÊNTICOS*

In 1965, the military regime closed the existing political parties and imposed a two-party system. Supporters of the regime joined the

National Renewal Alliance (ARENA), whereas those who opposed the military formed the Brazilian Democratic Movement (MDB). The objective of the reform was to guarantee a legislative majority for the regime while upholding a façade of democratic legitimacy (Melhem 1998). A progressive faction within the MDB did not accept this expendable role and decided to use congressional privileges to denounce the regime. In the 1970s, this faction advocated for participatory channels for popular participation in MDB municipal governments. This section examines this militant arm of the legal opposition party, the political practices it rejected, and the type of municipal government it endorsed.

As an umbrella opposition party, the MDB included a wide range of political views, from conservatives who did not join the ARENA because of personal grievances to former members of the PCB. There was, however, a known divide between a majority of moderate, experienced politicians and a minority of more radical, mainly young and inexperienced party members. The former group was in control of the party; the two party presidents and three head secretaries in the authoritarian period were moderate members previously active in the Social Democratic Party (PSD) of Vargas and Kubitschek (Motta 2007). The latter group was one of the leading proponents of participatory democracy in Brazil; its composition and name changed with each legislative election. The 1967 cohort was called *imaturos* (immatures); the 1971 group was known as *autênticos* (authentics); the defying deputies elected in 1974 were referred to as the *neo-autênticos*; and in 1979 the more progressive faction of the MDB was called *tendência popular* (popular tendency) (Kinzo 1988). Today the group is generally remembered simply as MBD *autênticos*.

In the years following the coup, *imaturos* openly attacked the military in congressional speeches, attempted to create a commission for popular mobilization, and participated in various campaigns and protests against the government. The group was mainly comprised of young deputies without previous political experience other than in student movements and in political journalism. According to Marcio Moreira Alves (1973), a journalist and well-known *imaturo*,

> A handful of congressmen, elected by the large cities where elections were free of the voting-booth control enforced in the interior, had decided to test the limit of the constitutional guarantees the

military had left standing as a token to international—and especially American—liberal opinion. We fired off denunciations, launched congressional investigations, and covered with our immunity all sorts of protest movements, mostly student demonstrations and workers strikes. Our connections with leftist movements were varied, but we shared a common hate for the regime and the justifying role it had assigned us. (14)

The continuing defiance of this group irritated the military, which in 1968 requested congress to revoke the mandate of Moreira Alves. In an unexpected reaction against the regime, two-thirds of congress voted against Moreira Alves's impeachment; a political crisis ensued and ended with the enactment of the infamous AI-5. Moreira Alves felt forced to leave the country, and numerous deputies had their mandates revoked (Motta 2007). Upon his return nineteen years later, he wrote a book about the participatory administration of the city of Lages. The book went through nine printings. He also wrote news pieces on the topic and participated in public debates on participatory democracy (Alves 1980a, 1980b, 1983).

The confrontational spirit of the *imaturos* was renewed by MDB deputies elected in 1971—the *autênticos*. After a poor performance in the 1970s election, wherein null votes summed to more than MDB votes, the party decided to move away from its overly moderate position. In 1971, the MDB appointed Pedroso Horta as the party leader in congress; a deputy with a more aggressive stance, Horta supported the combative deputies who now constituted 25 percent of the party, some forty deputies (Kinzo 1988). It is difficult to ascribe the group a homogenous ideology. According to Motta (2007), "many of the *autênticos* did not have previous political experience; they were mainly professionals disgruntled with the authoritarian regime who were offered the chance to run for Congress in a period where it was difficult to find more experienced candidates" (290). Kinzo (1988) argued that the most marked characteristics of the group were its members' young age, lack of experience in the pre-1964 political scenario, and courage to confront the military regime.

In spite of lacking a cohesive ideological framework, *autênticos* grew as a distinct force within the MDB throughout the 1970s. The group's most renowned action was an attempt to boycott the staged presidential elections of 1973. Initially a widely supported plan within the party, the plot was later abandoned by moderate leaders; on the election, twenty-three *autêntico* deputies absented from voting and issued a statement calling for real democracy. Attempts to gain space within the party hierarchy were equally unsuccessful. Efforts were not in vain, however. The daring attitude of *autênticos* helped the party to regain the respect of the electorate, and the MDB began to be seen as a real opposition party. Sensing the moment, the party leadership decided to devote more efforts to the 1974 legislative elections, which included drafting a campaign manual that included proposals for socioeconomic issues and advocating for more political participation. The elaboration of the proposal counted on the help of researchers associated with the Brazilian Centre of Analysis and Planning (CEBRAP), a research center that brought together intellectuals forcedly retired from universities. Results were positive: the party won sixteen out of the twenty-two senate seats in dispute and increased its representation in the federal chamber from 87 to 160 seats (Kinzo 1988).

The group of *autênticos* was reinforced with some thirty deputies elected with the support of trade unions and student movements; the fresh impetus of these *neo-autênticos* at times clashed with the more restrained deputies elected in 1971. The 1974 election also brought to the MDB a group of hardheaded deputies. Pejoratively called "pragmatics" and *adesistas* (those who adhere to), these politicians were concerned with winning elections and defending the economic interests of their constituency; the struggle for democracy did not really concern them. In the following years, there were numerous quarrels between *autênticos*, moderates, pragmatics, and *adesistas* deputies (Kinzo 1988). Most interesting, these groups espoused different views of municipal politics.

During the military regime, mayoral elections were the only direct executive elections, with the exception of state capitals and cities with hydro and mineral resources where governors appointed mayors. In the mid- to late 1970s, the MDB began to focus on municipal elections in hopes that victories in this sphere would strengthen the party and spur the democratization process. According to MDB president Ulysses Guimarães, these were the only elections with "representative authenticity" and offered a chance to reform the political system "from the bottom up" ("MDB quer reforma através do município," 1974). This broad vision presented by Guimarães comprised distinct views on the role of municipal politics.

Pragmatics created efficient "electoral machines" in the states of São Paulo and Rio de Janeiro. In the former, Orestes Quércia, the ambitious mayor of the city of Campinas (1969–1973) organized an encompassing web of more than two hundred municipal party chapters. "Quércia took advantage of local dissensions within the ARENA, thus managing to attract dissident elements from this party in order to create the MDB in town. Thus, most of these local branches merely reflected local disputes and had little to do with opposition attitudes towards national politics" (Kinzo 1988, 34).

His administration focused on modernization and economic development ("A tese de Campinas no Congresso de Itanhaem," 1973). On the three-year anniversary of his administration, a half-page advertisement in an important newspaper celebrated the accomplishments of "Quércia's Planned Administration": "We managed to bring together all of the city's problems into one City Master Plan. The precise fulfillment of all planned tasks led to numerous grandiose public works, which solves today's problems and leaves the city ready for the year 2000" ("Campinas Cidade Planejada para o ano 2000," 1972). Visible infrastructure projects were the most marked characteristic of Quércia's governments. The shrewd politician became senator in 1974 and state governor in 1987; in the latter post he became known for building highways.

In 1974, the MDB also elected twenty federal deputies supported by Rio de Janeiro Governor Chagas Freitas (Kinzo 1988). Freitas was an established conservative politician who supported the military coup but joined the MDB when he realized his state's ARENA was controlled by one of his rivals. Freitas led a large clientelist network entrenched in the state bureaucracy; in Rio de Janeiro, *chagismo* (derived from Chagas) became synonymous with clientelism. Freitas used his network to gain the MDB majority in the state assembly and became the only MDB indirectly elected governor of the time. This position allowed him "to consolidate an 'electoral-party machine' that largely depended on access to the state public administration as well as a receptive dialogue with the military" (Melhem 1998, 95). Freitas was later replaced by other traditional politicians from the MDB moderate caucus (Melhem 1998).

In contrast with these pragmatic and clientelist strategies, *autênticos* advocated a participatory approach to municipal government. Though present in various states, *autênticos* of Rio Grande do Sul and

Pernambuco were particularly recognized for their activism (Melhem 1998). The weakening of the party in the early 1970s was marked by national seminars organized in the capitals of these states, Porto Alegre and Recife. Final reports of these seminars included daring statements against the regime; the "Letter of Recife" even called for a new constituent assembly—an intrepid act frowned on by the party's leadership ("MDB quer assembléia constituinte," 1971). The party's first think tank was founded in Porto Alegre in 1973. The Institute for Political, Economic and Social Studies (Instituto de Estudos Políticos, Econômicos e Sociais, IEPES) organized seminars and debates with students, intellectuals, and party members, and published a series of documents and studies.

In 1976, the IEPES published a sixty-one-page booklet titled "Political Formation Course for Mayors and Municipal Representatives." The second chapter, authored by Senator André Franco Montoro, discussed the theoretical foundations of participatory democracy, which was defined as a "model of democratic organization funded not only in popular 'representation' but also in organized and active 'participation' of social groups in matters of their interest" (Instituto de Estudos Políticos 1976, 18). Montoro argued that instruments of participatory democracy could be created at the local level, in the work sphere, the educational system, the structure of political parties, and in professional and consumer co-ops. He concluded calling paternalist "all assistance plans carried out without the cooperation of their beneficiaries" (28).

In 1976, the MDB prepared two booklets containing the party's electoral strategies and political program for municipal government. The original idea was to have only one booklet, but the moderate leadership edited out the sections on direct popular participation included by *neo-autênticos*, who in response wrote and distributed a second booklet (Braga 1976). The booklet approved by the party leadership, issued in São Paulo, only made one mention of participation. Quoting principles approved in a national convention in that same year, the document discussed the "right to participation." "It is not sufficient to recognize community members' right to receive social benefits. In order to recognize an individual's personal dignity, it is necessary to recognize and ensure his right to actively participate in the solution of problems that affect him. Therefore, the substitution of 'paternalism' by 'participation' is an imperative of modern social policy" (Movimento Democrático Brasileiro

1976a, 1). Although unambiguously supportive of popular participation, this document was reticent on the subject in comparison to the second pamphlet.

The party directory of Pernambuco published the second pamphlet titled "A Municipal Government of the Opposition," which was conceived as an "instrument for the construction of a popular municipal administration" (Movimento Democrático Brasileiro 1976b, 1). After a long list of criticisms of the regime, the document set three goals for a government of opposition: to defend the cause of municipalities vis-à-vis state and national governments; to establish an efficient administrative structure; and "to strengthen the various forms of popular participation in [municipal] administration" (15). In discussing these goals in detail, the authors argued public spending should focus on attending to the basic needs of the population in deprived neighborhoods and rural areas, and not "in façade sumptuous public works and road projects" (18). Moreover, the document raised the question, "What must be done in order to have the population begin to decide about the social priorities to be taken into account in municipal budgets and programs, the utilization of urban areas, [and the management of] transport, housing, and health?" (21).

The proposed answer was, "It is necessary that all democrats and everyone who wishes to participate in the struggle for a DEMOCRACY WITH POPULAR PARTICIPATION help to strengthen base community organizations, such as party neighborhood chapters, neighborhood associations, football clubs, samba clubs, religious associations, urban and rural unions, etc." (23, emphasis in the original). The next section of the document added, "An administration fundamentally oriented toward [underprivileged] neighborhoods and rural areas . . . must mobilize its population for the most varied forms of participation. These forms of participation may vary from the organization of meetings, debates, and conferences about the city's problems to the direct involvement in the most varied tasks of municipal agencies" (24–25). The document emphasized the importance of the party city and neighborhood chapters. Contrary to clientelist approaches, in this view local chapters were not meant to serve as the main intermediaries between citizens and the government. "The population must learn how to use community organizations to pressure local and municipal administrations to carry out public works that satisfy their necessities. The main functions of city and neighborhood chapters must be to stimulate and promote this type of participation" (24). In the view of *autênticos*, a municipal government of the opposition had to create channels for participation and help communities to organize in order to take advantage of them.

The MDB also relied on *autêntico* militants in São Paulo. In this state, intellectuals associated with the CEBRAP collaborated with the MDB and regularly contributed to the political magazines *Opinião* and *Movimento*. In the months preceding the 1976 municipal elections, these magazines published numerous articles advocating for local-level participatory democracy and showing support for the combative arm of the MDB. In July and August, *Opinião* published pieces by intellectuals Braz José de Araujo and José Álvaro Moisés; whereas Araujo drew on political science classics in order to argue for the importance of local level democracy, Moisés reviewed some episodes of Brazilian political history warning against the risk of elites using old political practices to co-op emerging social movements into clientelist networks (Araujo 1976; Moisés 1976).

In September, *Opinião* published a large article, "MDB and the Local Question." The piece presented a summary of debates and works produced by the IEPES. The first part reproduced sections of the training course booklet discussed above. The second part discussed two models for organizing participation in municipal governments that fundamentally altered the structure of representative institutions. In the first model, city councilors would be replaced by ward delegates; each neighborhood would have a directory, whose leaders would form a political council that would decide on the agenda the ward delegate had to defend at the city hall. Thus, instead of a mandate to represent a constituency, delegates, as the term implies, would defend a pre-determined agenda. The second proposal regarded the creation of Municipal Councils that would count on the participation of mayors and their secretariats, city councilors, representative of the city staff, and the leaders of the main community associations. The proposal acknowledged that councils would have a de jure consultative role but suggested that MDB mayors should make them de facto decision-making bodies. In this proposal, community leaders were granted a role equivalent to that of elected officials, visibly disempowering the latter. It was recognized that these were hard goals to achieve; against them "stand not only the country's current institutional framework, but also decades of conventional political tradition." The piece ends with a call for those on the side of democracy to start participatory initiatives ("O MDB e a Questão Local," 1976).

In an editorial piece ten days before the election, *Opinião* discussed the history of municipal governments from the colonial period to the present day and concluded that the satisfaction of the aspirations of the popular classes depended "much more on the opening of channels of participation in decision making processes at the local municipal level, as well as the central government, than any possible alteration in formal institutional models" ("O município da oligarquia a nossos dias," 1976). The issue printed three days before the election brought three pages of denunciations of the way ARENA and MDB moderates conducted campaigns. The MDB leadership was accused of "reproducing the tradition of *politicagem* [politicking] that characterized [the country's] institutional life before 1964, with all its authoritarian and paternalist components" ("MDB Projeto e Campanha," 1976).

The magazine *Movimento* also spurred debate about local-level participatory democracy. In June and September of 1976, the magazine published summaries of IEPES texts discussing the Municipal Council proposal described above ("MDB. O que fazer nas prefeituras?" 1976; "O MDB e as Prefeituras" 1976). Another article in the same month endorsed the candidacy of an *autêntico* who promised to allow communities to decide the priority of public works in their neighborhoods ("Em defesa dos interesses populares" 1976). Yet another piece described the MDB administration in the city of Americana, which had already created forty community committees. According to the mayor of the city, "We get together with [these committees] and try to hear their suggestions. 'What do you want first? Water, sewage, playground, or football field?' They answer, and then we decide what do to" ("O Poder do MDB" 1976).

On election day, the cover of *Movimento* read, "After Elections. The MDB Strategy: Participation in the Cities." The central article discussed the fact that from 1822 to 1930 municipal autonomy was coupled with the political power of landed oligarchies to the detriment of the popular classes. The Vargas government centralized power at the federal level, and soon after the country witnessed the emergence of a movement for municipal autonomy. This movement, according to the article, was different in that it did not represent the interests of the oligarchies but the interest of the emerging popular sector. The military regime centralized power even further and almost completely eliminated municipal autonomy. The piece concluded that MDB mayors should come together to demand democratization and municipal autonomy while starting to open channels for popular participation in their own cities ("A participação popular e a autonomia dos municípios" 1976).

In the weeks following the municipal election, MDB politicians promised to follow through with the participatory project. The elected mayor of Feira de Santana, Bahia, relied on the campaigning efforts of 155 neighborhood committees organized by *autêntico* militants; he now promised that these committees would decide the city's spending priorities ("Governo com as bases em Feira de Santana" 1976). The twenty-four-year-old Geraldo Alckmin, elected mayor of Pindamonhangaba, São Paulo, planned to govern the city in collaboration with varied types of civil associations "in order to take advantage of the benefits of what is called participatory democracy." According to the young mayor, a municipal council was still a far-fetched dream, but there were small steps that could be taken in that direction ("Pindamonhangaba" 1976). In the city of Piracicaba, São Paulo, Herrmann Netto described his election as "a popular victory, not a populist one—a victory of the working-class neighborhoods" ("76 votos dão vitória ao MDB em Piracicaba" 1976). He became responsible for one of the best-known participatory administrations of the MDB, which included attempts to create a municipal council (DelPicchia 1982). Chapter 3 examines the model *autêntico* municipal administration: the city of Lages.

ECCLESIAL BASE COMMUNITIES

The ecclesial base communities (CEBs) organized by the Catholic Church under the influence of the Second Vatican Council and Liberation Theology played a crucial role in the emergence of participatory democracy in Brazil. CEBs encouraged citizens to participate in local politics and helped to delegitimize patron-client relations, clientelist networks, and populist politicians. CEBs also created community organizational structures that facilitated political mobilization. This section starts with a brief review of the Catholic Church's "preferential option for the poor," a topic already extensively explored in the literature, and then discusses the format of CEBs and the magnitude of the phenomenon in Brazil. Next, attention is paid to the type of political participation encouraged in these communities; this is done through an analysis of interclergy correspondence and pedagogical material used by CEBs.

For most of its history, the Catholic Church in Brazil sided with political elites, although never exerting over them as much influence as it did in other Latin American countries. From 1920 to 1950, the Brazilian Church followed the neo-Christendom doctrine that focused on the dissemination of Catholic values in the social sphere of degraded modern societies. In this period, the Church organized numerous movements tasked with promoting Catholic values and thwarting the spread of communist ideals. The main objective was to regain political influence by expanding its role in social institutions. The Church supported Vargas's dictatorial corporatist approach and in return received important concessions in the media and education fields. By the early 1950s, Vargas's power was fading away, communism remained a threat, urbanization was diffusing secular values, and Protestantism and Spiritism were on the rise (Mainwaring 1986).

In 1958, the Vatican under the leadership of Pope John XXIII initiated institutional changes that offered the Brazilian Church an alternative. In 1962, the Second Vatican Council established a new doctrine that "emphasized the Church's social mission, affirmed the importance of the laity in the Church, encouraged greater co-responsibility within the Church, developed the notion of the Church as the people of God, called for ecumenical dialogue, changed the liturgy to make it more accessible, and introduced a host of other changes" (Mainwaring 1986, 43). One of the fundamental changes brought by the Second Vatican was the encouragement of more interactions between the clergy and the people, replacing what were typically rigid hierarchical relationships, especially in Latin America (Mainwaring 1986).

In the 1950s, Brazil witnessed the emergence of new social groups and increasing demands for political inclusion. The Brazilian Catholic Church was part of this process. Krischke (2010) explained that in this period the Church became fairly autonomous from the state and civil society, and its political actions can neither be seen as the immediate expression of class interests nor as the unrelenting steps of an isolated institution. Instead, the Church was embedded in a political dialectal process, where it generated and propagated ideas that influenced the polity but also absorbed and reacted to external ideological currents. The National Conference of Brazilian Bishops (Conferência Nacional dos Bispos do Brasil, CNBB), created in 1952, became the steering body of the Brazilian Church and served as an umbrella for a variety of Catholic groups and movements.[1]

In the early 1960s, with the radical polarization of politics, groups within the CNBB and Catholic movements took different sides. In 1964, conservative bishops supported the military coup, some members of youth groups joined Marxist guerrillas, and the majority of bishops and Catholic groups chose a position in between these two extremes (Krischke 2010). The military regime subdued the more politicized Catholic movements, and in the years following the coup conservative bishops led the CNBB. In 1968, Latin American bishops met at the Episcopal Conference of Medellin and committed to putting into practice the mandates of the Second Vatican Council. Repression escalated in 1969 after the enactment of the AI-5. The Church finally took an unambiguous stand against the regime and started to denounce human rights abuses; progressive bishops regained the leadership of the CNBB and began to promote the formation of CEBs (Sader 1988).

An earlier, less known, but very significant CNBB initiative was the Movimento de Educação de Base (MEB, Base Education Movement), whose official mission was to combat illiteracy in the north, northeast, and center regions of the country. Created in 1961, the MEB was a partnership between the CNBB and the federal government, both interested in increasing their influence vis-à-vis the growing communist groups. However, from the beginning there was a consensus that a holistic approach to education would be adopted and courses would not simply focus on formal literacy. Beginning in 1963, the MEB adopted Paulo Freire's methodology, which focused on the empowerment of oppressed groups. As a result, students learned not only how to read and write but also why they had been kept illiterate for so long. The latter aspect, conscientização, became the core of the MEB's efforts, as teachers were increasingly recruited from radical youth church groups. Following the military coup, the MEB was slowly dismantled and eventually replaced by another initiative more in line with the government's ideology. By

the end of the decade, a portion of MEB militants began to aid in organizing CEBs, which also devoted much attention to *conscientização*
(Dawson 2002).

The CEBs were a pastoral effort to reach, proselytize, and assist the
poor. They have been defined as "small, freely forming associations of
ordinary Catholics, who meet on a regular basis to deepen their knowledge of the Gospel, to reflect on community needs and seek adequate
solution to those needs, to celebrate victories and share defeats together
in the Eucharist, and to spread the Word of God" (Hewitt 1986, 17). The
devotional activities of CEBs included Bible study circles and charity
work. Gatherings called *celebrações* (celebrations) were a type of informal mass led by lay leaders and involved social fraternization. Craft skills
workshops and literacy courses were some of the more practical activities organized by CEBs. Literacy programs used Paulo Freire's method of
popular education, wherein teachers were meant to facilitate the exchange
of experience-based knowledge existent in any group of individuals.
Activities guided toward *conscientização*, "consist of somewhat more
in-depth discussion and debate regarding the reality of social, economic
and political oppression . . . conducted with direct reference to Scripture
or . . . to specially prepared pedagogical material" (Hewitt 1991, 43). The
CEBs organized two types of community actions: joint-labor projects
called *mutirões*, which involved the creation of various types of cooperatives and the construction of houses, schools, or parochial houses; and
the coordination of *reivindicacões*, the act of collectively demanding a
social service or public work (Hewitt 1991).

Not all CEBs carried out all types of activities, and even when they
did, not all members participated in everything. Drawing on empirical
work with groups in São Paulo, Hewitt (1991, 47) created five ideal types
of CEBs according to their emphasis on devotional and political work;
type one is "simple devotional groups," whereas type five is "politically
oriented." In a 1984 sample of twenty-two CEBs, 50 percent had Bible
study circles, 86 percent organized reflection and discussion groups, and
45 percent carried out community actions (Hewitt 1991, 45). In a sample
of 275 members of these twenty-two CEBs, 18 percent never participated in Bible studies, and 49 percent never joined consciousness-raising
activities (48). Half of Hewitt's sample was located in low-income neighborhoods and the other half was in more affluent middle-class areas.

Although limited to twenty-two CEBs in one city, this is the most complete study of its kind and illustrates the diversity of these groups.

The informal character and diversity of these groups make it difficult to estimate the number of CEBs there were in Brazil in the 1970s. Groups in remote rural areas were unlikely to appear in official reports; and if they did, the question is how to differentiate between CEBs and groups of Catholics who gather informally to worship. Moreover, any estimate of CEBs must be multiplied by an estimate of the number of members per CEB in order to arrive at a rough number of how many individuals participated in these groups. In 1974, the Church's statistic center estimated that there were forty thousand CEBs in Brazil. In 1980, the same center updated the estimate to eighty thousand groups (Hewitt 1991, 17). In 1981, Friar Betto, one of the main promoters of the popular Church, in a short and widely distributed book on the basics of CEBs, multiplied those figures by an average of twenty to thirty individuals per group, and suggested that at least two million Brazilians participated in CEBs (Betto 1981, 17). Thereafter, this estimate appeared in numerous other publications. A later study indicates that Friar Betto was not completely off the mark. In 1994, the Datafolha Institute carried a survey on voting behavior according to religious affiliation in which 1.8 percent of the representative sample was categorized as CEB members (Pierucci and Prandy 1996, 216). In the 1991 census, 1.8 percent of the population constituted 2.64 million inhabitants; in the 1980 census, 1.8 percent of the population represented 2.14 million inhabitants (Instituto Brasileiro de Geografia e Estatística 1997).

In 1994, research pointed to the existence of approximately one hundred thousand ecclesiastical communities out of which 39 percent can be categorized as what Hewitt called "simple devotional groups" without any participation in social or political movements, whereas 42 percent participated in movements and struggles for improved living conditions (Valle and Pitta 1994, 59–60). The authors warned against dividing ecclesiastical communities between political and devotional groups. The study found that the frequency of masses was positively correlated with the organization of community actions, which suggested that the divide was between active and inactive communities. This study also pointed out that two-thirds of CEBs were in rural areas, 17 percent in urban peripheries, and only 12 percent in cities (49). The prevalence of CEBs in rural areas was common wisdom, showed in early studies (Demo and Calsing 1977, 20), but challenged by Hewitt (1991). Recent studies considered the early 1980s the peak of CEBs (Burdick 2004; Lesbaupin 1997; Levy 2000); in this case, 1990s statistics are likely to be an underestimation of the phenomenon in the late 1970s and early 1980s.

Notwithstanding the impossibility of arriving at a precise number of CEB members, the significant magnitude of the phenomenon is undeniable. For comparative purposes, 3,104 civic associations were created in São Paulo and Rio de Janeiro in the 1970s, a large increase from the previous decade (Santos 1994) and yet only a fraction of the estimated number of CEBs in the country in that period. The well-known Porto Alegre participatory budgeting engaged approximately 1.3 percent of the city's urban population in its peak year, which helps to gauge the magnitude of the 1.8 percent figure (Fedozzi 2007, 23). The CEBs constituted a civil society organizational structure hitherto unseen in the country.

Specific forms of political participation were advocated at CEBs. In the 1970s and 1980s, participation was discussed at three levels within the Church. At a conceptual level, participation was an integral part of a body of literature known as Liberation Theology. With more practical purposes in mind, bishops and clergymen discussed how to support political participation in their dioceses and parishes. At the local level, CEB leaders educated community members about the importance of being politically active. Although debates at these three levels were largely concomitant and often intertwined, they were only loosely connected. Liberation theologians argue that CEBs epitomized the type of church they espoused, and CEB leaders often incorporated notions from Liberation theologians in their teachings, but not every CEB leader was an adept of Liberation Theology and not every Liberation theologian was directly involved with CEBs. Likewise, not all CNBB bishops who welcomed the directives of the Second Vatican Council directly engaged with Liberation Theology. The Brazilian Catholic Church in this period is best described as a permissive institutional context that allowed for innovative thinking and practices that developed side-by-side in a mutually reinforcing manner.

Following the Second Vatican Council and the Episcopal Conference of Medellín, a group of Latin American theologians began to write texts articulating a new vision for the Catholic Church. At the core of this new

vision was the idea that the poor were being exploited by an unjust economic and political system and that it was the role of the Church to support their liberation from oppressive structures. This literature became
known as Liberation Theology. Some of its main exponents included
Peruvian Gustavo Gutierrez and Brazilian Leonardo Boff. The idea that
an unjust political economic system barred poor people from improving their lives and that collective action was the necessary response
brought these theorists close to Marxism. Nevertheless, Liberation theologians most often avoided using the concept of class and preferred a less
provocative term, "the poor." Though theologians acknowledged that at
times the Church had served the status quo, they refused to see it as the
"opium of the masses," and insisted instead on the liberating role it could
play (Camurça 2007).

Liberation theologians were prolific in the 1970s and 1980s. In
Brazil, the religious press Editora Vozes was the publisher of most of
their books and the journals *Tempo e Presença* and *Revista Eclesiástica
Brasileira*, the main specialized journals. Articles, books, and conference proceedings usually had as their central theme the discussion of
the objectives and characteristics of the new church, referred to as the
"church of the people" or the "grassroots church." CEBs were the most
concrete realization of this vision; they represented a break with old
hierarchical relations and the typical neglect of social injustices. CEBs
symbolized the Church going to the poor to serve them. Therefore,
Liberation theologians' writings about the CEBs were the exposition of a
project, a vision for a new church.

In a 1980 conference on base communities, Boff made a presentation later published as the "Theological Characteristics of a Grassroots
Church." The following passages illustrate how his view of the struggle for
a more just society began with the construction of a new church.

> The great virtues of the Catholic saint are obedience, ecclesiastical
> submissiveness, humility, and total reference to the church. . . . The
> prophets and reformers, the people who criticize the existing power
> relations in the church and call for mobilization, are subjected to all
> sorts of symbolic violence. . . . There is a contradiction between an
> unsymmetrically structured ecclesiastical religious sphere on the
> one hand and the figure and message of Christ and the apostles on

the other. The religious interest of the grassroots level is to make its own quest for liberation self-legitimizing. It seeks to delegitimize and denaturalize the domination under which it is suffering. The ecclesiastical sphere can offer this legitimation. . . . It may do so because it understands the righteousness of their struggle, or because it sees their struggle to be in conformity with the ideas and ideals of the gospel message.

These grassroots communities signify a break with the old monopoly of social and religious power, and the inauguration of a new social and religious process involving the restructuring of the church and society. (Boff 1980, 131–34)

Boff and other Liberation theologians saw the process of liberation within the Church and in society as intrinsically related and mutually reinforcing and CEBs as the main driver of this process.

More practical debates about the organization and promotion of CEBs are found in documents circulated among bishops and clergymen. The twenty-eight documents found in the archival research for this study offer valuable insights into the goals and concerns at this level of the church structure. The oldest of these papers is the outcome declaration of a 1969 conference on the organization of CEBs. The six-page document offered a detailed explanation of how CEBs are the continuation of the Church and a form of renovating it, followed by specific instructions of how to create a CEB and what types of activities to organize. At the end of the document, there was an example of a community structure: "12 families form a base community, 20 CEBs form a Community Center, and 15 Community Centers form a Communitarian Center" (Seminário Central do Ipiranga 1969, April 30, 5). This conference was likely one of the first efforts to begin to actively promote CEBs.

Some of these documents were written as chronicles of regional clusters of the CNBB to their brothers elsewhere, usually signed by a bishop or archbishop. They offered descriptions of efforts to organize CEBs, which usually began with approaching the most active members of the parish and encouraging them to become *animadores* (community organizers). According to these accounts, communities started as Bible study groups and only some evolved into active CEBs. The "poor" of each letter varied according to the socioeconomic characteristics of the region. A letter from the state of Goiás talked about a CEB of rural workers (Bispos do Centro Oeste 1973), a bishop visiting the state of Acre reported on the local Church's incipient political work with indigenous groups (Christo 1977), and a document issued in the state capital of Santa Catarina talked about rural exodus and growing shantytowns (CNBB Regional Sul 4 1981).

The final reports of meetings of the permanent council of the CNBB in 1981 and 1982 demonstrate the Church's concern with promoting political participation without becoming involved in party politics or reducing CEBs to social movements. This was a dominant debate during the democratization period. The 1981 letter explained, "although the Church is not involved in party politics, it has the political task of showing the important values of organization within a society" (CNBB 1981, 2). A definition of democracy is offered later in the document, "true democracy is a process that improves the living conditions of the people and allows their *full participation in public decision-making*" (3, emphasis mine). The 1982 document focused on the relationship between CEBs and social movements; it argued that CEBs must focus on their broad objective of supporting various types of social and political organization (CNBB 1982).

Theological arguments and intraclergy discussions were adapted to accessible booklets and pamphlets used by lay leaders in CEB meetings. Archival research for this book included the collection and analysis of 136 of these booklets from eighteen states and fifty-eight cities, printed between 1973 and 1993. Eleven do not have information about location; two-thirds were issued before 1984; and twenty-three do not have the year of publication. Few were professionally printed; most are photocopies of handmade and handwritten originals. Three features confirm that these booklets were used as education material: the use of simple language and illustrations (some are in the format of a comic strip); the first pages bring instructions of "how to use this booklet in your community"; and the last pages present "questions to debate with your group." The most common themes are political participation, equality (bosses versus workers, men versus women, clergy versus followers), the history of political exclusion in Brazil, the difference between principled politics and politicking, and the importance of the vote and reasons for not selling it.

In 1977, the Diocese of São Mateus, which encompassed the town of Boa Esperança, published as a booklet a popular version of the outcome document of a CNBB conference in that same year, titled "Christian Demands of a Political Order." The first pages remind the reader that Jesus was a humble servant of the people. It then goes on to discuss the role of the state, the notion of common good, and the role of political participation. The following passage illustrates how religion, politics, and community organization are woven together in these brochures.

> It is important to live in community. An isolated and lonely person is unhappy. The youth always organize strolls, football games, meetings, and dances. In the chapel, Christians come together to pray and worship the Lord. In labor unions, workers unite to struggle for their rights. . . . In chapter six of the Gospel of Saint Mark, which talks about the multiplication of bread, Jesus asks the people to organize in groups. This shows how important it is for the people and for every person to organize. If workers form a large union, they will have more strength to demand their rights. A Gospel group that reflects and debates is more likely to solve community problems. . . . When people partake in these groups, they are in a way trying to organize society. This is a form of political action. (Diocese de São Mateus 1977, 9–10)

In the same booklet, a chapter is devoted to participation. Government actions that prevented political participation were listed, and the following lessons were drawn:

> The government makes us lose the habit, interest, and wish to participate. It makes participation look like it is not important. We end up paying attention only to soap operas, football, and lottery. We discuss only unimportant things. As a result, we don't learn to have an opinion about things. The government decides everything without taking our interests into consideration. And so we cannot contribute to the construction of the common good. We see things that are wrong, but we can't do anything about them. People who remain outside of things, outside of politics, are depoliticized, and alienated. There is a lack of political formation. The Church has the right and the duty to collaborate in the political formation of the people, so that they can truly participate in the construction of a more just and fair nation. (24)

This chapter on participation ends offering two questions for group debate. "How can we have political participation? Why do workers spend their lives constructing buildings but never manage to have a house?" (24).

A booklet published in 1981 by the diocese of Juazeiro, Bahia, summarizes the history of political exclusion in the Brazil from colonial times to the date of publication. The First Republic is characterized in the following way:

> The people can already vote. But, how? "Encabrestado" [haltered like an animal]. The participation of the People in politics depends on the CORONÉIS of the interior, who get to choose the candidates in which the People must vote. The People vote in exchange for favor. . . . The Republic does not care about the interests of small farmers. (Diocese de Juazeiro 1981, 22, emphasis in the original)

Concerning the Vargas era, the booklet tells that "the People were cheated on by POPULISMO, which is a government based on beautiful speeches and promises about social reforms that never come about" (24). At the end, the booklet reminds readers that politics with a "P" is a struggle for the common good and concerns everyone; party politics is simply politics with a "p." Elections are a predominant theme in this sample of education material. In 1982, the year of a municipal election, a group in Piracicaba, São Paulo, published five booklets on the topic. The core message was to choose candidates carefully and refrain from exchanging votes for favors or gifts. The fifth issue of the series emphasized that "elections are neither the beginning nor the end but only a moment in the democratic process. The continuation [of the process] depends on us. If you don't water a little plant, will it grow?" The questions offered for debate were "What are the forms of political participation in your neighborhood, at work, at school, others?" (Equipe Caderno Debate 1982).

The theme of different types of politics is also discussed in a 1982 handwritten booklet issued in the state of Mato Grosso, which includes a table distinguishing *política* (politics) and *politicagem* (politicking). The former is defined as "to work in favor of the community and the search for the good of all," whereas the latter is, "to deceive the people, buy votes, make fake promises, and embezzle public money" (CNBB Regional Extremo Oeste 1982, 5). This volume also describes the "rights and duties of people in a democracy: (1) to elect leaders and representatives, (2) to inspect the activities of elected politics, and (3) to participate in the execution [of public projects]" (19). To inspect the activities meant organizing to debate the needs of the community and to then attempt to influence decision-making. To participate in the execution involved safeguarding public property and partaking in self-construction projects. The idea that political participation involved engagement in communal projects is often found in this material. For example, a 1981 issue printed in Ji-Paraná, Rondônia, promoted the idea of creating small farmer cooperatives to purchase inputs and food for a better price and sell their produce without intermediaries (Ji-Paraná 1982).

The participatory administration of Boa Esperança had as its main goal to create favorable economic conditions for small farmers. In this small town of the State of Espírito Santo, the organizational structure of CEBs became the structure of the participatory initiative, and lay leaders within these communities became the delegates to the city's community development council. Moreover, most of the city staff heading the project were politically trained at the CEBs. The prominence of CEBs in the region was due to in part to an active young bishop trained under the Second Vatican Council and influenced by Liberation Theology.

THE NEW UNIONISM MOVEMENT

The new unionism movement played a very significant role in fostering a participatory ideology in Brazil. This movement started in the early 1970s, in the industrial periphery of São Paulo, with a group of metalworkers who refused to accept the limits imposed on union activities by the corporatist framework established in the 1940s. They demanded a democratic, bottom-up union structure that would allow factory floor workers to participate in negotiations. This vision spread beyond São Paulo and became a current within the national labor movement. In 1983, this movement succeeded in founding a national central labor union with the aspired democratic structure. Moreover, new unionism, together with the grassroots arm of the Catholic Church, was one of the foundational blocks of the PT, which became an avid promoter of participatory democracy.

Brazilian unionism played an important role in the development of democratic ideals. From 1888 to 1930, numerous strikes and a few incipient labor organizations in Rio de Janeiro and São Paulo marked the beginning of the Brazilian labor movement. Initially fuelled by anarchist immigrants, the movement was engulfed by the PCB in the 1920s. In 1930, the Liberal Alliance rose to power without the support of communists or labor movements, and therefore felt free to crash strikes and begin an incorporation project aimed at creating "a legalized and institutionalized labor movement that was depoliticized, controlled, and penetrated by the state" (Collier and Collier 1991, 163). In the first years of the Vargas era, the newly created Ministry of Labor crafted an institutional framework that dismantled politically oriented unions. During his authoritarian period (1937–1945), Vargas erected "the most full-blown system of corporatism in Latin America," wherein economic policies were highly centralized and the labor movement subjected to strict controls (Collier and Collier 1991, 186).

The 1942 labor code known as Consolidated Labor Laws (CLT) created an organizational structure that allowed only one union per sector per geographical area, usually municipalities. All workers paid an obligatory syndical tax. Membership was not mandatory but advantageous, since it allowed access to social services. Federations grouped unions of the same sector in a larger geographic area, usually states. A confederation grouped all federations of a sector. There could be no unions outside this structure, no links between unions of different sectors, and no communication between unions in the same sector other than through the institutional hierarchy. Rural workers' unions were proscribed. The Ministry of Labor controlled unions' financial activity through mandatory reports and had the authority to declare strikes illegal. Moreover, "the state was given the right to 'intervene' in unions, that is, to seize its headquarters, take charge of its funds, and install a new leadership" (Collier and Collier 1991, 187). The Ministry also controlled union leadership. At the local level, the Ministry chose the directories responsible for electing union officers. At the federations, each union had one vote, regardless of its size, which made it easier to sideline rebellious movements in larger unions. The same was true for confederations. Finally, union leaders were required to make an "ideological oath" in which they swore not to subscribe to ideologies incompatible with the interests of the nation. The oath served as grounds to removing any objectionable leader (Collier and Collier 1991).

In the 1945–1964 period, the CLT was not legally abolished but overlooked as populist leaders tried to gain the support of increasingly more autonomous unions. During this period, the PSD and the Brazilian Labor Party (PTB) governed the country. According to Schmitter (1971), in an initial phase, "the permanence of the PTB, with its unofficial hold on the Labor Ministry, as a partner in the ruling coalition, meant a continuation of the past policies of preemptive cooptation and paternalism" (130). This relationship changed beginning in 1952, with the Ministry becoming increasingly more responsive to workers' demands. Communist groups played an important role in the strengthening of the labor unions. From 1945 to 1947, the PCB performed well in the legislative elections and gained influence in the labor movement, where it advocated for more union autonomy. Despite the party's moderate rhetoric, its advances became wearisome for the federal government, who banned the party in 1947 (Skidmore 1967). Illegal and under the influence of an international doctrine that argued that the development of democratic capitalism was a step toward a socialist revolution, the PCB opted for infiltrating formal politics in order to influence the country's development and regain its legality. The PCB gained control over numerous unions and was capable of influencing the vote of workers in favor of allies in legal parties, usually the PTB. Some criticized the party for validating and profiting from the bureaucratic apparatus controlling unions (Garcia 1986).

In the mid-1950s, the PCB split over party doctrines, and dissident groups focused on a new type of work with the labor movement. "They were particularly concerned with promoting union autonomy from government and the revitalization of grassroots participation within unions" (Collier and Collier 1991, 549). Marxist groups to the left of the PCB also began to promote mass-based unionism. In reaction, a group of right-wing *pelegos* organized an anticommunist union movement. In the early 1960s, the labor movement was divided between the leftists in the PCB and the PTB willing to work within the system, radical reformers, and *pelegos*. Most of the members of the first two groups joined the new national organization called General Workers Command (Comando Geral dos Trabalhadores, CGT), which played a major role in the political polarization that led to the military coup.

In 1964, the military revived the corporatist union apparatus and repressed leftist leaders. In the first two years of the regime, the Ministry of Labor replaced the heads of 382 unions, forty-five federations, and four confederations. In the first five years of the regime, 108 union leaders and deputies representing the labor movement had mandates revoked and political rights suspended. A law passed in 1965 mandated that annual wage increases were to be determined by an index published by the Ministry of Labor; this regulation preempted wage disputes, the main task of unions. After two years of intense repression, the regime allowed union activity to resume but then violently crushed strikes in 1968, which led to years of inactivity in the labor movement (Almeida 1983).

In 1973, a new labor movement rekindled in São Paulo; at first it was called *authentic unionism*, but later it became known as *new unionism*. From 1940 to 1970, the percentage of unionized workers increased only from 8 percent to 13 percent; however, in absolute terms, urban unionized workers increased 3.5 times from 1960 to 1978 (Almeida 1983, 193–94). Whereas in the period of 1930–1960 unions represented mainly workers in state-owned services and primary industries, in the 1970s "heavy industry workers—auto, metal, mechanic, steel, and petrol—were the backbone of the syndical movement" (Almeida 1983, 196). These workers were highly concentrated in the São Paulo industrial belt called the ABCD region, comprised of the cities of Santo André, São Bernardo do Campo, São Caetano, and Diadema. For example, in 1978 the city of São Paulo had four hundred thousand metalworkers, while the small towns of the ABCD region had 205 thousand metalworkers, of which eighty thousand worked in the three auto factories in São Bernardo, the heart of the new labor movement (Moisés 1982, 15). The ABCD region workers were young and highly trained, with an above-average educational level; most had not participated in union activity in the pre-1964 period (Moisés 1982).

Besides these sociodemographic characteristics, the new unionism movement had new aspirations. Specific wage and working condition demands fuelled the groundbreaking strikes of the late 1970s.[2] However, organizational changes were a key concern for the new unionism. According to Moisés, a scholar with close connections with the movement,

The question of organization at the factory level is the main focus of labor groups such as the Oposição Sindical, which are primarily interested in strengthening the bases of the labor movement. In order to create an effective process of grass-roots mobilization, the leaders of the Oposição Sindical faction are trying to organize *comissões de fábrica* (factory commissions). . . . Since these commissions are not officially recognized by labor legislation, their leaders must rely on support or tolerance from labor unions and leaders that function within a structure which does little to stimulate those rank-and-file groups. (Moisés 1979, 59)

It is worth reminding that the CLT authorized only one union per sector per city, and therefore factory floor organization had never been legally allowed. In this context, the idea presented below by then president of the metalworkers union of São Bernardo and Diadema was rather radical. In 1979, when asked about the ideal union organizational structure, Luis Inácio "Lula" da Silva replied,

The way I see it is as follows: a company with, for example, 50 sections, should have 50 elected union delegates. This of course would be in a different union structure. This way you could have a union convention made up entirely of union delegates. . . . These delegates could choose the union leadership. They would be the guys who would be in daily contact with the workers, talking about their problems, and in all their statements they would be representing the workers of their section. You could have meetings with the delegates of a particular company to discuss the specific problems of that company, and once a month we could have a general meeting of the delegates to take a united position for the metalworkers as a whole. (quoted in Garcia and Harding 1979, 96)

Lula's view was representative of a faction within the São Bernardo metalworkers union. When he was elected union president in 1972, his election slate put forward a nine-point program that included advocacy for the creation of a bottom-up structure of representation, wherein each set number of workers would have the right to send a delegate to consultations (Almeida 1975, 75, n26). The outcome document of the III Congress of Workers in the Metal, Mechanic, and Electric Industries of São Bernardo and Diadema also identified the creation of a new union organizational structure as one of the main goals of workers' struggle ("Resoluções" 1978).

The new unionism of the ABCD region developed into an organized faction within the national labor movement known as Syndical Opposition (Oposição Sindical), the short form for "workers in opposition to the syndical structure." Members of this faction gathered in state and national congresses and promoted their ideas through numerous pamphlets and bulletins. In 1981, Syndical Opposition printed a booklet describing the experience of three unions that succeeded in organizations' factory commissions. The piece described the formation of these commissions discussed the achieved results and shortcomings and called on workers to promote the idea. "[Factory] commissions are the seed for a grass-roots, independent, and representative unionism," the booklet concluded (Oposição Sindical Metalúrgica 1981, 60).

The confrontational approach of Syndical Opposition clashed with the moderate reforms espoused by a heterogeneous faction of the national labor movement called Syndical Union (União Sindical). This faction included members of the PCB as well as conservative trade unionists. The unifying characteristic of this group was their willingness to work from within the existing institutional structure, where many of them held posts. In 1981, a massive collective of unions around the country culminated in the First National Conference of the Working Class (Conferência Nacional da Classe Trabalhadora), the largest union gathering ever organized in the country. The conference brought together 5,036 delegates, representing 1,091 unions from 23 out of 25 states (Central Única dos Trabalhadores 1984, 33). The event was organized in a democratic fashion with regular communication from organizers to individual unions, a set process for choosing delegates in local assemblies, and a clear voting system at the conference. The majority of delegates voted in favor of repeating the event in the following year and establishing a subgroup in charge of planning the central labor organization, which was to be called the Unified Workers' Central (Central Única dos Trabalhadores, CUT). In the following year, however, moderate unionists withdrew from both resolutions, proposing instead smaller gatherings with the representatives of the official confederations and federations, who would draft a proposal for the new organization (Central Única dos Trabalhadores 1984; Keck 1984).

Adherents of the new unionism harshly criticized the undemocratic attitude of moderates. A document that represents Syndical Opposition's view described the situation as follows,

> Bloc 1 [moderates] has a project for a CUT established within the current syndical structure, under the control of the confederations and federations. Bloc 2 [syndical opposition] has a project for a CUT grounded on workers base organizations, controlled by base organizations: unions, factory commissions, base delegates, etc. We defend a CUT built on the extensive participation of workers organized in their working places, unions, states, and at the national level. (Central Única dos Trabalhadores 1984, 65)

The Syndical Opposition went ahead with the original plan, held the congress, and founded CUT.

In 1979, the military abolished the two-party system. The new unionism movement and the CUT became the main pillars of a new workers' party. According to Keck (1992), "the idea of a workers' party was first launched officially as a resolution of the São Paulo State Metalworkers' Congress in Lins, São Paulo, in January 1979. The Lins resolution on party politics called for Brazilian workers to overcome their marginalization by uniting to form an internally democratic party" (67). The PT was founded in 1980, after a herculean effort to satisfy the requirements imposed by the party reform. The 1982 legislative and municipal elections were the party's first test. The outcome was very unfavorable: the PT elected eight federal deputies, ten state deputies, and two mayors (Meneguello 1989, 125). The mayoral victories were in a small town in the northern state of Maranhão and Diadema in the ABCD region. The new mayor of Diadema, Gílson Menezes, was a metalworker and leader of the new unionism movement who had been fired in strikes of the late 1970s. The PT of Diadema was composed of new unionists and Marxists, both supporting participation but in somewhat different ways.

THE PARTICIPATORY MOVEMENTS examined in this chapter started with a critique of the lack of representativeness of their institutional contexts and the development of proposals for how to create bottom-up organization structures that would allow the participation of ordinary members. It was also understood that the democratization of their institutions would help to pave the way for the democratization of society. In this process, movements took a clear stand against partial and controlled forms of participation and social relationships marked by hierarchy and authority. MDB *autênticos* advocated for a true opposition party and developed programs to govern cities in a participatory manner, breaking away from the clientelist practices other party factions adopted.

The reform of municipal administrations was seen as the first step in the reform of the political party system. Progressive clergy and Liberation theologians argued the Church had to reinvent itself and break with a past of neglect to social injustices. In this view, the CEBs represented "a new way of being Church," and would contribute to the construction of a more just society. The new unionism movement urged a break with institutional restraints on workers' organization, and struggled for a grassroots labor movement based on factory commissions. The call for the democratization of unions evolved into a unified workers' central and a workers' party.

The members of participatory movements often overlapped; factory workers were also the residents of a certain community, which was the constituency of a certain candidate. These movements were mutually reinforcing and often deliberately supported each other. Most notably, the Catholic Church played an important role helping to organize the labor movement. Catholic groups known as *pastorais* worked much like CEBs but were issue-based instead of being organized around local communities. The Workers' Pastoral (Pastoral Operária) led discussion groups just like the ones at CEBs; the education material was similar, but more focused on topics pertaining to the reality of factory workers. Furthermore, CEBs in the ABCD region supported strike efforts, for example, fundraising money and food to help workers who had strike days deducted from their salary. The higher echelons of the Church also supported the new unionism. In a telling episode in 1980, the military accused São Paulo Bishop Paulo Evaristo Arns of inciting the strikes of the ABCD region. The government claimed the Church did not support such unlawful demonstrations. Days later the CNBB issued a document endorsing the strikes (Moisés 1982). In another example, the bishop of São Bernardo was one of the speakers of the conference that founded the CUT. In his remarks, the bishop acknowledged that the Church had wronged workers in the past but stated that it was now on their side (Central Única dos Trabalhadores 1984).

In an initial phase, the MDB *autênticos* and the intellectuals associated with the group saw the new unionism movement as a fundamental advance toward democratization, while unionized workers found among *autênticos* the best candidates to represent their interests. As democratization advanced, some MDB members wanted their party to become the voice of social movements, whereas workers started to envision their own party. This break was mirrored in intellectual circles, where new groups began to form according to views on the autonomy of popular movements.

It is not possible to understand these participatory movements outside the context of the partial and controlled political incorporation of the 1930–1964 period and the closure of formal channels for political participation following the 1964 coup. The former weakened traditional elites and spurred the organization of new social groups, some of which were granted rights (e.g., urban workers) and others that had to mobilize to fight for rights (e.g., peasants). Though limited, these political incorporations opened the party system to outside contenders, making electoral processes more than simply elite arrangements. These partial gains in participation were taken away by the military in 1964. As a pendulum that comes back stronger after being thrown in the opposite direction, the movements that emerged in the 1970s were no longer content with having their interests and needs included in the political agenda: they demanded that ordinary citizens have the means to directly participate in decision-making processes.

CHAPTER THREE

MDB *Autênticos* in Lages

This chapter examines how MDB *autênticos* put their participatory ideals into practice in a land of *coronéis*. The case study of Lages brings together images of the traditional Brazilian hinterland ruled by *coronéis* and those of a rapidly growing city without adequate infrastructure. The socioeconomic formation of the city provided the ideal condition for a limited access order: very high levels of land concentration. The dominant elite coalition intermittently ran the city from 1889 to 1972. Intra-elite disputes pitched brothers, cousins, and in-laws against each other, with no interference from the outside. New roads and industrialization policies brought to the city investors who invested in new economic activities, which created jobs that attracted migrants, all of whom contributed to the fragmentation of the dominant elite coalition. Industrialists and organized labor were the first to challenge the existing elite arrangement. In the early 1970s, a populist politician capitalized on the weakness of the dominant coalition and became the first nonelite mayor of Lages. He aimed to build a clientelist party to replace traditional patron-client relations. His vice mayor, however, was an *autêntico* who created a mass radical party, won the succeeding election, and brought to his team people with experience in the MEB and other social movements. This team of young politicians, imbued with participatory ideals, launched several initiatives to include subordinate classes and their interests in public administration, including a form of participatory budgeting. The first three sections of this chapter examine the socioeconomic basis of the limited access order, its working, and the beginning of the transition toward a more open access order. The format and intent of these initiatives, their partial successes, and the opposition they faced are discussed in the three subsequent sections.

SOCIOECONOMIC FORMATION

The Portuguese crown's concern with defending the colony from Spanish invasion and the transit of cattle herds were the two main factors spurring the occupation of the southern state of Santa Catarina. The lines dividing Portuguese and Spanish colonies in South America were unclear and provoked disputes that lasted almost four hundred years. In the eighteenth century, the Portuguese crown tried to address the overpopulation of the islands of Azores and Madeira and the vulnerability of the uninhabited south of Brazil by moving people from the former to the latter. In 1756, the crown sponsored the migration of five thousand Portuguese families from those islands to Santa Catarina (Cunha 1982, 8). Efforts to colonize the region continued in the subsequent century with the settlement of Italians, Germans, Poles, and other Europeans.

The patterns of occupation and the economic activities of each part of the state led to distinct social formations. On the southeastern coast, the first settlers and the Portuguese families from Azores and Madeira engaged predominately in subsistence farming, fishing, and the manufacturing of basic products for internal consumption. The type of soil, the abundance of crustaceans, the isolation from economic centers, and Azoreans' tradition of family farming prevented the development of large-scale agriculture (Lago 1968). In the northeast, Blumenau and Joinville started to stand out as technologically advanced areas with primary industries (mate herb tea, sugar cane liquor, timber, textiles, leather) in the second half of the nineteenth century. Geography favored the early industrialization of these cities, located in a region known as the Itajaí Valley, close to Curitiba and São Paulo, with fluvial routes to the interior and an international port. German migrants in this region had experience with industrial activities and founded family industries, the best known being the Hering brothers' textile factory (Cunha 1982). In the end of nineteenth century, the republican movement thrived in this region; Blumenau was the political base of Hercílio Luz, one of the most important politicians of the First Republic.

The plateau of Santa Catarina had a distinct formation. The main city of the region, Lages, was founded in 1776 to defend the territory from Spanish invasions and to serve as a provision post along the route connecting the ranches of the south and the Sorocaba (São Paulo) livestock market serving the gold mining region (Peixer 2002). Cattle dealers and muleteers slowly occupied the settlement attracted by the possibility of owning land in a region with natural grazing fields and unclaimed salvage livestock. According to a respected local historian, "From its foundation until around 1920 . . . livestock was Lages' exclusive economic pillar. First as a resting stop for cattle dealers; then with the trading of horses, donkeys, and mules; after with the commerce of leather and dried beef; and finally, with the raising of livestock sold to slaughterhouses in Rio Grande do Sul and in the coast of Santa Catarina" (Costa 1982, 1497). In 1939, the city of Lages was responsible for close to 60 percent of the cattle production in the state (Cunha 1982, 156).

The Lages plateau had the highest concentration of land ownership in the state. In 1817, a public land inventory listed only fifty-six farms in an enormous region that today includes Lages and neighboring cities (Costa 1982, 1478). In 1950, 44 percent of the state's farms with between one hundred and one thousand hectares were in Lages, whereas only 8 percent of the farms between ten and one hundred hectares were in the region (Peluso Júnior 1991). In 1966, after the first wave of urbanization and industrialization, land was still fairly concentrated; holdings with up to one hundred hectares occupied 18 percent of the arable land, while holdings with more than one thousand hectares occupied 30 percent of the land (Costa 1982, 1501). The economic and political elite of *coronéis* that emerged out of this pattern of occupation governed the city until the 1960s. It is possible to link many of the most influential families in the first half of the twentieth century to those fifty-six farms listed in the 1817 inventory.

Peluso Júnior (1949) explored in detail the operation of one of the large cattle farms in the region and described their social organization as comprising three groups. Peons were in charge of the cattle and did not receive a salary for this job, only payments for sporadic services such as the building of a fence or occasional work on the rancher's fields. "The floor of the house in which he lives, the land he works, and the field where he keeps a few cows of his own constitute the landowner's remuneration for his labor" (1387). The second group was constituted of tenants settled away from the center of the farm. In this case, the exchange with the rancher was also in kind: a portion of their crops for the use of the land. The third group was the rancher's family. Male children received fifty calves on their tenth birthday; eventually they would build a house within their father's land as a way to secure the occupation of large estates. The rancher was, above all, "the boss of a social group that in him finds support whenever in need of comfort and protection, which traditionally should be provided by large land owners" (1390). The children of the peons often became the peons of the new generation of ranchers. Demographic data and qualitative studies also point out the existence of small contingents of subsistence farms, especially in the less favorable mountainous terrains (Martendal, Calazans, Silva, and Sartori 1982; Peixer 2002; Peluso Júnior 1991).

The subaltern group of peons, tenants, and subsistence farmers formed a social group known as *caboclo*. Literally, the term means a person of mixed white and aboriginal descent. The *caboclo* of the Santa Catarina plateau, however, had a mixed ethnic formation that included African slaves brought with the first settlers, natives from the Botocutos and Kaigáng nations, and Italian and German migrants from the east of the state. Despite ethnic diversity, throughout two hundred years of living and working in this region, a culture with specific symbols and rituals developed. Unfortunately, the *caboclo* culture was delegated an inferior character in the history of the region. The *caboclo* is rarely present in official local history, and the rare mentions usually associate the group with backwardness (Peixer 2002). The most complete work on the history of Lages neglects the *caboclo* culture. The chapter "Cultural Evolution" focuses on classic music groups, jazz bands, orchestras, and choirs. Brief mentions of *caboclo* customs and beliefs are found in the "Folklore" chapter (Costa 1982, 1596–1622).

The uprising of a movement of *caboclos* led by a messianic leader is one of the best-known events in the history of Santa Catarina. The center of the Contestado War (1912–1916) was Curitibanos, the second largest city in the plateau, which at the time had a larger number of subsistence farmers than Lages. Destitute farmers, who believed a man with mystic powers led them, demanded the reestablishing of the monarchy. During the First Republic similar uprisings took place across the country (e.g., the Canudos Rebellion in the state of Bahia). In Curitibanos, what triggered the rebellion was the construction of a railroad that introduced a capitalist logic to land dealings, which disrupted traditional patterns of patron-client relations. Unequal by definition, these relations became more erratic and violent. The demand for the restoration of the monarchy may be understood as the idealization of an era when patron-client relations were grounded on the moral values of paternalism (Diacon 1990). We can also think of the Contestado War as a consequence of the initial crumbling of the economic basis of the limited access order in a time when new participatory channels had not yet been opened and violent insurgence was one of the few alternatives. As in other similar cases, federal troops massacred insurgents. The military campaign was accompanied by propaganda that depicted the movement as a revolt of fanatics, indolent and idle *caboclos* (Munarim 1990). To this date, people in the region reject the denomination *caboclo*, which they see as pejorative, and prefer terms such as "popular groups" or "Brazilians" (Peixer 2002, citing Geraldo Löcks 1999).[1]

A central preoccupation of the 1970s participatory administration was to promote the valorization of the *caboclo* culture. This social class was never part of local or state politics, dominated by local cattle ranchers and industrialists of the Itajaí Valley. The team in charge of the participatory administration tried to bring *caboclos* and their concerns to the fore of the city's social and development agenda. The objective was to improve the living conditions of rural families, allowing them to preserve their life style, avoiding rural exodus. Whereas much of the literature on participatory democracy focuses on initiatives in fast-growing urban centers, the pioneer experience of Lages was devoted to rural *caboclo* citizens.

LIMITED ACCESS ORDER: THE PLATEAU AND ITAJAÍ VALLEY ELITES

In Santa Catarina, the Proclamation of the Republic (1889) and subsequent conflicts brought to power a reformist elite imbued with the ideology of the revolution and allied with the *coronéis* of the Lages region. The appointed governor of the new regime was Lauro Müller, a military official from the Itajaí Valley. Established politicians from the former conservative and liberal parties swiftly showed their support for the revolution, and many joined the Republican Party (Partido Republicano). The new governor, however, isolated the old elites, filling legislative and administrative posts with "genuine republicans," who represented the urban, industrialist, and commercial classes (Meirinho 2009). Dissatisfied, members of the old elites joined the party of disgruntled monarchists and federalists. In 1893, a federalist revolt roared in the southern state of Rio Grande do Sul, involving Santa Catarina, whose capital came under the control of federalist forces. In September 1893, Desterro was declared the provisory capital of a new federal union. In April 1894, federal forces regained control of the city and launched a gruesome retaliating campaign that included the summary execution of federalist leaders (Meirinho 2009; Neckel 2003).

Hercílio Luz, a republican from Blumenau led the resistance to the federalist occupation and became the new governor in 1895. He was one of the most important political leaders of the time, and his followers were known as *hercilistas*. Lauro Müller was the other very influential republican politician, and his comrades were nicknamed *lauristas*. In 1898, the two republicans supported São Paulo's opposition to the candidacy of Campos Salles for the presidency. The lingering federalists campaigned for Salles and gained a considerable number of votes for the future president. Salle's political strategy rested on peaceful alliances with governors, and neither the president nor Hercílio would benefit from clashes. However, Salles had to reward federalists' campaigning efforts. The solution was the creation of a new party in 1902 that brought together *hercilistas*, *lauristas*, and federalists (Cherem 2001). The Santa Catarina Republican Party (Partido Republicano Catarinense, PRC) became the umbrella party of the dominant elite coalition—the organization that facilitated intra-elite negotiations and helped to avoid violent struggle. At the turn of the twentieth century the urban elite was at the top of the elite hierarchy.

In the Region of Lages, the transition to the Republic consolidated the political influence of landed families. The most powerful clan in the city branched off from Laureano José Ramos (1777–1862). In 1868, the Emperor Don Pedro II nominated Vidal Ramos, Laureano's son, lieutenant of the local regiment of the National Guard, in 1894 President Prudent promoted him to the post of *coronel*, and later he became the president of the city's Republican Party. In 1895, Vidal Ramos Junior,

Vidal's son, was the only candidate in the first municipal election in Lages. In the 1894 state elections, Hercílio and Lauro appealed to the political support of the Ramos in the Plateau. Vidal Júnior guaranteed the support of Lages and two neighboring cities, and soon after became Lauro's vice governor. Lauro resigned to serve in a ministry in Rio de Janeiro, and Vidal Júnior became governor (1902–1906). He was also governor from 1910 to 1914 and then became one of the three state senators until 1928. His son, the lawyer Nereu Ramos, made his debut in political life in the state legislature in 1912 (Costa 1982; Peixer 2002).

The 1922 presidential elections divided republican parties across the country between those supporting Arthur Bernardes, the incumbent president's candidate, and those backing Nilo Peçanha, the candidate of a dissident group. Senator Vidal Ramos Júnior and his son Nereu headed Peçanha's campaign in the state, aggravating previous disagreements with Hercílio, current governor and as such a supporter of the status quo. Bernardes won and ostracized the dissidents. In 1926, after the death of Hercílio (1924) and Lauro (1926), the Konder brothers of Itajaí rose to the top of the party, galvanizing authentic republicans and further isolating the Ramos family. Adolto Konder became governor in that same year. In the last two years of the decade, republicans nationwide were again divided between the incumbent president's candidate, Julio Prestes, and the opposition leader, Getúlio Vargas. The Konders backed Prestes whereas the Ramos founded Santa Catarina's Liberal Alliance and supported the Vargas candidacy (Lenzi 1983). With Vargas's ascent to power, the powerful plateau families moved to the top of the elite hierarchy in the state.

In Lages, Belisário Ramos, Vidal Júnior's brother, ran the city from 1902 to 1922. In these twenty years, his son Aristiliano Ramos and son-in-law Otacílio Costa served as deputies for prolonged periods. The Costa family was very influential and tied to the Ramos family by marriage. In 1923, Otacílio Costa became mayor, now as the leader of an opposition group to his father-in-law. In 1927, Caetano Costa, also from the opposition group, replaced Otacílio Costa. Despite intraelite disputes, the city continued to be run until 1977 by a Ramos, a Costa, someone directly appointed by a Ramos in the state government, or a politician publicly supported by the Ramos family (Costa 1982; Peixer 2002).

TOWARD AN OPEN ACCESS ORDER: THE LUMBER SHOP AND *CABOCLO* WORKERS

In the early 1930s, the brothers Vidal Júnior and Belisário retired, and their sons, Nereu and Aristiliano, respectively, became the political leaders of the Ramos clan. In 1935, both cousins wanted the Liberal Alliance's nomination for state governor.[2] The gentlemen's solution for this intra-elite dispute was simple: the party leadership sent a telegram to Vargas asking him to choose one of the two cousins. Thirty-five party leaders signed the message, thirty-three of whom were official *colonels* of the National Guard. Vargas picked Nereu and soon after Aristiliano became the candidate of the opposition party. The pre-elections negotiations involved intrigues, threats, and bribes. Nereu won and remained governor until 1945 (Lenzi 1983).

The discord between Nereu and Aristiliano had an impact on Lages. In 1930, the cousins, leaders of the victorious revolution, appointed Colonel Octávio Silveira Filho for mayor. In the mayoral election of 1935, Aristiliano backed the candidacy of a cousin on his side of the dispute, Henrique Ramos Júnior, while Nereu supported the name of his brother Celso Ramos. Henrique won and headed the city until 1937, when Vargas's coup endowed the governor with new authoritarian powers. Nereu discharged Henrique and appointed his comrade Idalécio Arruda, and later his younger brother, the second Vidal Ramos Júnior (Lenzi 1977; Peixer 2002). Subaltern classes remained excluded from these intra-elite disputes.

In 1945, Vargas's authoritarian regime ended, and the political elites reorganized. Santa Catarina followed the national trend wherein the "ins" in Vargas's period formed the Social Democratic Party (PSD) and the "outs" grouped in the National Democratic Unions (UDN). Nereu's clan and the Costa family became the leaders of the PSD, while Aristiliano's branch and most of the coastal elite enlisted in the UDN. Saulo Ramos, Nereu and Aristiliano's uncle, founded the Brazilian Labor Party (PTB) in the state. Saulo was a doctor trained in Rio de Janeiro, where he entered Vargas's inner circle. He practiced medicine in the state's capital and was popular in low-income areas where he did unpaid work (Peixer 2002).

Whereas intra-elite disputes between Ramos and a few other influential families continued to mark Lages politics during the Vargas period, the city's socioeconomic context dramatically changed, leading to the emergence of new social and economic groups that would challenge the limited access order controlled by the landed oligarchy. During the First World War, logging became an increasingly significant activity in the state. Initially in the northeast coast, logging moved toward the plateau, partially because of fast deforestation, but also spurred by the construction of new roads. The revenue generated by logging in Santa Catarina increased almost fivefold between 1910 and 1920 (Cunha 1982, 148). In the 1930s, timber became the number one export of the state. The Second World War increased the demand for wood, and in 1942 the product represented 38 percent of Santa Catarina's exports (CEAG/SC 1980, 184). By the 1950s, "cattle farming stopped being the [Lages Region's] principal activity; the lumber factory, as unit of production, began to compete with the ranch" (CEAG/SC 1980, 187).

The lumber factory was the symbol of the new economy, but the formation of new social groups was a consequence of a number of interrelated socioeconomic processes. First, Lages's transport infrastructure improved. Until the 1920s, precarious roads connected the city to the capital and other states; livestock was sold alive and herded to slaughterhouses. The "Second Construction Battalion," an army-run construction company that also employed civilians, was stationed in Lages between 1934 and 1970. In this period, the battalion built and improved roads connecting the city to the state capital and to the neighboring states. The new roads attracted logging entrepreneurs and contributed to the emerging of the new economic activity. The construction company also brought with it a considerable contingent of workers and wage jobs. According to the general in charge of the Battalion, in 1952 approximately eight hundred troopers and sixteen hundred civilians worked in road building and related activities (Lenzi 1977, 126–27), two thousand two hundred workers in a population estimated at 35,598 people (Peixer 2002, 17).

Writing in 1949, Peluso Júnior noted that improvements in the transport infrastructure were making agriculture more attractive; some peons were becoming tenants hoping that the sale of their produce in newly accessible markets could improve their livelihood. The continuous portioning of large farms and the progressive change in the type of land usage was making it increasingly difficult for the descendants of peons to find positions in the same occupation. As a result, Peluso Júnior (1949) noted, the new generation had to look for land elsewhere or engage in different economic activities. The more accessible, economically striving, and only partially occupied plateau also attracted the descendants of the migrants workers settled in the east of the state and in the state of Rio Grande do Sul.

The Second World War and national policies promoting import substitution encouraged the transformation of raw wood into furniture, paper, carton, and wood pulp. In the first decades of the activity, numerous small lumber shops provided raw material for low-technology factories. An observer of the time described production as predatory, very labor intensive, and extremely wasteful (Lago 1968). In 1962, however, this industry was responsible for 27 percent of the state's industrial output (Lago 1968, 307), and much of it was concentrated in the region of Lages: 46 percent of the state production in 1959, and 78 percent in 1970 (CEAG/SC 1980, 187). The largest paper factory in the state was located in the district of Otacílio Costa in Lages. In 1962, this factory alone employed 450 people, had an industrial village with 250 workers' houses, and provided basic social services to the family of employees (Lago 1968, 309).

These changes fostered outside migration to the Lages region and an exodus from rural zones to the urban perimeter of the city. The rural and urban populations dramatically increased between 1940 and 1970. Whereas rural dwellers increased by 51 percent, the urban population increased by tenfold. The percentage of urban inhabitants rose from 31 to 75 percent of the total population, which increased from 27 thousand to 112 thousand inhabitants in the same thirty-year period (Peixer 2002, 17). This profound socioeconomic transformation fuelled the emergence of new social groups and new types of social relationships, "the *caboclo*-peon, from a patrimonial work relationship, starts to experience, in the lumber shop, a binary, vertical, modern, and capitalist type of work relationship ... the *caboclo*-small grower no longer sells the excess of his subsistence production, now he sells labor power for money" (Munarim 1990, 97). Munarim also captured an aspect of this transformation that helps us to understand the format of the participatory initiatives implemented in the late 1970s. According to Munarim, although freed from patrimonial bonds, the employee of the Lages lumber shop remained a rural person. "He continues to live in rural areas, even if his house is now in a village" (98). His religion, cultural practices, eating and dressing customs did not alter. Most importantly, this *caboclo*-worker preserved the subservience to authority typical of patron-client relationships. As viewed below, the participatory administration put great emphasis on activities aimed at increasing the self-esteem of *caboclo* people; this was seen by the team in charge of the administration, which included Munarim, as an essential step in the process of political emancipation of excluded groups.

Mayoral elections resumed in 1951. The outsider elite of logging entrepreneurs grouped in the PTB. The *caboclo*-worker class remained without organic political representation. The traditional and the new elites began to compete for the vote of this class, using old patrimonial tactics as well as new clientelist and populist political strategies. Nereu's clan won the five municipal elections between 1951 and 1968. Neverthe-less, these electoral victories were more costly than the political arrange-ments that had crowned Ramos and Costas in the previous decades. The PSD had to form alliances with the PTB and include members of the new elite in its ranks. The party's 1951 candidate was a lawyer born outside the region, and in 1960 the elected mayor was the son of an industrial-ist (Lenzi 1977). In rural areas, political allegiance was no longer simply exchanged for patronage. A considerable portion of peons and subsis-tence farmers were now wageworkers in lumber factories and relatively independent from patrons. In many cases, PSD candidates had to buy votes, and stories are told of farmers that went bankrupt selling cattle and land in order to "invest in votes" (Munarim 1990, 94). Traditional rural families remained a powerful political force, but their ability to deny access to political and economic activities had considerably decreased by the late 1950s.

The industrialization and urbanization processes that altered the socioeconomic formation of Lages and weakened the political power of the Ramos family occurred while the most prominent members of the clan enjoyed two decades of uncontested rule in the state government. This paradox begs for clarification. The parsimonious explanation here is that political groups in this period did not have a development agenda. Intra-elite disputes merely decided who shared the spoils of govern-ment. In the first three decades of the twentieth century, the only policy question dividing the coastal and the plateau elites regarded taxation; coastal politicians favored taxing property, while the large landowners of Lages pushed for taxation of exports (Neckel 2003). Development debates are largely absent in the state's political literature for the first half of the century. The focus of this literature is on intra-elite disputes. A review of the economic literature of Santa Catarina points out that the two main interpretations of the state's economic development agree that external forces fuelled industrialization between 1930 and 1950 (Michels 1998).

In the 1950s, as the externally promoted industrialization started to lose momentum, a group of influential developmentalist intellectuals advocated that the state government had to lead the industrialization process and guarantee the economic prosperity of Santa Catarina. Both the coast and the plateau elites embraced this ideology. Irineu Bornhausen, political leader of the Itajaí Valley, launched the first state-sponsored industrialization scheme in the early 1950s, which was continued by Celso Ramos in his 1961–1966 administration. At this point, Vidal Ramos Júnior, the Ramos running Lages, had already sold his cattle and invested in lumber production. The military regime endorsed the state-led industrialization policies of the Santa Catarina elites. Between 1950 and 1980, coastal and plateau politicians took turns in the state government, all promoting industrialization (Michels 1998). The *caboclo* did not figure in this development plan; culturally subdued, politically unorganized, and economically vulnerable, this class was expected to adapt to the new times.

Following the 1964 coup d'état, most UDN politicians nationwide joined the National Renewal Alliance (ARENA), but in Lages the regime's party was staffed mainly by former PSD members—demonstrating once again the ability of Nereu's clan to land on the "right side" of the "revolution" (Silva 1994). A former UDN member and founder of the local MDB chapter explained that "we supported the 1964 revolution thinking we would come to power, but to our surprise the military chose the PSD, so we joined the opposition" (Celson Anderson de Souza, personal communication, December 14, 2010). The Lages MDB also included a large portion of the PTB, the Ramos of Aristiliano's side, and young professionals educated and politicized in state capitals (Andrade 1996b).

In 1972, MDB's Juarez Furtado defeated the Costa candidate running for ARENA. Born and raised in Lages, his pre-1964 political affiliation was with the PSD. Furtado was educated in law in Curitiba and worked as a labor lawyer in his hometown, which gained him the support of urban workers. Although running for the MDB, he counted on the public support of members of Nereu's side, who were discontented with the ARENA candidate. Tellingly, his role model in the MDB was Quércia, the pragmatic mayor of Campinas, who created a wide clientelist network in the state of São Paulo. Furtado's MDB was a clientelist party organized around *sub-diretórios*, that is, party neighborhood chapters that assiduously campaigned for the party's candidates during election years in return for priority treatment by the elected administration. This political strategy inhibited broad and autonomous popular political engagement since only *sub-diretórios* leaders could negotiate favors. In Quércia's style, the Furtado administration was marked by visible infrastructure projects, including two industrial districts and a modernizing discourse that appealed to most sectors without challenging the established elites (Peixer 2002; Silva 1994).

THE DIRCEU CARNEIRO TEAM: A RADICAL MASS PARTY

Dirceu Carneiro, Furtado's vice mayor and secretary of public works, had a more radical ideal of democracy. Carneiro grew up on a farm in the plateau, moved to Lages to complete his secondary schooling, and then left for Porto Alegre to study architecture. The historical perspective presented in the architecture program and his active involvement in the city's vigorous organized opposition to the military regime influenced his political thoughts. In 1971, Carneiro returned to Lages and joined the MDB; soon after, he became the party's general secretary, and then the vice mayor of the first MDB administration. Furtado envisioned a politico-technical administration, and thought an architect would complement his skills (Silva 1994). Carneiro attributed his rapid political rise to his ability to communicate with people in the rural areas, where the party was weak (personal communication, December 13, 2010). By 1973, the two had become political opponents. Furtado regretted having the architect as his vice mayor; "it would have been better to have chosen people we knew from the party, from the city" (quoted in Silva 1994, 77). Carneiro affirmed that the labor lawyer was conservative and unwilling to break with clientelist practices.

While Furtado focused on urban projects in the central part of town, Carneiro started to mobilize the rural neighborhoods. The landmark of the city's participatory approach was an initiative called Viva Your Neighborhood, launched by Carneiro while Furtado was in Europe (Quinteiro 1991). On set dates, the Secretariat of Public Works would send a large portion of its equipment and personnel to a specific neighborhood; there, municipal workers and residents would work together on self-construction projects called *mutirão*, which addressed immediate infrastructure and maintenance problems. According to Carneiro, besides being an efficient work strategy, these collective actions "animated the people in the neighborhoods." In 1976, Carneiro was elected mayor with more than twice the number of votes of the ARENA candidate (Costa 1982, 1372).

The "Dirceu Carneiro Team" is the name used to refer to the enthusiastic group of cabinet secretaries, department heads, and community organizers that worked in the 1977–1982 municipal administration of Lages. The team's main concern and motivation was to promote a new type of political culture and practice. Although Furtado's clientelist party incorporated new urban groups and factory workers, and marked a significant step away from the reign of *coronéis* toward a more open access order, team members simply saw the continuing exclusion of *caboclos*. Carneiro noted that among team members there was "an intense preoccupation with doing things differently from the status quo." The Dirceu Carneiro Team fits the category of a radical mass party that brought together elite and middle-class members who tried to mobilize subaltern groups with the goal of furthering democratization. In this context, the furthering democratization meant creating channels for the direct participation of the rural poor in public administration, which first required the *conscientização* of *caboclos*. Although it is not possible to assign the Dirceu Carneiro Team a coherent ideology, there are noteworthy political-cultural traits that help to understand its emphasis on popular participation.

Carneiro's years spent at university in Porto Alegre introduced him to political life, and subsequent trips to the city helped to shape his political ideals. Carneiro partook in several meetings organized by MBD's Institute for Political and Social Studies (IEPES). In 1976, Carneiro and some of his secretaries attended a regional meeting for MDB candidates for municipal government. The principles and strategies of the group were listed in a document in which popular participation is one of the foundations for municipal government:

Today, one of the central questions confronting the [MDB] is the *creation and strengthening of mechanisms for effective popular participation in the municipal administrations of the party.* . . . The municipal technocracy is necessary in the elaboration of budgets, programs and projects, but in an [MDB] administration, it should never be in charge of making any decisions, it should simply provide technical advice. . . . The effective popular participation in the decision making at the municipal level is not only a viable possibility, but indispensable in the formulation of a truly democratic government program. (PMDB 1981a, 95–96)

According to Andrade (1996a), "the then candidate Dirceu and his team adopted almost in its totality the guidelines set in this document" (80). The text was later used as the grounding paper for the First National Seminar of PMDB Mayors in 1981, and was printed in the *Revista do PMDB*, followed by a description of Carneiro's government, introduced as "an example of the creative implementation of PMDB's program" (PMDB 1981b, 103). Carneiro was the model administrator espoused by *autênticos*.

Many in the Team were not closely affiliated with the MDB, and their source of motivation rested elsewhere. "The truth is that there wasn't a unique and complete theoretical project, well-elaborated intellectually, around which [these] intellectuals/militants gathered" (Munarim 1990, 157). Most members belonged to the middle class, were recently graduated from university, originally from the region, inexperienced in Lages politics, but had a history of involvement with student movements in the 1960s (Quinteiro 1991) or some other form of resistance to the military regime (Silva Neto 1995). According to two interviewees, the Team's view of the interior of the country was influenced by Leal's famous book on *coronelismo* and municipal administration, widely read by the group. The state governor accused the Team of being Marxist, which at that time only contributed to their popularity. Although some saw Cuba as an inspiring example, a clear Marxist doctrine was absent (Paulo Tarso, Mayor's aide in the Dirceu Carneiro administration, personal communication, December 16, 2011).

Researchers and interviewees pointed out that the single unifying principle of the Team was a strong belief in the knowledge and political potential of the popular classes. A researcher and former member of the Team described the group as, "a group of young intellectuals, 'agents of the middle class' who made an 'option' for the popular classes . . . [they] repudiated the manipulation of people and tried in their day-to-day living and being with people to value them, to help them to turn to themselves, to believe in their strength, in their capacity to interpret and change reality" (Quinteiro 1991, 136–37). Another Team member mentioned in his master's thesis an "almost blind belief in the capacity of the 'oppressed people' to organize themselves and confront the dominant forces" (Munarim 1990, 158).

During the military regime, numerous leftist militants became involved in adult literary campaigns inspired in the Paulo Freire's popular education method, which was seen as a tool for "consciousness raising." The term "popular education" and the name Paulo Freire are recurrent in oral and written depictions of the participatory administration, but never in a systematic or elaborated way. The ideals of the grassroots arm of the Catholic Church also played a role in motivating the group. The most experienced Team member was known as Professor Manuel. In the early 1960s, Manuel and his wife Sonia were active in the political life of São Paulo, where they participated in a theology seminar guided by the doctrine of the Second Vatican Council and in a movement for public education reform led by Dom Paulo Evaristo Arns (Quinteiro 1991). In the same decade, they moved to Lages and became teachers. Furtado brought them to the department of education, and in the Carneiro years Manuel became the head of the department. The former vice mayor explained that much of what they did in Lages was based on principles Manuel brought with him to Lages (Celso Andrade de Souza, personal communication, December 14, 2010). The former director of the cultural department, who had previously worked in adult education programs, referred to Manuel as the "guru" of the Team (Valmor Beltrani, personal communication, December 20, 2010). According to a local researcher and lay religious leader, CEBs were not yet organized in the city in this period (Geraldo Löcks, personal communication, December 16, 2010).

A marked attribute of the Team was its devotion to the work being done. The conviction in new political practices motivated these young public administrators to work long days. An interviewee reported having undergone a tenfold income decrease in order to join the administration, "and I didn't think twice about it" (Valmor Beltrani, personal communication, December 20, 2010). Carneiro reported having to order his secretaries to go home and rest. Every written description of the experiment transpires a feeling of enthusiasm and anticipation that seems to have been present in most of Dirceu's mandate. The 1979 national electoral reform that allowed for the creation of new political parties also extended the mandate of current mayors from four to six years. The energy of the Team is reported to have declined in these two additional years. Only a couple of members of the Team remained involved in party politics after the administration.

THE PARTICIPATORY ADMINISTRATION

Carneiro explained that the first challenge of the participatory administration was to surmount party politics lines that impeded them from reaching communities associated with the PSD. The solution was to pick schools as the central public spaces for organizing community activities. The neutral image of the school and the respected position of teachers allowed for the broad mobilization of the city's population. Whereas Furtado privileged efforts to create party neighborhood chapters, the frontline workers of the new administration assisted people in organizing varied kinds of "base organizations"—namely, agriculture centers, parent-teacher associations, mothers' clubs, small business owners' associations, rural youth groups, community gardens, and neighborhood associations. The mayor and his secretaries had an open-door policy to leaders of all representative associations, which constituted a change from the clientelist logic where only community leaders loyal to the party were recognized as legitimate interlocutors. For this reason, party colleagues criticized Carneiro for working with people who had campaigned against them.

The administration's effort to mobilize the population to participate in political life relied heavily on the work of the education and culture departments. The objectives were to promote an education based on people's practical experiences and to organize activities that helped to unearth local customs and history. The Education Department included gardening, construction, and basket weaving in the curriculum of rural primary schools. Parents were regularly invited to teach these classes as a way of calling attention to the knowledge existing within the culture, customs, and everyday practices of oppressed groups—a core component of Paulo Freire's method. The Culture Department worked with teachers in the preparation of annual plays that presented important chapters in the history of Lages as told from the perspective of subaltern groups. The Department also organized periodic gatherings in rural schools as a way of recovering local customs and stories. These activities extolled the hitherto denigrated *caboclo* culture, and as such constituted a key aspect of the *conscientização* process that would empower them to take advantage of opportunities to actively participate in the city's political life.

The Gralha Azul, a marionette theater group, also drew on local cultural themes in their numerous plays. The former director of the Secretariat of Culture explained that this cultural agenda was not inspired by romantic ideas of the past or a nationalist outlook. Instead, the work was based on the conviction that people had the right to express themselves, the right to access culture, and that it was of vital importance to preserve the local cultural heritage. Thus, the secretariat promoted activities that rescued local culture, allowing audiences not used to artistic languages to recognize themselves in the works presented and even to participate in it. The Gralha Azul sang a song that typified this thought: "You can do tomorrow as we do today" (Valmor Beltrani, personal communication, December 20, 2010).

The knowledge, skills, histories, and stories uncovered by the various cultural and educational programs soon demanded a place to be better showcased. The Mostra do Campos (Field Fairs) were annual events organized in each of the city's seven districts. At these fairs, communities displayed the produce of the year's harvest, animals, machinery, and artwork—all accompanied by melodies of local musicians, the rhymes of uninhibited poets, and freshly cooked food. The preparation for these events mobilized all the recently created associations, each working on specific tasks, coordinating with the remaining organizations and district organizers, who in turn discussed a multitude of matters with the city's secretaries. The administration supported the event from a distance, allowing organizational structures to form. According to the education secretary who preceded Professor Manuel, within the first three years it was already possible to notice improvements in community groups' organizational skills (Martendal 1982). A participant researcher concluded that in these fairs, "the *knowledges* [sic] of local culture were valued, increasing the desire to learn and share them. Those who participate in this process felt valued in one way or another. As a result, the self-esteem of these historically marginalized and exploited peasants was elevated" (Silveira 2004, 100).

The Team also implemented participatory programs focused on social and economic problems. Twenty-one agriculture centers were formed and worked as small farmer cooperatives. The primary incentive for forming these groups was the opportunity to use city-owned tractors for a third of the price charged by commercial services. In order to have access to the machines, farmers had to organize themselves to purchase and store diesel, make minor repairs, pay for the cost of tractor drivers, and fairly share the use of the equipment. The goal of this program was to prevent the bankruptcy of small farmers who were unable to access machinery (Alves 1980b). The centers also housed the rural youth groups and served as central community spaces.

The *mutirão* (self-construction project) was the best-known program of Lages. By the late 1970s, the city had become predominantly urban, and squatter homes had mounted everywhere. The federal low-income housing project required applicants to have an income above the average of most squatters. Carneiro's team decided to work with the ineligible families. The administration divided a large plot of public land into 960 lots and had social workers select the families most in need. The mayor then passed a law authorizing city personnel to do free demolition and free transport of debris for any construction site, as long as all material was donated to the *mutirão*. The future residents topped the recycled debris with traditional construction methods, for example, clay roof tiles, and some nonsubstitutable materials were provided by the city, for example, doorknobs. Groups of twenty families worked together in the construction of each other's homes. The administration provided technical assistance for the construction of sewage and water pipes, and technical guidance for volunteers. Further, Carneiro demanded that municipal employees contribute one day per year of volunteer work in the *mutirão* (Alves 1980b).

It is remarkable to note the precursory participatory budgeting installed in Lages. In the beginning, Carneiro's Team allocated 5 percent of the budget for special projects and called upon community leaders to be active in the Viva Your Neighborhood to help decide how best to use these resources. This structure became more complex as the number of base organizations increased. Popular Councils were created to represent neighborhoods' concerns. Councils had, on average, fifteen members from various "work fronts"; for example, associations concerned with health formed the "health work front" and would elect delegates to neighborhood councils. Council representatives were subsequently invited to participate in the preparation of the municipal budget and the elaboration of the city's master plan (Quinteiro 1991).

The administration distributed pamphlets explaining that "in Lages, as we draft the city's budget, people in rural and urban areas are organizing and meeting with executive representatives. Together they discuss, vote and make decisions about the use of the public funds." In 1982, the Team wanted to make their innovations official and so began issuing decrees known as "popular laws." Law number 550, Section V, created the Cabinet of Planning and Coordination (GAPLAN), responsible for linking together the various departments and projects of the municipal administration. Article 51 describes how the cabinet should operate:

> In the implementation and execution of projects in the sphere of responsibility here outlined, the GAPLAN must submit projects of future works to popular and democratic consultation, specially matters regarding the municipal public budget, urban planning, and legislation of social interest . . . using for this purpose assemblies of associations and organizations duly constituted by the people. (Alves 1980b, Annex 1)

The Team's disregard for the municipal legislative chamber is patently clear in this proposal. A "popular and democratic consultation" did not involve elected representatives; instead, the new executive body had to interact directly with civil society associations about essentially every matter of municipal public administration.

Actual implementation of the participatory budgeting process seems to have been timid. The close cooperation between administration and popular associations created a largely consensual atmosphere, and community leaders' participation was limited to comments and suggestions on proposals elaborated by the secretariats (Ferreira 1991). Ultimately, the 1982 electoral defeat prevented continued evolution of the participatory budgeting and the other initiatives here described.

THE 1982 ELECTIONS: OLD AND NEW POLITICS

The MDB lost the 1982 municipal elections to a PSD candidate well connected with the city's traditional elite. "The new mayor [assumed the position] willing to liquidate the innovative experience implemented in the city" (Ferreira 1991, 29). One of his first moves was to fire the technical staff identified with the previous administration (Andrade 1996b). The still weak neighborhood associations slowly crumbled and were replaced by organizations connected with the new mayor's political party. What is more, a similar outcome would have likely resulted had the former Mayor Furtado, the PMBD's candidate, won the election (Silva 1994).

Several factors contributed to the Team's inability to elect a successor. The "Dirceu Carneiro Team" became a political group isolated from the rest of the party. Ferreira (1991) attributed this disregard for the party as a sign of the group's political naiveté, pointing to its majority of non-politicians convinced of the supremacy of the popular organization. The Team worked predominately with the most needy sectors of society, the population of urban peripheries and especially the *caboclo* population in rural areas. Little attention was paid to organized workers' unions and the middle class of the city's center. The former kept corporatist ties with the PSD while the latter was generally disgruntled with Carneiro's lack of attention to urban developments (Silva 1994).

Furtado, then PMDB president, continued to organize the party's base during Carneiro's years. He was helped by municipal representatives who feared that direct citizen participation was going to undermine their role as political brokers. When the party convention arrived in 1982, Furtado was able to maneuver things according to his preferences (Silva 1994). Carneiro avoided direct confrontation with the party's president because by now he was focused on his nomination for federal deputy, which would be hard for him to obtain if Furtado opposed it or decided to run for the position himself. There is a known rumor about a tacit agreement among the party's leadership: "the city goes back to Furtado in exchange for Carneiro's ascension" (Silva 1994, 129). Franscisco Küster, the former secretary of agriculture, and, for many, the natural candidate of the Team, was hit in the crossfire and forced to the sideline. During the electoral campaign, Carneiro and Furtado did not publicly support each other's candidacy, and neither aided Küster's bid for the state legislative chamber.

Interviewees reported that tensions within the Team began around 1980 with the arrival of the "ideological tourists." News about this defying democratic experiment spread quickly in 1970s' authoritarian Brazil. Militants and intellectuals from all over the country came to Santa Catarina to see the experiment firsthand.[3] After a tour of the projects, visitors would sit with Carneiro and his team for a question-and-answer period; questions were often theoretical and enquired about the meaning and long-term goals of the participatory administration. It was in these meetings that the Team learned that their political orientations were dissimilar. Carneiro frequently failed to provide the leftist political-programmatic answers that some of his aides expected, either because of lack of theoretical knowledge or for unwillingness to openly ascribe to a particular ideology; eventually Carneiro stopped attending these meetings. An additional and related point of friction within the Team regarded the possibility of joining the recently created PT. Some in the Team felt that PT's program was in line with what they had been doing, but the discussion became taboo (Quinteiro 1991). Tensions escalated with Carneiro's inaction regarding the selection of a successor, which led a portion of the Team to unsuccessfully try to launch the candidacy of the secretary of urban services.

Meanwhile, the restored PSD organized a concerted effort to crush what the state governor pejoratively called a "little Marxist republic." In the two years preceding the municipal election, the PSD state government first attacked the city by encouraging the dismemberment of the two districts with cellulose factories, considerably reducing the administration's revenue (Ferreira 1991). Moreover, the governor financed a parallel administration in the form of a regional superintendence. According to one journalist, three thousand employees staffed this regional administration, while the city had 1,788 people on its entire payroll (Nelson Zambom quoted in Quinteiro 1991, 206 n30). A good example of the financial might of the state government was in the housing area. In the *mutirão* project, people had to pay for the land and some construction costs in installments that never amounted to more than 10 percent of a family's income. The PSD candidate promised to write off everyone's debt (Andrade 1996b); in the weeks preceding the election, the state government inaugurated a popular housing complex much larger than the sum of all the houses built by the people in the previous six years (Ferreira 1991, 27).[4] In the end, the PSD candidate won the elections in a close race. Carneiro moved to the country's capital. The Team dispersed.

THE SOCIOECONOMIC FORMATION of Santa Catarina led to the emergence of an economically and politically hegemonic class of cattle farmers in the Plateau of Lages, who shared the control of the state with the industrial elite of the Itajaí Valley. The politically excluded class of Lages was comprised of peons and rural workers whose interests were neglected in state-level politics and in the consecutive municipal governments of the Ramos family. Culturally, the identity of the *caboclo* was relegated an inferior status that led many to avoid the categorization. Economic changes in the 1930s–1950s period weakened the dominant elite, fuelled the emergence of new social and economic groups, transformed peons into wage earning *caboclos*, and spurred the fast growth of rural and poor urban neighborhoods.

In this new socioeconomic context, a populist politician nonmember of the traditional elites managed to become mayor and headed an administration focused on visible urbanistic projects. Furtado's attempt to build a strong clientelist network was obstructed by his vice mayor and other militants influenced by participatory ideals promoted at the IEPES, the values espoused by the progressive arm of the Catholic Church, and notions of popular education. The participatory administration of Lages had an unequivocal objective: to include, strengthen, and benefit subaltern classes hitherto barred from politics. The design of the participatory initiatives followed this rationale. In order to mobilize a society without a previous history of popular mobilization, the Team found it necessary first to promote the value of the *caboclo* culture and boost the self-esteem of this social group. Participatory initiatives focused on culture and education as much as social and economic problems, an approach that is not seen in current participatory administrations.

The Dirceu Carneiro Team had plenty of *political will*, but it was a politically weak group trying to galvanize the most disenfranchised class against a still-powerful economic elite. A class alliance with middle-class groups could have increased the odds of participatory innovations, but the obstacle was a populist leader trying to forge a broad coalition among the upper classes. The separation of the two industrial districts was a PSD strategy to split *caboclos* and urban workers and avoid an alliance that could have further weakened the traditional elite. The PSD also used the sizable investments of the regional superintendence to persuade citizens of the benefits of supporting the governor's party. Thus, participatory democracy had to compete with other forms of political inclusion, which although less democratic from a normative standpoint, may be more effective in the achievement of material necessities, as the case of popular housing illustrated well. In the end, old tactics prevailed.[5]

Notwithstanding the disappointing electoral result and the dismantlement of much of the participatory structure, the Dirceu Carneiro Team accomplished the extraordinary deed of initiating participatory democracy in a period of political repression, in a land of *coronéis*. The news of this defiant group of administrators quickly spread across Brazil, a country that had lived for almost twenty years under a technocratic military dictatorship. Alves's reports of the city's innovative programs were read throughout the country, inciting interest and admiration. Moraes's (1983) documentary about the Lages initiative circulated the country stimulating debates. Buses full of visitors from all parts of the country came to the city to witness the experiment (Quinteiro 1991). Paulo Freire himself came to see the practice of popular education. National television news programs highlighted the successes of the southern town. Short articles and studies helped to further disseminate the democratic practices of Lages (Ferreira 1991; Martendal 1982; PMDB 1981b; Silva 1981). Carneiro and his aides shared their experiences during public events. In 1983, in São Paulo, more than two hundred people watched a panel discussion with Carneiro, Alves, Moraes, two scholars, and the secretary of interior of the state of São Paulo. The last was quoted as saying, "the democratic experience of Lages is a model for all of Brazil." The hosting newspaper described the event in a half-page piece in its Sunday issue. The title of the article read, "Lages, a pioneer experience"; the subtitle was, "São Paulo plans to implement Santa Catarina's model of 'participatory democracy'"

("Lajes, experiência pioneira," Alves 1983). Contrary to the Diadema PT, the Dirceu Carneiro Team was not part of a party committed to participatory democracy, nor could they directly build on this experience and create a pragmatic approach to the inclusion of citizen participation in public administration. Nevertheless, this short-lived initiative made a valuable contribution to the inception of participatory democracy in Brazil.

CHAPTER FOUR

CEBs in Boa Esperança

This chapter shows how a pragmatic mayor used the CEB's organizational structure and its leaders to build a participatory structure to save the town from bankruptcy. In sharp contrast with Lages, the state of Espírito Santo has the lowest level of land concentration in the country. The state's dominant elite coalition was composed of two groups: plantation owners of a small part of the state and merchants who controlled the trade of coffee produced by family farmers across the state. Through various intra-elite arrangements, some more peaceful than others, these groups retained the control of the state to the detriment of the subordinate classes, whose main group was family farmers. With deficient physical infrastructure and little capital, industrialization evolved slowly, and the weak industrialist class joined plantation owners in an uneasy alliance that only had an opposition to family agriculture in common. A populist leader emerged to capitalize on the state's neglected small farmers. Once elected governor, his populist rhetoric actually translated into programs and policies for family farming, some of the first in the state's history. A federal program, however, offered incentives for small coffee growers to sell their land to cattle ranchers and eucalyptus farmers. And the 1964 coup d'état sidelined the populist governor and family farming. In a part of the state where militant bishops had fuelled an active CEB network, the mayor called on these already organized citizens and launched a participatory administration that made family farming feasible. The first three sections of this chapter examine the socioeconomic basis of the limited access order, its workings, and the beginning of the transition toward a more open access order. The format and intent of this participatory administration, its partial successes, and the obstacles it faced are the topics of the three subsequent sections.

SOCIOECONOMIC FORMATION

The state of Espírito Santo has always faced insurmountable challenges to economic development. In 1535, the Portuguese settler endowed with this part of the colony was a high-ranked soldier with limited resources, not a wealthy nobleman. The indigenous populations of the region did not easily yield to friendly barter or forced labor. In 1547, three native nations united to destroy the Portuguese settlement; the colonizers had to start over in an easier-to-defend island they named Vitória, the present state capital. In the late seventeenth century, gold was found in a neighboring region, but the province did not benefit from it. The Portuguese crown considered the inhospitable jungles of Espírito Santo a great natural defense for the gold mines, and in 1704 passed a decree forbidding the opening of routes in the province (Oliveira 1975). According to one source, 85 percent of the territory of the province was still virgin forest in 1850 (Borgo, Rosa, and Pacheco 1996, 14).

Espírito Santo followed the main economic cycles of the country—*pau-brasil* (lumber), sugar, and coffee—but the aforementioned factors made the province a latecomer. The coffee expansion started in Rio de Janeiro and São Paulo in the last decades of the eighteenth century and peaked in the 1860s and 1910s, respectively. In Espírito Santo, production began in the 1820s, and then grew slowly until the 1960s. The lack of transport and commerce infrastructure hindered the expansion of coffee farming. The other key factor was the absence of a labor force. In Espírito Santo, the expansion of coffee coincided with the ban on the slave trade (1850) and the abolition of slavery (1888). São Paulo invested heavily on programs to bring migrant workers from Europe but Espírito Santo did not have as much capital (Silva 1995). In times of high coffee prices the state-sponsored immigrants who settled in holdings offered by the government (twenty-five hectares) or became tenants in large plantations (Dadalto 2003, 55–57). Saletto (1996) noted that the sharecropping contracts were very attractive due to plantation owners' desperate need for labor, but most settlers worked as tenants only for the necessary number of years to save money to start their own farm. Government policies made it easy to regulate the tenure of illegally occupied land. Settlers without land titles, known as *posseiros*, could occupy land, start producing, and pay for it years later. In 1888, 62 percent of the land of the state was occupied by *posseiros* (Saletto 1996, 117). In 1920, the average size of landholdings in Espírito Santo (sixty-one hectares) was the second smallest of all states in the country (Saletto 1996, 139). In 1966, 54 percent of arable land was divided in plots of up to one hundred hectares (Instituto Brasileiro de Geografia e Estatística 1970c, 24); the average for the country was 18 percent (Instituto Brasileiro de Geografia e Estatística 1970a, 85). This pattern of colonization and land occupation prevented the formation of a politically hegemonic landowning class in Espírito Santo.

Regional economic variations created distinct economic elites and supported specific types of social domination. The south of the state was the agriculture frontier of Rio de Janeiro's coffee growers; in the mid-1800s, large plantations with slave workforces entered the export-oriented economy centered in neighboring states. Harvests were transported to Rio de Janeiro's port and did not generate tax revenues for Espírito do Santo. Southern plantation owners formed an economic elite that remained influential for most of the twentieth century, although the end of slavery and the volatility of coffee prices forced some to hire tenants and sell parts of their land (Silva 1995). The specialized literature refers to the plantation owners of the south as the classic Brazilian *coronéis*.

The center and north of the state was a distinct socioeconomic region. The capital Vitória comprised the government bureaucracy, military corps, liberal professionals, and the import-export houses in charge of the coffee trade. The interior of the central region included traditional families with large estates acquired during colonial times and small growers (Silva 1995). In the north, the coastal city of São Mateus developed independent economic activities: the growing of cassava in large plantations, the production of cassava flour in numerous small industries, and the commercialization of the product in the city's port (Nardoto and Lima 2001). São Mateus was not the basis of a single political class; large landowners tended to support their southern counterparts whereas industrialists were more inclined to back politicians from Vitória.

The northwest region was colonized only in the twentieth century. Government programs to expand the agriculture frontier and logging companies spurred the deforestation of the region, displacing indigenous populations and making possible the settlement of small growers. Initially, settlers were Italian immigrants and freed slaves (Osório, Bravin, and Santanna 1999). In the middle of the century, new settlers arrived, mostly the descendants of immigrants established in the center and south of the state and Brazilians from neighboring states (Dadalto 2003). In 1890, Italians settlers founded a village called Nova Venécia (New Venice) seventy kilometers from São Mateus (Egler 1962, 159). In the same decade an entrepreneur founded an estate called Boa Esperança across the river from Nova Venécia, which later became a town with the same name (Nardoto and Lima 2001, 158). The first mass in Boa Esperança was celebrated in 1940, the village became a district of São Mateus in 1949, and in 1964 the district became an autonomous municipality (Azevedo and Kohlz, n.d.). Small coffee farms were the principal unit of production in the region. Although always present, logging was predatory, in the hands of foreign companies, and did not constitute an organized economy activity until the 1960s (Borgo et al. 1996).

A network of merchants brought the economies of the central and north regions together. The *vendeiro*, owner of the local store called the *venda*, was the local boss in these regions. He bought the production of small growers and sold them kerosene, salt, wheat, and other items farmers could not produce themselves. Farmers could buy overpriced products on credit, and that required them to sell their next harvest to the *vendeiro* to whom they were indebted. In personal accounts, Italian settlers repeatedly mentioned the fact that *vendeiros* had cargo animals to fetch the coffee harvested (Vilaça and Dadalto 2003). One can imagine how arduous it was to transport the year's crop without animals or vehicles. The *vendeiro* also played a patrimonial role, offering counseling and aid in time of need, baptizing the children of settlers, and solving local disputes. According to an observer of the time, *vendeiros* often exerted more authority than the priest, and disagreements between the two could disrupt peace in the community (Silva 1995, citing Ernst Wagemann 1949). According to another early observer, "Generally, famers in Espírito Santo are desolately dependent on merchants, the zonal political bosses who tie farmers through anticipated credit, making themselves bankers, and subduing entire municipalities—becoming rich while the poor farmer heroically struggles to obtain the indispensable for his maintenance" (Torres Filho 1913, as quoted in Saletto 1996, 146). Saletto (1996) classified the *vendeiro*-settler relationship as a type of "primitive accumulation," wherein capital appropriated workers' surplus without being directly involved in the production process. Silva (1995) and authors drawing on her work (Hees and Franco 2003; Vasconcellos 1995) classified the phenomenon as Espírito Santo's distinct type of *coronelismo*.

It is important not to exaggerate the social influence of *vendeiros* by simply equating them with *coronéis*. Small growers owned their land and did not grow only coffee. The climate and topography of the center and north regions were not propitious for coffee (Bittencourt 1987a); much of the harvest of the state was sold as low quality grains (Saletto 1996). However, the virgin soil and the climate were favorable to a number of other crops. In 1920, 78 percent of landholdings grew coffee, 86 percent grew corn, and 77 percent grew beans (Saletto 1996, 139–40). In 1966, the amount of land used for growing corn, beans, and rice equaled the amount dedicated to coffee (Instituto Brasileiro de Geografia e Estatística 1970c, 25). Polenta made out of corn was the staple food of Italian immigrants, and rice and beans is the most basic everyday food in Brazil. According to Rocha and Morandi (1991), smallholdings produced most of the food products necessary for their maintenance and adapted their consumption patterns in times of low coffee prices. Moreover, immigrants' accounts indicate that family holdings would often have some livestock and that in some locations it was possible to choose between two or more *vendeiros* (Vilaça and Dadalto 2003). Since small farmers' livelihood only partially depended on coffee, *vendeiros* could not exert the same control over farmers as *coronéis* had over subdued workers.

Notwithstanding this necessary qualification, the merchant network connecting local *vendeiros* to import-export houses in Vitória sustained the most influential political elite of the state. This was a closed political system not accessible to small farmers. The easy access to land in Espírito Santo was due to the fact that the merchant elite had a monopoly over commerce, not production, and were therefore interested in spurring production and consumption (Saletto 1996). Entry in the economic system was open only at the bottom of the pyramid that sustained the merchant network. This socioeconomic context helped to determine the format and objective of Boa Esperança participatory programs, which were mainly focused on making small farming a lucrative and autonomous economic activity.

LIMITED ACCESS ORDER: THE MERCANTILE AND PLANTATION ELITES

Following the Proclamation of the Republic, the elites of Espírito Santo regrouped in two political parties. One of them brought together plantation owners of all three regions of the state, while the other included the mercantile class, the small urban middle classes, and a large portion of the military and bureaucratic establishment. In spite of the distinct economic and regional base of the two parties, negotiation and accommodation were more common than confrontation. The national republican leadership appointed a plantation politician to the state government. However, disputes within the republican leadership brought to power the party of the mercantile class (Silva 1995). The leader of the party, Moniz Freire, a journalist from Vitória, governed the state from 1892 to 1896 and from 1900 to 1904. Henrique Coutinho, Freire's vice governor, led the state from 1904 to 1908. Coutinho had disagreements with his vice governor and expected successor, Freire's son-in-law, which generated a stalemate within the party. To prevent conflict, the party invited the bishop of the state to be the party's candidate. Don Fernando declined the offer but appointed his brother Jerônimo Monteiro to the position (Hees and Franco 2003).

The Monteiros were the most influential family in Espírito Santo in the first half of the twentieth century. Francisco de Souza Monteiro, a thriving merchant, bought some land in the south of the state in 1851 and soon after married the daughter of a prosperous tradesman. The dowry was a piece of land and a family of slaves. Francisco, his wife Henriqueta, and their slaves went on to build Monte Líbano, one of the most opulent plantations of Espírito Santo. Francisco became a *coronel* in control of local politics and very influential in the south region; he died at age forty-eight, leaving Henriqueta the control of the family. Of their five children, Jerônimo and Bernardino went to law school in São Paulo and later became involved in politics; Fernando went to seminary and became the state's Bishop (Vasconcellos 1995).

Support for the candidacy of the son of a southern *coronel* by the merchant class's party symbolized a truce between the state's political elites. The uncontestable political control of these two elites is illustrated in the 1908 election results: Jerônimo Monteiro received 7,989 votes, whereas the two other candidates together received 23 votes (Hees and Franco 2003, 54). Jerônimo and a leader of the mercantile class founded the Espírito Santo Republican (Partido Republicano Espírito Santense), which brought together the two dominant elites into one organization that would facilitate intra-elite negotiation. Jerônimo was governor between 1908 and 1912, managed to elect his successor, became state representative, and later senator. Bernadino Monteiro was elected senator in 1909 and then governor from 1916 to 1920. In 1919, Bernardino wanted to appoint his successor, but Jerônimo wanted the position back for himself or for an appointee of his. The brothers' old quarrels developed into conflict, and even shots (without victims). Bernardino won. The clan previously known as *monteiristas* became split between *bernardistas* and *jeronistas*. Bernardino was the representative of the mercantile class, while his brother was the preferred Monteiro of plantation owners. In 1924, an agreement between the two brothers led to the election of Florentino Avidos, their brother-in-law (Achiamé 2010).

In the First Republic, the mercantile class was at the top of the elite hierarchy and had more influence over the state's development agenda. "The basic priority of public funding was infrastructural build-up: the building of roads and bridges to transport the coffee production, investments in urban implements, and the construction of Vitória's port" (Silva 1995, 107–8). In turn, Jerônimo's government tried to spur industrialization and promote the diversification of crops, but results were meager. The state lacked infrastructure, capital, and skilled labor. Jerônimo used revenue from years of high coffee prices to invest in industrialization, but efforts were unsustainable in the absence of basic factors of production (Bittencourt 1987b). The interests of small farmers were not included in either program; due to the exploitative *vendeiro*–small farmer relationship at the local level, increased coffee sales did not directly entail improvement in the conditions of growers. In the 1920s, high coffee revenues helped to improve the infrastructure of the state. Toward the end of the decade, investments were yielding results, and Espírito Santo politicians were finally starting to participate in the inner circles of the national coffee elite led by São Paulo farmers (Achiamé 2010). Once again, Espírito Santo was late. The coffee elite was about to lose political control of the country.

TOWARD AN OPEN ACCESS ORDER:
SMALL FARMERS ENTER THE POLITICAL AGENDA

In 1930, *bernardistas* and *jeronistas* supported the federal government and president's choice for the upcoming election, whereas a minority of politicians excluded from the dominant elite coalition joined Vargas's Liberal Alliance. When it came time to choose a governor, the revolutionary elite could not come to a consensus about a name, mainly because their loyalties rested with distinct economic and regional groups. After standing out in the revolutionary campaign, Captain João Punaro Bley had become the military member of the tripartite provisional government. The Commerce Association of Vitória saw in Captain Bley a safe choice and suggested his name to President Vargas, who was pleased to appoint one of his military fellows (Achiamé 2010).

Bley appointed supporters of the Liberal Alliance to municipal governments, in some cases altering the local balance of power, in others simply bolstering already dominant families. Once elections were scheduled for 1934, Bley was in charge of organizing the PSD in the state, and for this, he reverted to old political practices. The uncle of Carlos Monteiro Linderberg, one of Bley's aides, was none other than Jerônimo Monteiro, who authorized his nephew to mobilize *coronéis* in the south (Achiamé 2010). A segment of the mercantile class also joined the PSD (Silva 1995). The opposition party gathered the political elites sidelined by the new regime, which included Jerônimo Filho, Jerônimo's son, and Nelson Monteiro, Bernardino's son. This opposition group was strong and threatened the incumbent governor's candidacy for the 1934 election. Bley managed to break the opposition coalition by sending a letter to Jerônimo Filho's mother, explaining that her son was supporting the candidacy of the son of a former political enemy of her husband. Jerônimo backed down.

Bley won the election and stayed in power throughout most of Vargas's authoritarian period (Achiamé 2010).

Although politically entangled with local elites, Bley managed to stay the course of the state's economic development according to Vargas's national strategies. The 1929 international crisis brutally affected the revenue of the state, which was almost solely reliant on coffee export taxes. Fiscal adjustment was therefore one of Bley's priorities. He created a state agency to supervise municipal administrations and investigate cases of mishandling of public resources, sending auditors to scrutinize the work of mayors around the state. Achiamé (2010) noted that this direct intervention in municipal affairs constituted a marked change from the First Republic, during which governors simply endorsed the most prominent local groups. Bley also made considerable investments in health and education; between 1930 and 1933, expenditure in education increased fourfold (Silva 1995, 120). The administration built new roads, reequipped the port, invested in the manufacturing of sugar, created a vocational agriculture school, and supported cattle farmers in the south of the state. Finally, the governor created a rural credit bank for small growers with the objective of fomenting cooperative agriculture. According to Silva (1995), development policies in this period were independent from impositions from the local oligarchy and in line with national industrializing strategies.

The composition of the major national parties in the 1945–1964 period followed national trends. Toward the end of the authoritarian regime, Vargas replaced Bley with Jones dos Santos Neves, a well-established politician from the São Mateus region, who had occupied important positions in government since the revolution. Jones's main task was to reconcile the elites and reorganize the PSD. Bley's assertive policies had made him unfit for the task. Neves was successful. The new PSD founded in 1945 included most of the mercantile and the large landowning elites, both the "ins" and "outs" of the Vargas period. The National Democratic Union grouped intellectuals, liberal professionals, and opponents of politicians included in the PSD. The Brazilian Labor Party (PTB) included leaders of urban sectors sympathetic to Vargas.

The particularities of the state's socioeconomic context are found in the characteristics of the minority parties. The Popular Representation

Party (Partido de Representação Popular, PRP) was born out of the fascist movement and initially led by Priest Ponciano Stenzel. First, the PRP appealed mostly to German and Italian migrants and their descendants, some of whom had previously supported fascists. The Catholic priest leader helped to boost the influence of the party in Italian towns where the Church was strong. The socioeconomic basis of the party was small growers, who for the first time had a political organization to represent their interests. The Progressive Social Party (Partido Social Progressista, PSP), founded by populist politicians of São Paulo, was also an important political group in the period. Leftist groups active in various parts of the country did not find fertile ground in Espírito Santo.

The new social group represented by the PRP and the new political practices of the PSP slowly became part of the state's political context, competing for space with traditional elites and their intra-elite maneuvers. In 1947, two PSD contenders disputed the gubernatorial elections. On the one hand, Carlos Lindenberg represented the traditional agriculture elite of the south of the state. In the campaign, he felt forced to reach out to small growers. One of his public notes stated that, "small growers should not pay any taxes . . . all taxes must be paid by the distributing centers" (quoted in Silva 1995, 235). This pledge drew the support of the PRP. On the other hand, the jurist Attilio Vivacqua represented the progressive forces within the PSD. Vivacqua's image of accomplished intellectual enthralled the emerging urban elites, but in the interior of the state his intricate proposal to reform state institutions did not have the same appeal as the "zero taxes" refrain. Lindenberg received 65 percent of the votes, and his coalition gained the two senate posts and half of the seats in the representative chamber. Old and new political groups shared the other half of the representative chamber (Silva 1995).

The 1950 election reaffirmed the political might of traditional elites and the efficacy of traditional practices. The Lindenberg administration was conservative and largely focused on responding to the agriculture class's demands and by doing so consolidated the political basis of the PSD. In the process, the PRP had its demands sidelined, which led it to join an unsuccessful anti-PSD coalition for the 1950 election. This time the PSD made an alliance with the PTB and launched a campaign appealing to poor urban workers. The PSD candidate Jones dos Santos Neves

became the new governor. Santos Neves followed an autonomous policy agenda informed by nationalist-developmentalist ideals of the time;
his authoritarian-technocratic approach was difficult to advance without
breaching political pacts.

In 1955, an opposition coalition representing the mercantile class, the
PRP of small growers and the PTB of the urban working class was finally
successful in winning a state election. Although a wealthy farmer, the
coalition candidate did not have family bonds with conservative groups;
instead of being known by a reputable last name, he went by "Chiquinho,"
an affectionate nickname for Francisco. Chiquinho was a federal representative in Rio de Janeiro between 1950 and 1955, at the peak of Vargas's populism in the country's capital and Adhemar de Barros's rise in
São Paulo. He learned the new style of doing politics and successfully
conveyed the image of a common man, a farmer, a father figure; his campaign included catchy jingles and for the first time a candidate visited
poor areas (Silva 1995). Whereas Santos Neves focused on industrialization projects, Chiquinho reoriented development policies toward small
growers and small agribusinesses.

The opposition coalition that elected Chiquinho became fragmented
and unable to forge an alliance for the 1958 elections, which allowed for
the return of Carlos Lindenberg as governor. In 1959, political forces representing industrial interests formed the Industrial Federation of Espírito
Santo (FINDES), which rapidly gained space within the PSD. The influence of industrialists within the PSD was visible in the selection of the
candidate for the 1962 election. While Lindenberg tried an alliance with
the PSP, the industrial faction successfully pushed the name of Neves, the
developmentalist governor who had previously displeased the traditional
landowning class (Silva 1995).

The 1962 election marked the end of intra-elite politics. On the one
hand, there was a PSD internally divided between the traditional elites
and the new industrialist groups; their candidate had already governed
the state and pushed industrialization. The party stubbornly refused
to make coalitions and trusted elite arrangements that had previously
won it numerous elections. On the other hand, the various opposition
parties representing the mercantile class and recently included political groups backed Chiquinho's candidacy. The alliance heavily invested
in populist tactics that had become even more prominent in the 1960

presidential elections. In the end, the coalition alliance won all major posts—governor, vice governor, and the senate seats—and reduced the PSD space in the legislative chamber (Silva 1995, 406). In government, Chiquinho turned the state apparatus toward small growers. The Credit and Rural Assistance Association of Espírito Santo replaced the FINDES as the most influential lobby group.

In 1964 the military came to power, and within two years Chiquinho was forced to resign. In the next two decades, the federal government and its appointed governors highhandedly sidelined small agriculture from the development agenda. Initiated soon before the 1964 coup, the eradication of coffee farms was a federal response to low prices of the product in international markets. The average price of a sack of coffee went from US$16 in 1945 to US$86 in 1954, leading to a 74 percent increase of the number of coffee trees in Espírito Santo between 1940 and 1960 (Rocha and Morandi 1991, 47). Overproduction soon made prices plunge. In 1962, a federal agency started to promote the eradication of low-productivity farms by paying a set price per burnt coffee tree. Espírito Santo was the most affected coffee-producing state because of the low productivity of its farms and overall low quality of its coffee. An estimated 54 percent of the state's coffee trees were burned between 1962 and 1966 (Rocha and Morandi 1991, 52).

Whereas in states with market-oriented agriculture the eradication program led to the diversification of production, in Espírito Santo eradication meant a profound change in the economic basis of the state. Seventy percent of the area freed by eradication became grazing fields. In the 1950s, grazing fields occupied 23 percent of the state's rural area; by 1970, the activity was using 55 percent of all available land. As a less labor-intensive activity than coffee farming, cattle farming absorbed only 13 percent of the 73,470 workers made unemployed by the eradication program (Rocha and Morandi 1991, 66, 58). The second economic activity spurred by the eradication program was logging and lumber production. Logging extraction increased almost fivefold between 1954 and 1974; from 1960 to 1975, the area used for forestry increased from 398 to 142,239 hectares (Rocha and Morandi 1991, 62, 72). Coffee farms ceased to be the predominant unit of production in Espírito Santo's rural area.

While the eradication program began before 1964, the military regime played an unequivocal role pushing industrialization and disregarding other development agendas. The authoritarian federal government, exclusively dedicated to the modernization of the country's social and economic structure, made industrialization the only development alternative for Espírito Santo. Numerous industrialization schemes and policies were implemented in the late 1960s and early 1970s. The main goal was to promote primary industries that could process local natural resources. Funds for these initiatives came from the state and federal government as well as private investors. The most notable initiatives included infrastructure projects, a development bank, federal tax cuts for new industries, the creation of industrial districts, and a fund to foment port activities and tourism. Large industries with mixed state and private capital also received numerous incentives (Bittencourt 1987b).[1]

The rapid shift in the economic basis of the state created grave social problems due to the inability of the industrial sector to absorb the newly available workforce and the lack of state capacity to provide the necessary social programs. Like many other state capitals in the country, Vitória received a rural exodus that it could not adequately accommodate. In the interior of the state, "the decline of traditional economic activities caused the stagnation and even the decay of a large number of municipalities" (Bittencourt 1987b, 208). Boa Esperança, in the northeast region, was one of these impoverished municipalities. In 1970, Boa Esperança had 11,387 inhabitants in an area of 344 square kilometers (Instituto Brasileiro de Geografia e Estatística 1970b, 16); out of the 695 land holdings, 486 had up to 50 hectares and 613 up to 100 hectares (Instituto Brasileiro de Geografia e Estatística 1970a, 134–35). Largely dependent on the production of coffee, Boa Esperança was one of the towns bankrupted by the eradication of coffee farms. According to the mayor responsible for the 1970s' participatory administration,

> The municipal economy consisted of 18 thousand cows and the logging of the remaining native timber. Houses lost their commercial value and commerce was reduced to a bar, a basic grocery store, and two little fabric stores.
>
> On average, ten flatbed trucks with wooden seats (*pau-de-arara*) left the city each month taking families to the states of Paraná, Rondônia, Mato Grosso, Goiás and Pará. Cattle ranchers planned to transform the downtown square into a cattle-loading station.

In this period, the State Financial Board advised the governor to abolish the municipality and reincorporate it to the city of São Mateus, due to its economic infeasibility. This news spread and all state secretariats had their doors closed to Boa Esperança, making matters worse for everyone.

Small and middle holdings were disappearing, sold to cattle ranchers for very low prices. In order to facilitate acquisitions, cattle farmers recklessly burnt fields, destroying planted areas, expelling men, and replaced them with cows.

This was the lamentable situation of [Boa Esperança] when we were elected to care for the town's fate, in the two-year administration of 1971–1972. There was only one way to save [the municipality]: guided by the hands of the Almighty, we began community work. This work was interrupted between 1973 and 1976 because my successor did not share this ideology. In 1977, again in control of the municipality's fate, we reactivated community work, and made it official in order to avoid future interruptions. (Covre 1980, 1–2)

Local-level participatory programs are commonly associated with burgeoning urban centers, but the pioneer participatory initiative examined below took place in a decayed rural town.

MAYOR COVRE AND CEB LEADERS: A COMMUNITY PARTY

Mayor Amaro Covre was the mind behind and the face of Boa Esperança's participatory administration, but an enthusiastic group of twelve inexperienced public servants was crucial for the success of the initiative, as Covre himself recognized. The project relied on the staff's ability to engage existing community leaders. The ecclesial base communities (CEBs) were very strong in the region of São Mateus and in the rural neighborhoods of Boa Esperança, and the leadership it formed became Covre's community organizers.

Amaro Covre grew up on a coffee farm in a region south of Boa Esperança. He started working in the farm at age eight and later was sent to a Marist school that "formed [his] spirit and forged [his] character" (Amaro Covre, personal communication, January 20–22, 2011).

His father had fifteen tenants, "all very well taken care of," and was never involved in politics. Three of his brothers and one of his sisters married the children of tenants—an astounding fact for those whose view of Latin America's countryside rely on the literary portrayals of Isabel Allende. In the late 1950s, Covre worked in state storage facilities and was personally responsible for burning 180 thousand sacks of coffee. This experience had a profound impact on his view of agriculture and the need to diversify production. In the mid-1960s, Covre helped to found the MDB of Boa Esperança and partook in political activities organized by the Brazilian Democratic Center (CEBRADE), an organization blacklisted by the military regime. One day, hours before leaving for a CEBRADE event in Rio de Janeiro, he received a phone call warning that he was going to be arrested at the airport. He cancelled the trip and later received a call from the governor offering to erase his dissenter background records if he left the MDB and joined the ARENA. Covre replied, "right away, where do I sign?" The "headache" was over.

Amaro Covre's most marked characteristic was pragmatism, which is exemplified in the fact that his administration had the very concrete aim of making family farming economically viable. This stands in contrast with Dirceu Carneiro's charismatic leadership and ideologically driven administration. This difference in the style and motivation of the two mayors did not have a dramatic impact on the implementation of participatory initiatives. As the next section shows, the two cities had similar successes and failures. This is in part due to the fact that both mayors counted on the help of a team of equally enthusiastic community organizers fully devoted to the participatory administration, but largely uninterested in party politics. The contrast will become sharper as we compare these two cities with Diadema, which was headed by a political party in the making.

Mayor Covre described his staff as a "small and multifaceted team." The vice mayor, Valdelino Zagotto, deceased by the time of this research, was a lay religious leader. Interviewees described Valdelino as a senior and esteemed citizen who won the administration the respect of more conventional groups. Valdelino's son Joelson was the mayor's aide. He eventually left the administration to follow his seminary studies in Paraná, but returned every summer to assist the team. The administrative head was Maria Motta, whose family was very active religiously; her testimony shed light on the slowly mutating nature of religious groups in the city. Another foot soldier was Teresinha Bergamin, the coordinator of one of the community centers. Teresinha described her work in Boa Esperança as directly linked with her Italian background, the community values in which she was raised, and her involvement in what she called a "very open Catholicism" (personal communication, January 25, 2010). The Social Assistance Department was staffed with two dedicated workers who received visits from citizens in need at home in the late hours and left dinners unfinished to attend requests from the mayor. Dulce Maria da Costa and Lidia Pasti Moreira mentioned working closely with church groups, although they were not personally involved with the Catholic Church (personal communications, January 21 and 22, 2011). Miguel Lorenzone, then in charge of public works, recalled that the top priority was to listen to community leaders' demands (personal communication, January 22, 2010).[2]

Oral depictions portrayed a young, very devoted and enthusiastic team. None of the interviewees had previous political or public service experience. Joelson participated in the diocese's Catholic youth groups and described this as the political experience that prepared him for the work with Mayor Covre. According to Joelson, "most of the people working with us [in the administration] had this same type of training" (personal communication, January 22, 2011). My assessment is that Joelson's assertion applies to two-thirds of the team. The topic of party politics did not naturally emerge in interviews, and when asked, interviewees had difficulty recollecting anything on the matter. The two Zagottos participated in the founding of the PT in the mid-1980s but eventually left the party and party politics. Miguel became the owner of a construction material store. After a career as a social worker in São Mateus, Maria considered running for the municipal legislature but decided to focus on her community work instead (personal communication, January 24, 2011). During our interview, she had to make calls to finish organizing that afternoon's meeting of a church-related community organization. Dulce and Lidia continued to work as social assistants for the municipal governments (personal communication, January 23, 2011). Teresinha moved to Vitória, where she continued to work with education and run volunteer social projects. All interviewees had fond memories of the Amaro Covre years and distaste for party politics.

It is difficult to specify the magnitude of CEBs because of insufficient data and the fact that groups had varying combinations of politically oriented and purely ecumenical activities. Nevertheless, it is possible to affirm with confidence that São Mateus and Boa Esperança had a strong CEB presence. The most comprehensive quantitative study on the subject found that Espírito Santo had thirty-two ecclesiastic communities per parish whereas the national average was sixteen (Valle and Pitta 1994, 45). A booklet printed in 1979 by the Diocese of São Mateus listed 456 communities in its thirteen parishes, thirty-five on average (45). The parish of Pinheiros, which at the time included Boa Esperança, had thirty-eight ecclesiastic communities (Diocese de São Mateus 1979, 3). However, the study by Valle and Pitta (1994) also noted that in the region including the states of Espírito Santo and Minas Gerais, only 41 percent of the ecclesial communities declared having socioeconomic activities, and an even lower 38 percent admitted to participation in political organizations (56). These averages are lower than most other regions of the country, and there is no data available for specific dioceses.

Nevertheless, the history of the Diocese of São Mateus attests to the outstandingly active and progressive character of the Church in this part of the country in the examined period. In a state that received large contingents of Italian and German migrants, Catholicism endured in spite of an underdeveloped Church infrastructure. Until the 1950s, the state of Espírito Santo was a diocese within the archdiocese of Rio de Janeiro. In 1937, the bishop of Vitória sent Priest Guilherme Schimitz to the parish of São Mateus. Schimitz reported having found the parish in a terrible condition: an unfinished church inhabited by bats, no parochial home, and insufficient candles for daily masses. He was responsible for the entire São Mateus region, which at the time covered almost a third of the state; horses and canoes were used to reach the villages, where malaria was a constant concern (Nardoto and Lima 2001).

In 1954, Italian Comboni missionaries arrived in São Mateus to support the Church's efforts in the region. In 1958, Vitória became an archdiocese and São Mateus one of its two dioceses. Comboni Priest José Maria Dalvit became São Mateus's first bishop, loyally assisted by Priest Aldo Gerna. Between 1962 and 1965, the two returned to Italy to participate in the Second Vatican Council and while there raised funds for their deprived diocese. Upon return, Don José worked to implement the Church's new vision. In the following years, he founded a training center for rural leaders, a seminary for priests and lay leaders, and a typography center, among other things. Don José's most popular maxim was "we have to help the people to help themselves" (Nardoto and Lima 2001, 415). Don José stepped down in 1970 due to ill health.

In 1971, Don José's loyal aide was made bishop of São Mateus. Don Aldo Gerna was an exemplary Liberation Theology leader. A novice in the years of the Second Vatican Council, he rapidly embraced the Church's "preferential option for poor." He rose in the Church hierarchy in the late 1960s, became an energetic advocate of social justice, promoted CEBs and unions, and helped to organize the Landless Workers' Movement (MST). In the 1980s, the Vatican scolded Don Aldo for his exaggerated attention to political questions, and displeased coronéis sent him two death threats because of his support for landless workers (personal communication, January 24, 2011).

In an interview, Don Aldo noted that when he became bishop the diocese still had very few priests, and the work in the communities was just starting. This gave him the chance to start almost from zero. Don Aldo did not face internal resistance since he ordained all the new clergy. He recalled mimeographing CEB booklets one by one and leading "political faith" study groups. "Fundamentally, participation was a requirement; if you participate in your community, you can receive the sacrament, if not, we will see [laugh].... People joked that I asked to see their union cards before giving them the communion." Don Aldo acknowledged that his forceful emphasis on social and political participation caused the disenchantment of a considerable number of followers who joined evangelical groups. He held Zagotto, the vice mayor of Boa Esperança, in high regard, "a religious leader much more than a politician." Don Aldo valued the work done by Mayor Covre but found it limited to economic objectives, as opposed to the more fundamental reforms Liberation Theology promoted. According to the former bishop, the Covre administration built on the work done by the Church but did not replace it because the goals of each project were different.

In Boa Esperança, CEBs and the associations involved in the participatory initiative seemed to have had a mutually reinforcing relationship. It is often difficult to distinguish them in written and oral descriptions of the experience. The confusion is at least in part due to the fact that Covre's team named neighborhood associations "base communities," without the "ecclesial." The only piece published on Boa Esperança's participatory administration is unclear on this topic. Writing in 1982, sociologist and activist Herbert de Souza states that

> In the last 10 years, some local leadership and the Church developed in this area a process of organization of base communities concerned with studying and solving the local population's problems. In November of 1971, the experience of the base communities gained a legal format, becoming a not-for-profit, non-partisan, non-religious civic association constituted by representatives of social, cultural, and economic organizations and community leaders: The Municipal Development Council of Boa Esperança. (Souza 1982, 104)

It is not possible to know whether "the experience of base communities" refers to CEBs or the lay base communities that Mayor Covre first tried to organized in 1971. In 1981, a news piece on Boa Esperança's initiative read as follows, "the base communities organized by the church played a fundamental role; in 1971, *they became* civil society organizations constituted by representatives of economic and cultural organizations and community leaders" (Tragtenberg 1981, emphasis added). These and other similar accounts, but especially Souza's widely read piece, have disseminated the idea that CEBs became the community organization of the participatory initiative.

An unpublished report of Boa Esperança's participatory administration by researchers of the Brazilian Institute of Municipal Administration (Instituto Brasilerio de Administração Municipal, IBAM) offers a contrasting view to Souza's piece. The report explains that "some of the base communities had been previously organized by work conducted by the Church and some local leaders, which made it easier to implement the mayor's plans" (Lobo, Oliveira, Lopes, Rocha, and Cortez 1984, 113). This attenuated version is more consistent with the testimonies of Don Aldo and the lay leaders in the administration. Maria Motta explained that ecclesial groups had been present for a long time, but slowly became more organized. In the rural parts of town, Catholic families routinely gathered in each other's houses to worship. Whenever a school was built, the same site became the area's center, and communal efforts were made to construct a church. The new church would bring together people from the various ecclesial communities.

Covre's team shrewdly based the five district centers of the participatory initiative in the main schools of the town, taking advantage of this preexisting organizational structure. Joelson Zagotto attested that the design of the participatory structure took into account the existence of already organized communities. In testimony collected by Souza (1982), an interviewee explained that in his district center, five of the eight community leaders were also CEB leaders. Teresinha Bergamin affirmed that CEBs and community leaders "were the same people." She noted that in the rural communities leaders had an encompassing role. Thus, the Boa Esperança participatory administration rested on synergy among a practical-minded mayor confident of the potential of community work, a diocese actively promoting political participation, a group of devoted public servants with experience in community organization acquired in Catholic circles, and a preexistent community organizational structure. As the next section shows, these social actors united to resist a national and state development agenda that neglected small growers.

THE PARTICIPATORY ADMINISTRATION

The participatory administration of Boa Esperança had as its main objective the creation of conditions that would allow for the permanence and prosperity of small growers, and in this way deter the rural exodus that threatened to bankrupt the city. Mayor Covre and his team designed a participatory structure based mainly on small growers. Education, health, culture, and agriculture programs branched from this participatory structure. Data suggests that the initiative achieved its main goals, but was only partially successful in promoting a participatory political culture.

The initiative rested on a clear structure. The city had five districts: Sobradinho, KM 20, Santo Antonio, Bela Vista, and Sede; each district had between four and ten base communities, totaling thirty-three communities. Each district had a Centro de Irradiação (Outreach Center) with an infrastructure that included a sports court, a social hall, a health clinic, a police station, and phone posts. Base communities usually used the local school as their communal space. Dirt roads connected communities to their respective Irradiation Centers, and paved roads connected the latter to the downtown core (Souza 1982).

The functioning of the participatory schema was equally clear. Base communities met bi-monthly to discuss local problems and needs. Elected community leaders met bi-monthly in the Irradiation Centers to debate the problems of each community and elaborate a program to attend the district's needs. The mayor and his team also attended these meetings. According to Covre (1980), "the objective of the Centro de Irradiação [was] to allow the families that constitute it to live in society, with all the necessary assistance, and provide conditions for the permanence of the rural men" (8). At the top of the participatory structure was the city's Development Council, "a not-for-profit civil society organization constituted by [community] leaders, the mayor, the vice mayor, legislative representatives, priests, pastors, union leaders, representatives of technical and credit agencies, principals of primary and secondary schools, the director of the hospital, the director of the sanitation unit, the police chief, the justice officer, and the public attorney" (Covre 1980, 9).

The Council met twice a month: once with the leaders of the Centro de Irradiação of the urban area and once with the leaders of the four rural districts. The tasks of the Council included "to bring together decisions made in the Centros de Irradiação in a single work plan that can attend to everyone at the Municipal level . . . [and] send this plan to the mayor and the legislative assembly in order for it to inform the elaboration of the budget and the use of funds from federal programs" (Covre 1980, 10). Another task of the Council was to engage with state and federal agencies operating in the city to ensure they worked in accordance with priorities determined by local communities.

According to Souza (1982), the Development Council created a new type of state-civil society relation wherein political power rested on the community and political parties were redundant. As the only published piece on the subject, it is worth quoting Souza's account in length.

The Council is in fact the sovereign assembly of the municipality, to which the mayor, the bureaucracy, and the legislative representatives are subjected. This power relation is exerted directly, every month.

Citizens elect legislative representatives as leaders of the communities to which they belong. They act in the Council as community leaders and in the legislative assembly as elected representatives; however, [in the latter] they *act according to decisions made in the Council.*

The mayor is a member of the Council and in charge of leading the meetings; however, *he submits himself to majority decisions just as all other members. . . . The bureaucracy is submitted to a double control, from the mayor and from the community, in monthly meetings where everyone's tasks are followed up and the veracity of information passed on to the mayor, legislative representatives, and the community is verified.*

Finally, current political parties more or less lose their function. Party divisions are in a way external to the reality of the municipality, and do not correspond to the diversity of interests concretely present in the city. . . . The contradictions existent within the community are not expressed in the form of an officially institutionalized political "opposition" removed from power; instead [contradictions] are resolved in assemblies that make decisions by simple majority. In Boa Esperança, PSD and MDB representatives are not distinguished by the differences of their respective parties, but in terms of the concrete performance of their duties as community leaders: the communities to which they belong, not party programs, determine their commitments and duties. (Souza 1982, 113, emphasis in the original)

Souza was closely involved in the experience, and his account is more optimistic than that of the authors of IBAM's unpublished report. Even if perhaps unintentionally confounding facts with visions, it is clear in Souza's description how the participatory administration of Boa Esperança attempted to create a form of direct democracy that disregarded the tenets of a representative system. In the Development Council, elected representatives and the mayor sat side-by-side with the delegates of Irradiation Centers, ignoring the distinction between formal representation and community advocacy.

The activities of the Irradiation Centers and the Development Council were focused on testing new crops and organizing cooperatives to commercialize products and share machinery. In the beginning of his mandate, Mayor Covre forwarded to the legislative chamber a municipal bill defining the use of the city's land according to quotas discussed with growers and cattle farmers. Although unconstitutional, the bill passed and set the following limits for land use: 20 percent for coffee, 32 percent for livestock, 10 percent for cassava, 8 percent for sugarcane, 10 percent for other crops, and 10 percent for preservation and reforestation (Lobo et al. 1984, 112). Moreover, four "experimental crops" were introduced in "testing fields" around Irradiation Centers: black pepper, soya, sorghum, and rubber. Toward the end of his mandate, Mayor Covre proposed the creation of a sugarcane biodiesel cooperative factory. Many advocates of family farming saw this project as a move toward monocropping and contrary to everything the administration had previously promoted. Don Aldo was a vocal opponent of the project. The administration thought the activity could be interspersed with other crops, and that the land usage law would impede monocropping. Private investors established the factory in the mid-1980s, already in a different administration.

The participatory administration also launched numerous other initiatives in other areas of government. Basic infrastructure in rural areas constituted an important element in the plan of avoiding rural exodus. The city opened or paved 320 kilometers of back roads. Electricity was also a main concern. The Development Council decided in favor of requesting those to be benefitted by the new electrical infrastructure to contribute with material or work so that funds transferred by the state government extended the service much further than forecasted. The administration built schools in rural communities and the aforementioned infrastructure of Irradiation Centers (Lobo et al. 1984, 115).

Shantytowns had already formed in the urban center by the beginning of the Covre period. The administration tried to address the need for popular housing in the same way as Lages: *mutirão*. The main difference between the two cities was that Amaro Covre was a PSD mayor and received state government funding. Resources were limited, however, and the participation of the population made projects much cheaper. Future residents were involved in every aspect of the project, from choosing suppliers to the actual building of the houses. The city hired the more skilled construction personnel, but the community did most of the construction work. In the end, the administration managed to save part of the money channeled by the state government. Mayor Covre then opened a savings account for each family and deposited their respective fraction of the saved funds; with the high interest rates of the period, the money paid for a considerable portion of the state-subsidized loans due within the next years. The idea of unused public funding was so absurd that federal inspectors came from Brasilia to investigate possible corruption schemes (Amaro Covre, personal communication, January 20–22, 2011).

Education programs also included community participation and took into account the rural vocation of the city. The administration created an agricultural vocational school in the urban center with the ambitious goal of training one agriculture technician per family. In the Irradiation Centers, fourteen youth groups received vocational training and support to organize social activities "by and for" rural teens (Lobo et al. 1984). Funds for this project also came from the state government. Finally, Volkswagen Kombis transported teachers to and from rural schools; this service was costly for the administration but was a priority because proximity to schools was one of the main pull factors of urban living.

The administration's Kombis also transported doctors and dentists to rural areas as part of an attempt to decentralize health care. The health post of each Irradiation Center had a nurse and a domestic economist whose work focused mainly on preventive health. In some districts, health post staff coordinated community gardens that brought together primary school students, youth, pregnant women, and anyone interested in learning about gardening and nutrition. Food harvested at the gardens went to the schools' kitchens. Toward the end of the administration, a Home Industry Community Cooperative was established. "The idea was to integrate house work with the local economy" (Lobo et al. 1984). Homemade products included soap, cheese, baskets, wine, and candy. The original project included setting up a large distribution network, but in the end only one store sold cooperatives' products. Women involved in the project expected to earn a steady income, and the small and sporadic returns from sales de-motivated them.

Every year a large field fair brought together all the Irradiation Centers. The idea was to promote amicable competition among the communities, share experiences with new crops and growing techniques, and offer an opportunity for community building. Music, food, and sports animated the event. Awards were given to the most productive Irradiation Center. Tenants and wageworkers that acquired land received "model worker" awards, and land titles were publicly handed with much ceremony (Covre 1980).

The participatory administration was successful in its main goal of making small farming a feasible economic activity. Agricultural censuses allow for indicative comparisons between Boa Esperança and its neighboring towns: São Mateus, to which it once belonged; Nova Venécia, the Italian settlement on the southern border; and Pinheiros, the northern neighbor. Table 4.1 shows that whereas in São Mateus and Pinheiros the percentage of small and median holdings dropped by half from 1970 to 1985, Boa Esperança and Nova Venécia witnessed only a 7 percent decrease. Noteworthy, Boa Esperança showed a reaction between 1975 and 1980, with a 3 percent rise. In the same period, São Mateus and Pinheiros continued on a descent, and Nova Venécia improved by less than 1 percent. In the mid-1980s, Boa Esperança and Nova Venécia still had more than a third of their land occupied by small and median farmers.

Table 4.2 shows that Boa Esperança was more effective than its neighbors in resisting the encroachment of cattle farms. In 1975, agriculture used 30 percent of the land and cattle farming used 69 percent; by 1985, agriculture occupied 56 percent of the land and cattle farming 41 percent. This 44 percent increase in the percentage of land used for agriculture was superior to that witnessed in São Mateus and Pinheiros, and close

Table 4.1. Percentage of Land Occupied by Plots between 10 and 100 Hectares

	1970	1975	1980	1985
Boa Esperança	42	34	37	35
São Mateus	41	25	20	18
Pinheiros	34	22	16	17
Nova Venécia	46	38	39	39

Source: Information compiled from agricultural censuses published by Instituto Brasileiro de Geografia e Estatística (1970a, 134–137; 1979, 162–165; 1983, 184–187; 1985, 218–21).

Table 4.2. Percentage of Land Use for Agriculture and for Cattle Farming, 1975–1985

	1975		1980		1985	
	Agric.	Cattle	Agric.	Cattle	Agric.	Cattle
Boa Esperança	30	69	47	46	56	41
São Mateus	30	43	22	37	34	27
Pinheiros	11	88	22	66	32	60
Nova Venécia	28	69	43	49	56	37

Source: Information compiled from agricultural censuses published by Instituto Brasileiro de Geografia e Estatística (1979, 146; 1983, 156; 1985, 186).

to the 46 percent achieved by Nova Venécia. Remarkably, Boa Esperança was the first of the four cities to turn the game around; in 1980, during the participatory administration, agriculture had already surpassed cattle farming.

One widely publicized figure about the success of the Amaro Covre administration was that during his tenure, Boa Esperança went from last place to the 33rd position in a ranking comparing the tax revenues of all fifty-five municipalities of Espírito Santo (Covre 1980, 15; Lobo et al. 1984, 136; Souza 1982, 119).[3] The authors do not provide dates or specific statistics but probably refer to the 1971–1972 Covre administration, because another study shows that in 1974 Boa Esperança made the 36th largest contribution to the state revenue (Garcia 2002, 33). It is possible to use the data in the latter study to calculate percentage changes in cities' contributions to the state revenue, and then plot these values against a common start point, isolating differences in cities' sizes. Figure 4.1 shows the evolution of the four cities in the period from 1978 to 1982, using ten as the common start point for 1977. Boa Esperança presented the best performance with an increase of 31 percent in the period. Nova Venécia had an accumulated increase of 7 percent. São Mateus and Pinheiros closed the period with small declines in their contribution to the state revenue.

Finally, Boa Esperança managed to avoid eucalyptus and pine plantations, the second activity spurred by the coffee eradication program of the 1960s. The 1970 and 1975 censuses do not even mention the city in the tables for this economic activity. Boa Esperança appears in the

Figure 4.1. Evolution of Boa Esperança's Contribution to State Revenue, 1978–1982

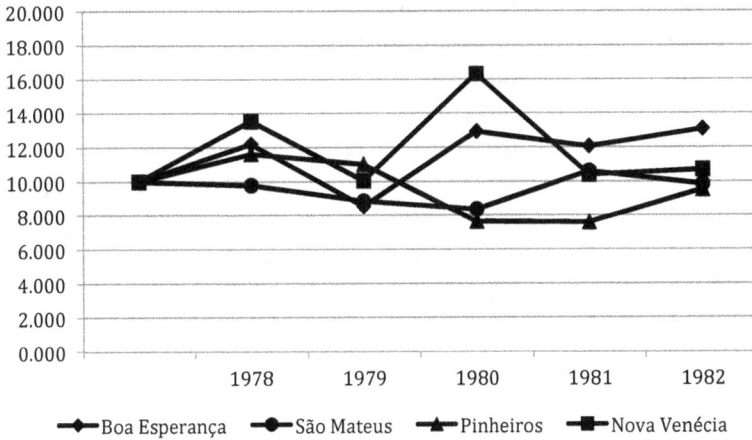

Source: Municipal participation indexes listed in Garcia (2002, 33), calculations by the author.

eucalyptus inventory only in 1985, with one planter with between one and two thousand trees. In the same year, Nova Venécia had 321,000 trees, Pinheiros had 464,000, and São Mateus close to 8 million eucalyptuses (Instituto Brasileiro de Geografia e Estatística 1985, 343). One interviewee described Boa Esperança as the frontier of numerous eucalyptus plantations surrounding it. In sum, the administration was successful in its main economic objective: preserving small scale farming and stopping the encroachment of cattle and eucalyptus farming.

SUCCESSIONAL ELECTIONS, PERSONAL DISPUTES, AND HIGH COFFEE PRICES

Mayor Covre's team's ability to build a long-lived participatory culture is more difficult to measure, and outcomes seem mixed on this front. Mayor Covre was elected for another three mandates between 1982 and 2008. According to Amaro Covre Júnior, the city goes through periods of mobilization and demobilization. In his father's tenures, citizens actively participate because they trust programs will deliver results, but successors come, discontinue programs associated with Mayor Covre's image, and people return to their private lives. Yet according to Júnior, organizations that gain strength during a Covre administration continue some activities through the demobilization period, but weak associations disband (personal communication, January 21, 2010). The motto of Covre's 2001–2008 administration was "Communitarian Administration: The population suggests, the City does. People decide, the City implements" (Prefeitura de Boa Esperança 2008). However, Mayor Covre acknowledged that participation never reached the same levels as in the 1978–1982 administration.

In the 1980s, coffee prices began to rise and once again became an economically viable alternative. Numerous small farmers decided to go back to the practice of producing a single cash crop in addition to subsistence crops. Mayor Covre strongly opposed this choice. He argued that dependence on monocropping led to ups and downs in the revenue of the municipal government and in the income of citizens that is detrimental to the city's economic development. In economic terms, there was no investment in town because in times of fat cows people save money for the next drop in coffee prices. Monocropping, moreover, does not require community organization since it can be easily sold to wholesale buyers, the contemporary equivalent of *vendeiros*. The participatory administration aimed at allowing citizens to keep their land and preserve their economic activity. It was successful, but participation became largely associated with specific economic goals.

In 1982, reelection was not permitted and none of Mayor Covre's aides stepped to the plate. The party nominated Etury Barros, who easily won the election with the support of the mayor. This, however, did not guarantee the continuity of Covre's policies. The participatory programs of the late 1970s as well as other initiatives implemented in the later mandates were often interrupted by his successors. In interviews and reports the subject of party politics does not appear as a key factor. Mayor Covre blamed lack of continuity on his successors' envy and desire to efface programs associated with his name. Another possible explanation is that Mayor Covre's forceful character and hands-on attitude made him an irreplaceable piece of participatory initiatives. He had a known contempt for legislative representatives, who accused him of wanting to run the show alone (Lobo et al. 1984). His argument was that he worked for the city, not for any one party.

The IBAM study called attention to the only aspect in which party politics seems to have been crucial: state funding. Written in 1984, the report noted that the funding of some of the participatory programs was drying up. In this period, municipalities were highly dependent on the goodwill of state governments to channel them funding. Covre's friendly relationship with the state government brought a considerable amount of resources to the city. In 1983, Espírito Santo elected a PMDB governor less willing to support PSD activities; funding for the decentralized health post was cut, for example (Lobo et al. 1984). During our interviews, Covre reported that he did not think highly of the 1988 constitution that decentralized power to the municipal level. Admittedly, his preferred strategy is to meet one-to-one with state officials, pitch an idea, and see how much support he can get. According to the mayor, this was always done in the name of the city and despite party politics.

Finally, team members contended that the participatory administration involved a process of *conscientização* that required time and should not have been interrupted. IBAM researchers noted challenges in the creation of a long-lasting participatory environment; their study pointed out that the participatory infrastructure built by the administration was not sufficient to install active participation. In some communities, organizations took advantage of the new participatory structure, but many other programs died once the city administration stopped actively promoting participation (Instituto Brasileiro de Administração Municipal 1984). A participatory culture did not develop in Boa Esperança.

In the little Espírito Santo town, participation remained associated with the image of one man. What connected the population with Mayor Covre was not patrimonial or clientelist bonds but confidence in his administrative competence. While the old elite regained Lages and Carneiro moved up the political ladder to become senator, Covre did not find resistance in being reelected mayor of Boa Esperança later in the decade. By then, however, his team had dispersed and, as examined in chapter 6, the Church was no longer forming political leadership. Furthermore, other politicians saw that participation was something closely associated with Covre's image and preferred not to boost the image of the already widely praised competitor. Though Covre managed to be reelected numerous times, he did not find a successor or party to give continuity to participatory projects. As the next chapter shows, this experience is in sharp contrast with the one in Diadema where participatory initiatives continued despite the fall of the mayor.

THE SOCIOECONOMIC FORMATION of Espírito Santo led to the emergence of two political and economic elites: large plantation owners in the south region and coffee merchants in the center and north regions. At the local level, the merchant network relied on unequal relations between powerful *vendeiros* and small farmers. The latter was not included in the political programs of either political elite until the 1950s. After the Vargas period, a new political party emerged and reached out to small farmers using the populist tactics common of the period. The traditional political elite coalition became fragmented as industrial interests permeated the rankings of the state government. The 1950s witnessed a battle between traditional politicians uneasily allied with new industrialists and populists rallying small farmers. In 1962, the latter won the state elections and started to guide government policies toward small farmer interests. The military regime sidelined this political project and put industrialists in charge of the state's development. The coffee eradication program further worsened the conditions of small farmers in the state. Small rural towns started decaying as land was sold to large cattle and eucalyptus farms, and idle workers migrated to other parts of the country.

The participatory administration of Boa Esperança had as its main goal to make small farming an economically viable activity. Mayor Covre took advantage of the organizational structure of CEBs and the experience of lay Catholic leaders to create a participatory structure that allowed for cooperation in the design and execution of government policies. Economic and culture activities were implemented with the goal of mobilizing small farmers to participate in production and sales cooperatives. From a purely economic perspective, the administration was successful. Data shows that the city performed considerably better than its neighbors. Results were less encouraging in terms of promoting a participatory culture. Participation in the city is instrumentally attached with economic results, which are trusted to an individual politician.

In spite of its shortcomings, the Boa Esperança participatory administration inspired mayors and activists around the country. Souza's chapter was included in a widely read book organized by José Álvaro Moisés and other scholars actively engaged in the democratization movement. Case studies written by IBAM researchers were discussed in seminars on municipal administration (Instituto Brasileiro de Administração Municipal 1984; Lobo et al. 1984). Mayor Covre talked about community participation in events planned by the IBAM, in a convention for Espírito Santo mayors, or in other forums organized by municipal governments around the country. Boa Esperança also received broad media attention, with newspaper articles covering the successes of the administration and the touring of the mayor. Headlines included "Boa Esperança Method Valid for the State" ("Metodo de Boa Esperança válido para o Estado," 1980); "The City of Democracy, Boa Esperança Proves that Power and People Can Walk Side-by-Side" (Caponi 1981); and "Community Administration Resuscitated Boa Esperança" (Tragtenberg 1981). The large television network Globo and other smaller channels also dedicated airtime to the initiative. Thirty years later, the name Boa Esperança "rings a bell" in activist and academic circles.

CHAPTER FIVE

The PT in Diadema

This chapter examines the Workers' Party's (PT) first participatory municipal administration in Brazil. Diadema is located in the industrial belt of one of the world's largest cities, São Paulo, the capital of a state with the same name, whose history is intertwined with Brazilian coffee. Politically and economically unimportant until the mid-nineteenth century, São Paulo became the richest state in the federation after coffee became the country's number one export. The divide between farmers, traders, and industrialists was much less marked in São Paulo than in Santa Catarina and Espírito Santo. Coffee growers were entrepreneurs directly involved in commerce, banking, and industry. The physical and financial infrastructure that facilitated coffee trade, and the capital it generated, impelled industrialization efforts. São Paulo had a distinct rapport with the federal government: if political relations were at times strained, economic interests were most often aligned. Thus, the dominant elite coalition in this state was more powerful and homogenous than in the other two. In São Paulo, industrialization did not cause the fragmentation of the elite coalition; it instead created a large urban working class. The state's working class was incorporated through the corporatist state in a controlled fashion, while a large portion of poor urban dwellers remained excluded. As a result, in São Paulo we witness less intra-elite dealings and more direct confrontation between juxtaposed groups: on the one side, an economic elite backed by the federal government, on the other side, urban workers and poor city dwellers. The latter groups had the choice to accept state co-optation, join the clientelist networks of populist leaders, or gather around a new radical mass party that promoted participatory democracy. The first three sections of this chapter examine the socioeconomic basis of the limited access order, its workings, and the beginning of the transition toward an open access order. The PT of Diadema, the party's first participatory administration, and the challenges it faced are discussed in the three subsequent sections.

SOCIOECONOMIC FORMATION

In 1554, Portuguese Jesuits founded the village of São Paulo dos Campos de Piratininga in a plateau seventy kilometers away from the coastline. During the colonial period, the province of São Paulo served as the base for expeditions to the unexplored interior and as a supplier of some subsistence crops for the rest of the colony. The poor quality of the soil was compensated by a privileged geographical location; waterways and favorable topography made all the neighboring regions accessible. The village of São Paulo was on the only feasible route connecting the south and the northeast of the colony. The village also had ready access to the Santos port. The Tietê River supported family agriculture, and later became a valuable source of hydroelectric energy (Prado Júnior 1975).

Due in part to these geographical conditions, São Paulo developed a commerce-based economy only indirectly involved with the agriculture export sector. In the first three centuries of colonization, the economy of the region was marked by "adventure capitalism."[1] Colonial scouts known as *bandeirantes* headed expeditions to the unexplored interior of the country in search for something that could be traded for luxury goods. Initially, the most profitable activity was the capture of natives sold as slaves to sugar plantations in the northeast. This activity became less lucrative with the introduction of African slaves, and the focus became the search for precious metals (Singer 1968). In the eighteenth century, the discovery of gold in a northern neighboring area led to the partial depopulation of the village, but also helped to spur trade, especially the commerce of mules and dried beef coming from the south to supply the mining region. In the nineteenth century, coffee became an increasingly lucrative crop and by 1840 it was the country's chief earner. The north of São Paulo was the first coffee-growing region, but most of this production was sold and taxed in Rio de Janeiro's port. By the 1860s, coffee farms had spread south and westwards, and improved transport infrastructure connected them to São Paulo's Santos port. In 1894, Santos surpassed Rio de Janeiro in coffee exports (Singer 1968).

A marked difference between São Paulo coffee growers and plantation owners elsewhere in the country was the former's direct involvement in the commercialization process. The city of São Paulo was the financial center where foreign and national capital changed hands and where most coffee growers resided. With the abolishment of slavery in 1888, the São Paulo government invested in the sponsoring of European migrant workers; 700,000 immigrants arrived in the state in the 1890s, more than 60 percent of all immigrants arriving in the country in that decade (Love 1980, 10). Although the objective of the migrant program was to supply workers for coffee farms, a significant group preferred to settle in the city and find opportunities in the emerging industries. The government also invested in energy, communication, and transport infrastructure. In the 1910s, the state became the largest industrial center of the country, responsible for 31.5 percent of Brazil's industrial production (Singer 1968, 48).

The southeast periphery of the city of São Paulo is known as the ABCD region because it comprises the cities of Santo André, São Bernardo, São Caetano, and Diadema. The first settlement in the region was the commune of Santo André da Borda do Campo founded in 1553 by *bandeirante* João Ramalho. São Bernardo and São Caetano were large estates owned and run by the Jesuit congregation of São Bento from the 1630s to the mid-1800s. Both were devoted to subsistence and cattle farming, and the more prosperous São Caetano also had a brickyard and a pottery factory. These farms were located in the margins of the road connecting São Paulo and the Santos port and largely depended on the commerce generated by it. Monks, slaves, bastard children, natives, and ethnically mixed individuals inhabited these estates. Diadema was a rural neighborhood of São Bernardo (Kenez 2001).

In the mid- to late 1800s, the coffee elite of São Paulo attempted to transform the ABCD region into a green belt that could feed the city. According to Alves (2001), the implicit idea was to create a boundary between the backward countryside and the modernizing city. Two colonial nuclei were created and received European migrant workers sponsored by the state government: São Caetano in 1847 and São Bernardo in 1893. The poor quality of the soil, agriculture pests, and the absence of transport infrastructure frustrated the original plans of the coffee elite. Most of the region became a poor enclave based on subsistence farming and logging. The inauguration of the railroad in 1868 meant prosperity for Santo André, where a train station was located, but brought further ruin to areas at the margin of the now abandoned road to Santos (Alves 2001). The plans for the green belt failed, but the region would later become the industrial belt of São Paulo.

LIMITED ACCESS ORDER: THE SÃO PAULO COFFEE ELITE

The Republican Party of São Paulo (Partido Republicano Paulista, PRP) was the umbrella political party for the dominant elite coalition of the First Republic period. The PRP was founded in 1873 with the chief goal of protecting the province's economic interests, which at the time meant the needs of the coffee exporting sector. The majority of PRP members were not steadfast abolitionists, but policies passed between 1884 and 1888 securing the entrance of cheap migrant labor allowed the party to portray itself as a champion of the victorious abolition movement. The abolition of slavery opened the way to the 1889 republican coup that put an end to the Empire and brought the PRP to power. All eleven state governors of the First Republic were from the PRP, and all received between 98 percent and 100 percent of cast votes (Love 1980, 143).

The interconnectedness of the agricultural and industrial sectors in São Paulo made elites more homogenous than in other states. Paulista coffee bosses were entrepreneurs also involved in commerce, banking, and industry. Coffee revenues fuelled investments in economic activities that supported the exporting sector (e.g., railroad companies) and responded to local needs (e.g., the textile industry). The political ideology in São Paulo was relatively uniform. Regardless of party affiliation or membership in cliques within parties, the Paulista elite wanted autonomy from the federal government, a market economy with special treatment for the coffee sector, the separation of church and state, and incentives for foreign capital investments. The Paulista elite might have been imbued with some liberal values and urban attitudes, but the representative system was based on patron-client networks just as in the rest of the country.

According to Love (1980), the PRP executive committee was constituted of *super coronéis* responsible for distributing patronage and securing party cohesion.

> Factional divisions within the PRP were offset in great measure by the continuity provided by the party's executive committee, a body that stood between the governor and the *coronéis*. The committee's authority derived from the power of party [bosses] (or their representatives) who sat on it. Through the [bosses], the committee also represented various zonal interests, and served the brokerage function of distributing patronage, including public works. (Love 1980, 115)

These *super coronéis* coordinated nominations between the party executive and local *coronéis* responsible for securing ballot results. Electoral competition was most often successfully avoided. "The PRP had organizational cohesion and discipline, and was clearly something more than an elaborate network of parentelas and clientelas; yet it had this side to it too, and party divisions, such as the 1901 and 1924 splits, were heavily influenced by patterns of family solidarity" (Love 1980, 115). In an incredible empirical effort to catalogue the Paulista elite in the First Republic, Love arrived at a list of 262 men and one woman who occupied important positions in government. This was a fairly homogeneous group: no one from the working class; only one landed immigrant and eleven sons of immigrants; 63 percent had a degree from the São Paulo Law School; 67 percent worked mainly in the capital city but owned farms in various parts of the state; 43 percent had a direct family relation with at least one other member of the group; and "more than a third of the whole elite formed a single complex of business and kinship ties" (Love 1980, 155). Family bonds were visible at the top of the political ladder; of the eleven governors in this period, only two did not have an immediate relative who occupied the same position (Love 1980).

In the mid-1920s, the cohesiveness of the Paulista elite started to deteriorate as a result of its diminishing political clout. In 1924, the state created an agency solely concerned with the coffee sector, the Coffee Institute. Planters welcomed the initiative until they realized the agency was not in their hands; only two of the five executive positions in the Institute were designated for planters. Competitions for these positions aggravated intra-elite tensions. Furthermore, low coffee prices in the early 1920s forced the government to borrow abroad and print money to guarantee an undervalued currency that could secure coffee sales. In order to address the ensuing debt and inflation, the government began to impose fiscal austerity measures in the second half of the decade, which fuelled further discontent with the established political class (Font 2010). In 1926, the increasing fragmentation of the Paulista elite led to the breakup of the PRP and the creation of the Democratic Party (Partido Democrata, PD). The founding members of PD were for the most part middle-class professionals from traditional coffee grower families. The party's liberal-democratic program defended certain institutional reforms such as the establishment of the secret vote. Otherwise the party's positions were similar to those of the PRP (Fausto 1972).

TOWARD AN OPEN ACCESS ORDER: CORPORATISM AND POPULISM

The 1930 Revolution deposed Paulistas from power both at the national and state level. The PD supported the Liberal Alliance and hoped to gain control of the state. The party's ambition was frustrated by the nomination of a *tenentista* governor who defended a centralized political system. The 1930–1945 period was marked by an incessant struggle between Paulista elites and Vargas's government, which included a failed armed revolt in 1932. Although the "communist threat" was the excuse used for the 1937 coup d'état, Vargas's main concern was the political strength of São Paulo. Likewise, Paulista elites' demands for a new constitution and respect for democratic principles was rhetoric aimed at regaining their lost political power (Codato 2010).

In the early 1930s, the emerging working class of São Paulo benefited from this unstable political scenario. The revolution did not count on active participation from the working class, at the time largely engulfed in the Brazilian Communist Party (PCB) (Collier and Collier 1991). Nevertheless, organized workers saw in the political crisis an opportunity to press for their demands. In Rio de Janeiro, manifestations were violently repressed. In São Paulo, however, *tenentistas* facing opposition for the state's elite tried to gain the support of the working class. According to Fausto (1972, 59), "*tenentistas* tried to channel [political] pressure and organize the [working] class . . . as a way of establishing a stable social basis" in the state. This *tenentista* attempt included support for a large textile workers strike as a way of attacking a politician from the traditional coffee party. Ultimately, coffee elite defeated *tenentistas*, and Vargas's corporatist apparatus encapsulated the labor movement.

In the economic sphere, the 1930s was marked by the decline of the coffee sector as the prices of the product never fully recovered from the 1929 international crisis. At the same time, the federal government began to play a direct role in promoting industrialization, which would make São Paulo an even stronger economic force. By the late 1920s, the state offered the best conditions for capital investment: it was located at the center of Brazil's internal market, and coffee exports had paid for the country's most developed infrastructure and sponsored a large contingent of immigrant workers. Moreover, state autonomy in the First Republic allowed the Paulista elite to invest in what by then was the country's most developed industry. Following the logic of capitalist development, São Paulo continued to grow, accumulate, and attract further investment (Singer 1968).

The National Steel Company, created in 1942, spurred the development of various manufacturing sectors, including the metal and auto industries. In the early 1950s, the federal government encouraged the production of auto parts for trucks assembled in the country by foreign firms. President Kubitschek (1955–1961) made the auto industry a core piece of his modernization plan, which also included the construction of a new capital in the inaccessible center of the country and the construction of new roads connecting major cities to it and to each other. Kubitschek created an agency that lobbied the world's largest auto companies to install manufacturers in the country; companies producing outside the country would not have access to the domestic market. This strategy was successful, and the auto industry became the symbol of industrialization in Brazil (Singer 2009).

Most auto companies established themselves in the ABCD region. In the first decades of the twentieth century, the downtown core of São Paulo housed commercial and financial enterprises; affluent families lived in the hilly area immediately next to it. Immigrant neighborhoods such as Mooca and Ipiranga housed the first industries. Far from downtown, the ABCD region supplied the city with coal, lumber, bricks, pottery, and furniture; a smaller number of factories produced chemicals, raw steel products, and tires. The closer to the train station the larger the number of industries; Santo André was the most industrial, São Bernardo was in the middle, and Diadema remained rural. In 1925, the road connecting São Paulo to the Santo port that cuts through the ABCD region was paved. In the industrializing efforts of the 1940s, this road became the main connection route between the capital, the port, and the east of the state, where important factories were located including the National Steel Company. Besides the favorable location, land in the ABCD region was more easily available than in the increasingly crowded city of São Paulo (Fonseca 2001).

Despite short-lived efforts toward grassroots mobilization, the mass of workers concentrated in the ABCD region was incorporated into political life mainly through corporatism and populism. The state corporatist structure has already been described in chapters 1 and 2. However, it is important to note that in São Paulo corporatist and populism were closely connected. According to French (1992), Vargas's 1945 electoral legislation "was systematically designed to enfranchise the working class and favor urban over rural voter registration and electoral participation" (111). This legislation maintained the literacy requirement for voting, made voting mandatory, and allowed group registration for employees of public offices and professional organizations. The goal was to undermine the political power of *coronéis* by reducing the weight of the vote of their dependents and subordinates. Nationwide, suffrage increased from 10 percent of the adult population in 1930 to 33 percent in 1945; in São Paulo, the "country's urban and industrial heart-land," the percentage of voters increased between 400 percent and 500 percent (French 1992, 129). This new legislation illustrates how intra-elite struggles lead to the inclusion of previously excluded socioeconomic groups, which contributes to the enlargement of the dominant elite coalition and consists in a significant step toward a more open access order (North, Wallis, and Weingast 2009). It also demonstrates that this sort of top-down incorporation is partial and controlled, and full incorporation will depend on the ability of subordinate groups to organize and demand full democratization.

In the first years of the democratic period there were two competing approaches to the electoral incorporation of urban workers: populism from above by the Brazilian Labor Party (PTB) that controlled the union structure and grassroots mobilization efforts by the Brazilian Communist Party (PCB), which infiltrated unions. Whereas the former relied on *pelegos* at the top of the union structure, the latter connected with workers increasingly discontented with the controlled union structure and poor living conditions. Vargas had the support of workers, but the PTB lacked local networks. The grassroots approach of the PCB was based on the organization of popular democratic committees (*comitês democráticos populares*, CDPs) in working-class neighborhoods; these nonpartisan PCB-led groups focused on the concrete needs of the poor, for example, garbage collection, and strengthened support for the party in the ABCD region. The PCB was also closely connected with workers' groups that began to demand union freedom and autonomy. "The PTB's greatest weakness in 1945 was precisely its inability to conceive of politics on such a participatory basis" (French 1992, 142). The PTB slowly lost ground to the PCB.

In 1947, workers displayed their electoral might. The PCB became the third largest party in the state assembly; the representative of the ABCD region, Armando Mazzo, a union leader in Santo André, was the party's most voted candidate, with four times the number of votes of the second most voted candidate, a labor lawyer. Furthermore, the PCB backed the gubernatorial candidacy of Adhemar de Barros, who was running for a small and unknown party. Barros won the election with twice as many votes in urban as rural areas. The grassroots approach to local level and factory mobilization was showing results (French 1992).

It did not take long for conservative forces to dismantle this political threat. In May 1947, the federal electoral court banned the PCB. The next day, the government passed a decree stating that unions had to be kept apart from political parties and social movements. PCB and other militant union leaders were removed from leadership posts. Adhemar de Barros, the PCB-backed governor, accepted the directives of the federal government and helped to demobilize the labor movement and the PCB. In the ABCD region, PCB members joined a small and unknown legal party in order to run in the municipal elections at the end of the year. In Santo André, union leader and PCB state deputy Armando Mazzo was elected mayor with 33 percent of the votes; communists also elected the largest number of city councilors. Santo André had a union leader mayor, thirteen city councilors representing workers interests, and CDPs organized in nine districts. The prospects for a participatory administration were very concrete, but none of these workers were inaugurated. Conservative parties appealed the PCB's victory, the São Paulo electoral court denied the plea, but the federal court accepted it. The inaugurated mayor was a member of a traditional family in the city. Soon after, PCB state deputies also had their mandates revoked. In the following two years, the international scenario of growing polarization served as an excuse to dismantle communist organizations and repress labor activists. In 1948, Santo André's elected but not inaugurated mayor was jailed for ninety days.

The coalescence of neighborhood committees, union activists, and a grassroots political party in power would not be repeated for another forty years. Populist leaders dominated the remainder of the 1945–1964 period in São Paulo. On the one side, there was Adhemar de Barros, "a charismatic, paternalistic leader with a mass lower-class following or clientele, bound together by 'the personalistic, particularistic ties' between the powerful leader and his 'dependent followers'" (French 1988, 3). Adhemar was governor from 1954 to 1967, mayor of São Paulo from 1961 to 1963, and again governor from 1963 to 1966. To achieve these electoral successes, "Adhemar could and did ally himself with just about every group at least twice" (French 1988, 2). On the other side, Jânio Quadros offered voters a different populist option. The eccentric schoolteacher presented himself as an outsider to the dirty realm of party politics, which he promised to clean up. His moralist rhetoric was particularly alluring to the state's growing middle class, but his personal style and campaign themes also attracted the popular classes. In the democratic period, Jânio was city councilor of São Paulo, state deputy, mayor, and governor. In 1961, he became president, but resigned in the same year. Populists Adhemar and Jânio were the two most influential politicians in the state, and local politics in the ABCD region was divided between *ademaristas* and *janistas* (Skidmore 1967).

In the 1950s, the process of seceding from São Bernardo marked politics in Diadema. In this period, municipalities had little financial autonomy; budgets largely depended on mayors' contact inside the state government and were usually spent at the urban core where influential families lived. Districts removed from the core were neglected, and many tried to secede. Municipalities resisted separations because they entailed a decrease in tax revenue. São André and São Bernardo used to be one municipality with the city center at the latter. The train station brought prosperity to Santo André, and it became the city center in 1938. São Bernardo did not want to be simply a disregarded district and managed to gain autonomy in 1945. The Anchieta highway made São Bernardo once again the economic center of the region. Ford, Mercedes-Benz, Volkswagen, and Scania established plants in São Bernardo between 1956 and 1962, leading to a population boom. Land by the highway was expensive, and workers lived mostly in the interior of the city in places like the neglected rural district of Diadema, which soon started to demand autonomy (Simões 1992). In some cases, the movement for political emancipation was a demand from organized citizens; in other instances it was the political move of a local boss (Moisés 1978).[2] Diadema was the latter case.

The political boss of Diadema was Evandro Esquível, a real estate agent, accountant, and teacher. His trades conferred on him the key features of a local boss: connections in the state capital and the ability to extend favors to local residents. He was known as "Professor Esquível," a title with a paternalist appeal.[3] Elected city councilor of São Bernardo in 1947, he managed to build a school and a small church in Diadema, feats that boosted his popularity. Esquível submitted the first plea for the political emancipation of Diadema in 1953, but it was not even put to a vote. At the time the mayor of São Bernardo was Tereza Delta, a politician who "represents the epitome of many established ideas about populism" (French 1992, 207). She emerged as a political leader in the city in the early 1940s and was rapidly brought into the clientelist network of Governor Barros. As a mayor closely connected with the governor, Delta was capable of outright ignoring Diadema's plea. Five years later a state deputy persuaded Esquível to pass to the side of by-now Governor Jânio in exchange for backing for the secession. The deal worked. Diadema was emancipated in 1958 (Simões 1992).

Municipal governments for the following two decades were dominated by *janista* Esquível and Lauro Michels, a real estate agent and cattle farmer, locally influential and well connected with the *ademarista* network in São Bernardo and São Paulo. Since reelection was not allowed, the two took turns in power: Esquível from 1960 to 1962; Michels from 1964 to 1968; Esquível again from 1969 to 1972; legally barred from running in 1972, Michels successfully endorsed Ricardo Putz, the mayor from 1973 to 1976; and Michels came back from 1977 to 1982. Elections in this period were a contest between local *janista* and *ademarista* political networks, which were led by middle-class politicians disconnected from the reality of factory workers. Clientelist networks facilitated the exchange of favors among voters, political intermediaries, politicians, and officials in the state government. Ideological commitments were absent, and whether a politician joined the MDB or the ARENA was largely accidental (Draghichevich 2001; Simões 1992).

Diadema drastically changed in the decades that Esquível and Michels ran the city. The population increased almost nineteen-fold, from 12,287 inhabitants in 1960 to 228,663 in 1980 (Instituto Brasileiro de Geografia e Estatística 1960, 82; 1982, 110). In the same period, Santo André's population doubled, São Bernardo's increased five-fold, and São Caetano's grew 40 percent (Instituto Brasileiro de Geografia e Estatística 1960, 82; 1982, 116). Whereas at the time of political emancipation Diadema had a seventieth of São Bernardo's inhabitants, in 1980 it had slightly more than half of the population of its neighboring town. Migrants came mainly from the interior of the state and from the drought-affected northeast of the country (Fonseca 2001). Population growth was not accompanied by economic development and investment in social services. As a late industrializer in comparison to its neighbors, the city did not attract as many major companies; for example, instead of large plants of multinational auto companies the city had small to medium auto parts factories. Poor infrastructure made the city less appealing to the well-paid workers of the major companies in the region, and even those working in the few larger companies of Diadema often lived elsewhere. Diadema became a dormitory town for factory workers with average to low earnings, and the home of small to medium industries that did not bring as much in tax revenues.

Municipal administrations tried to reverse this scenario by investing available resources on infrastructure at the urban downtown core. The argument was that new industries would bring economic development. According to this view, public works in rural areas with fast growing shantytowns was a shortsighted idea. Esquível's and Michels' properties and networks in the downtown area certainty made it easier for them to support this view. The city slowly succeeded in attracting industries that established themselves in the downtown area and in major transport routes, but this did not bring significant improvements to neighborhoods entirely constituted of shantytowns. Shantytowns only became a concern when they occupied land that could be used more profitably; in these cases the policy was to relocate poor residents to more distant areas. The exception seems to have been the Putz administration, during which some modest but concrete efforts were made to ameliorate the conditions of certain poor areas (Draghichevich 2001; Simões 1992).

In the early 1980s, Diadema was known as the "poor cousin" of the ABCD region. At this time, in the four cities of the region, between 52 percent and 57 percent of the adult population was economically active; of these, between 51 percent and 56 percent were employed in industrial activities (Instituto Brasileiro de Geografia e Estatística 1983b, 227, 230, 234, 237). In terms of educational level, 3 percent of Diadema's total population had finished secondary education, and 6 percent had an elementary school degree (eight years), whereas in the other three cities these figures varied between 8.5 and 12 percent and 11 and 13 percent, respectively (Instituto Brasileiro de Geografia e Estatística 1982, 621, 624). As Table 5.1 shows, 60 percent of Diadema households had an income between one and five times the amount set as the legal minimum monthly salary for a full-time worker; in the other cities only between 33 and 40 percent of families were in this income bracket. Whereas in the other three cities between 52 and 56 percent of families earned between

Table 5.1. Percentage of Households According to the Number of Minimum Monthly Salaries

	Up to 1	1 to 2	2 to 5	5 to 10	10 to 20	>20
Santo André	2.8	7	32.6	33.6	17.2	5.4
São Bernardo	2.5	7.7	30.5	30	20.6	7.4
São Caetano	2.1	5.7	27.2	33.5	22.4	7.8
Diadema	2.7	13.1	46.7	27.4	7.1	1.1

Source: Instituto Brasileiro de Geografia e Estatística (1983a, 82–83, 88–89). In all four cases, the categories "no income" and "no response" add to approximately 1.5 percent.

five and ten times the minimum monthly wage, only 34 percent of Diadema households had this income. Considerably fewer Diadema households were in categories of "10 to 20 times" and "more than 20 times" the minimum wage. In terms of social indicators, in 1981 the infant mortality rate per thousand live births in Diadema was 87.9, whereas the average of the other cities was 42.3 (Simões 1992, 68). This socioeconomic inequality among ABCD cities fuelled tensions between the Marxist faction of the Diadema PT and the party's leadership. The former accused the latter of neglecting the city's real problems and of giving excessive attention to the concerns of "bourgeois" party members from São Bernando and São Paulo.

THE PT IN DIADEMA: NEW UNIONISTS AND MARXISTS

In the 1982 mayoral election, union leader Gilson Menezes defeated Michels' vice mayor, former Mayor Putz, and a candidate associated with Professor Esquível. The eleven-year-old Gilson Menezes moved to São Paulo from the interior of Bahia in 1959. In his youth, Gilson worked in small factories, then worked for Mercedes-Benz, and in 1973 was hired as a toolmaker in the Scania plant in São Bernardo. His union activity started with recruiting members, giving legal aid to youth interns, and serving in the factory's accident prevention commission. In 1977, the metalworkers union organized a protest to contest the rate used to adjust salaries. Gilson's mobilization job at Scania impressed the union's president, Lula, who invited the toolmaker to join his slate for that year's election. In May 1978, Gilson became part of the twenty-four-member board of directors leading the Metal, Mechanic, and Electric Workers Union of São Bernardo and Diadema—the heart and mind of the new unionism movement. In the same month, he led a large strike at Scania, the first of a series that marked the late 1970s (Batista 2004).

Gilson participated in the foundation of the PT and was in charge of organizing the party in Diadema. He had never participated in party politics, although as a union leader he supported the candidacy of MDB *autênticos*. Gilson became the president of the Diadema PT and was unanimously chosen as the party's candidate for the 1982 municipal elections. He used the word *mutirão* to describe his electoral campaign. He and his colleagues trained volunteer leaders who organized groups that went canvassing door to door (Batista 2004). One of these volunteers said they worked like Jehovah's Witnesses, "but instead of Jesus Christ, we handed out a PT star and a program we made" (Justino 1997). At the core of the political program was the proposal to create popular councils that would break away from the city's traditional politics. The campaign was aided by an electoral regulation that forced voters to choose governors and mayors from the same party; the PT candidate for the state was Lula, the esteemed union leader of the region.[4] Gilson won by a small voting margin, and the PT elected six out of seventeen city councilors (Meneguello 1989; Simões 1992).

In 1982, the PT did not have a defined, much less tested idea of how to govern a city. Cesar (2002) examined the varied and evolving meanings of key terms in the party's political program, such as workers, democracy, and socialism. In what concerns local-level participation, the two first documents of the party presented statements that did not make clear the relationship between society's base organizations and the party's nuclei. Both were exalted as vitally important, but the role of each was not defined. The Letter of Principles (Carta de Princípios) issued in 1979 stated that

> As a political organization aiming at increasing the degree of mobilization, organization, and consciousness of the masses, and seeking to strengthen the political and ideological independence of the popular sectors, especially workers, the PT will promote a broad debate about its theses and proposals, which should include: the leadership of popular sectors, even if not members of the party, [and] all militants, bringing to the interior of the party debates propositions from any organized sector in the society considered relevant based on the objectives of the PT. The PT declares itself committed to and engaged in the task of introducing popular interests in the political scenario. . . . With this aim, the Workers' Party plans to implement its militants' nuclei in all work places, unions, neighborhoods, municipalities, and regions. (Partido dos Trabalhadores 1979)

This document was written by a small group of union leaders associated with Marxist groups, who were accused by others involved in the process of creating the party of trying to play a vanguard role (Keck 1992). The Manifesto published on the occasion of the official creation of the party was equally ambivalent.

> The PT does not want to be active only during elections, but also, and mainly in the day-to-day of all workers, only in this way will it be possible to build a new type of democracy rooted on society's base organizations and on majority decisions. This is why we want a broad party open to all, committed to the workers' cause and [the party's] program. As a consequence, we want to build a democratic internal structure based on collective decisions and program directives decided at the base. (Partido dos Trabalhadores 1980)

These documents did not explain whether a PT administration should give priority to proposals put forward by the organized base of the party, the nuclei, or to demands coming from organized groups allied with but not inside of the party. Another document issued in 1982, the Electoral Letter (Carta Eleitoral), discussed in more detail the relationship between elected officials and the party's *diretórios* (city chapters); in short, the mandate was of the party, not of elected individuals who must always subject projects to the approval of the *diretórios*. The document was mute on the question of the relationship with other organized groups in society.[5] Members of the Diadema PT issued and signed a local version of the document, wherein the subordination of elected officials to the *diretório* was reinstated (Simões 1992).

The PT team elected in Diadema was in some ways similar to the Dirceu Carneiro Team and Mayor Covre's staff. "A group of young leaders (the elected mayor and councilors all had less than 35 years of age), skilled and semi-skilled factory workers, with primary or secondary education levels, zero legislative experience, who until then had played a subordinate or not very expressive role in local politics" (Simões 1992, 90). In spite of these similarities, the team had distinct ideological backgrounds and different visions of how the party should govern. Studies of the formation of the PT identified workers associated with the new unionism movement as the most numerous and influential group within the party; intellectuals, professionals, MDB politicians,

CEB members, and Marxist groups were important but less prominent actors in the process (Cesar 2002; Keck 1992; Meneguello 1989). The PT in Diadema was more equally divided between new unionists and Marxists.

THE PARTICIPATORY ADMINISTRATION

During the electoral campaign, differences within the party were shrouded by Gilson's ambiguous speeches. After the election they became irreconcilable. Marxists expected the local *diretório* to be in charge of appointing the *heads of departments*. Gilson refused to renounce his prerogatives on the matter, a fight ensued, and the mayor had his way. A few months later, the Marxist faction won the *diretório* elections and gained control of the Diadema PT. From then on there were practically two PTs. On one side were Gilson and eight heads of departments chosen by him, including his chief of staff, Juracy Magalhães, a former co-worker and also member of the board of directors of the Metalworkers Union in the 1978–1982 term. Another two members of the same board of directors were now the first secretary of the PT and the president of the São Paulo *diretório*, which facilitated the relationship between Gilson and the party leadership outside Diadema. Three heads of departments were from São Paulo. On the other side were the leadership of the *diretório*, the heads of two departments, and four of the six PT city councilors who now joined the opposition in denouncing and attacking the mayor. The vice mayor, a Catholic lawyer esteemed for defending shantytown dwellers, and the two remaining councilors remained neutral, picking sides for each battle (Keck 1984; Simões 1992).

The numerous quarrels that marked the entire administration sprang mainly from four related disagreements. First, Marxists accused Gilson of exerting too much direct authority and succumbing to the bureaucracy instead of following the party's directives; they claimed that solving problems in an ad hoc fashion without consultation was a clientelist practice. Gilson responded that militants were unaware of the concrete challenges involved in running a city. Gilson adopted a realistic approach of trying to learn how the administration worked before implementing changes

(Pinto 1985). Second, Marxists criticized the administration for being populist, that is, trying to please everyone and not defending workers' interests. Gilson replied to this recurring criticizing by stating, "I am not the mayor of the PT, I'm the mayor of Diadema," to which one of the PT opposition councilors replied, "Gilson was elected by the majority, but he was elected by the PT. . . . The working class voted for a class-based political program, and Gilson must commit himself to this" (Simões 1992, 121). Third, the PT opposition resented Gilson for bringing administrators and staff from outside of Diadema. This decision intensified local bitterness toward the "intellectuals of São Paulo" and "bourgeois workers of São Bernardo" (Keck 1992). This disgruntlement was grounded on the idea that São Bernardo workers, such as Gilson and his colleagues, were well paid, and their priorities differed from that of the poor workers of Diadema. Finally, the two groups disagreed on the format of popular councils. In Gilson's words, "people told me they had to be PT councils, but I said they would be popular councils" (personal communication, March 17, 2011). Marxists wanted councils working within the party structure and limited to "politically qualified" members. Gilson's team supported the idea of neighborhood community councils open to all residents. Gilson pushed his model, but his own party heavily undermined his efforts.

In the weeks following the 1982 election, Gilson made numerous public announcements about the creation of popular councils in Diadema ("Em Diadema, conselhos populares," 1982; "Gilson já começa a delinear seu trabalho," 1982). However, if being at the epicenter of the new unionism movement guaranteed a political leadership committed to participatory democracy, it did not mean that the neighborhoods were organized and ready to participate. In fact, there was little popular organization in Diadema. Most of the neighborhoods did not have any organized group. Some areas had the more traditional Society of Friends of the Neighborhood (SABs), which were usually part of the clientelist network of a politician. The city's shantytowns had some incipient community organization resultant from the spread of a Santo André movement for the defense of shantytown dwellers. This movement was supported by CEBs, which were better organized in Santo André than in any other ABCD city. According to the testimony of a local historian and militant,

CEBs formed some of the most active citizens in Diadema, but they were relatively few and did not form a community organizational structure as they did in Santo André (Valdo Ruviado, personal communication, May 10, 2011). Therefore, the Menezes administration also faced the challenge of having to mobilize the population to take advantage of the participatory channels being created.

The first popular council was created in the neighborhood of Eldorado by the initiative of some of its residents, but this was an exception. This region had a history of popular organization due to its location next to a water reservoir that had recently become an area of environmental preservation. The first meeting was held days after Gilson's inauguration and gathered 250 residents ("Conselho vai fiscalizar o novo prefeito," 1983). The Planning Department received representatives of the Eldorado Popular Council every Monday to discuss the area's challenges. Nevertheless, the Council failed to become an established participatory channel because of divergent interests within the area: shantytown dwellers did not want to be removed; low-income families wanted rights to the land they had settled without papers; middle-class families wanted the environmental preservation of the land and the consequent valorization of their properties, which required removing shacks and illegal occupations. Each group saw the other as a problem. Once the administration became divided, these groups picked allies within the PT. Ultimately, militants associated with the *diretório* came to dominate the Eldorado Council. As a result, the mayor came to see it as a "nest of the opposition" and systematically disregarded their demands, which led to the demobilization of the Council (Pinto 1985; Simões 1992).

The second attempt to create popular councils was the Internal Urbanization Commissions (Commissões Internas de Urbanização, CIUs) of shantytowns. The Planning Department was headed and staffed by technical personnel from the São Paulo PT who advocated for "pedagogic participation"; these *técnicos de fora* (outsider technicians) believed that the process of learning to organize and deliberate was as important as the solving of the problems at hand. The Department created the Program for the Urbanization of Shantytowns (Programa de Urbanização de Favelas, PUF). CIU members were responsible for organizing their neighborhoods and discussing their priorities; a PUF *técnico* helped them to draft a diagram of how shacks could be reallocated in order to allow for the construction of infrastructure, for example, light posts, asphalted streets, sewage pipes. The diagram had to be approved by both residents and the directorship of the PUF. Once that was done, residents were in charge of demolishing and rebuilding shacks according to the diagram, then the city came in and built the agreed-upon infrastructure. CIUs also sent representatives to the Municipal Commission of Shantytown Dwellers (Comissão Municipal de Favelados, CMF), which met regularly with the Planning Department to discuss broader urbanization issues (Santos 2009; Simões 1992).

The head of the Planning Department, Amir Khair, was politically savvy and managed to keep his department largely isolated from PT internal conflicts.[6] Nevertheless, the department's emphasis on "pedagogic participation" eventually clashed with the mayor's priorities. The CMF became a much-disputed political space since on the Commission's agenda was nothing less than land tenure matters, which in Brazil is a thorny legal issue (Holston 2008). In an initial moment, militants with CEB experience dominated the space in a slightly forceful fashion, but after some time other members began to challenge their authority and managed to gain voice. Landowners associated to SABs asked their respective city councilors to intervene in their favor. As a consequence shantytown dwellers had to come together in the CMF to oppose the influence of SABs. In sum, this was a very politicized and time-consuming process.

The *técnicos de fora* regarded clashes between popular groups as democracy in the making, and even celebrated the existence of struggle for the leadership of the CMF. In their view, this was proof that groups were learning to organize and participate. Mayor Gilson, however, had opposition from all sides and few results to show as the end of his second year in office approached. A 1984 survey showed that a small fraction of the population participated in any of the initiatives, and the majority demanded more actions from the government (Santos 2009). The mayor was further haunted by the fact that Diadema, as the first PT administration, was responsible for proving to the public that the PT could govern. Pressured to show some results, Gilson unilaterally decided to move the PUF to a department that he believed would be more expedient. Debates and fights ensued, but the mayor pushed the change through. Amir Khair quit the administration. The PUF continued to involve the participation of shantytown residents but in a much less politicized, consultative manner (Draghichevich 2001; Santos 2009; Simões 1992). This conflict between the ideal of participation and efficient administration "would plague all future PT administrations as well" (Keck 1992, 210).

The Gilson Menezes administration launched a participatory budgeting process in 1984 that discussed the expenditures for the third year of the PT mandate. The plan was to implement the process in the first year, but internal disputes made Gilson wait. The initiative was called Popular Council (Conselho Popular), probably because Gilson had promised councils during the campaign and felt pressure to deliver them, but their sole purpose was to discuss the budget. The structure of the process was similar to the participatory budgeting established in Porto Alegre in 1989. In the first half of the month, meetings were held in various districts of the city (eleven in 1984, and seventeen from then on). In these meetings, city staff explained the budgetary process, and residents elected delegates to the Council, four per district in 1984, five in 1985, and ten in 1986. In the first year there was a great emphasis on explaining to the population that only a small portion of the total budget could be used for new investments (10 percent in 1985). Delegates met at the Council and discussed the priorities for the available funds. The city's technical personnel helped citizens to draft an investment plan, which was then subjected to approval of the city council (as required per law). Delegates were encouraged to inspect the execution of the investment plan ("População discute o orçamento de Diadema," 1984; Prefeitura do Município de Diadema 1984, 1985, 1986a, 1987a).

Given the low organizational level of the city and the delicate political scenario, the Popular Council developed slowly and did not achieve the aspired levels of participation. According to Simões (1992), in the first year the process was closely controlled by the overzealous chief of staff, who made sure that the Council was not hijacked by the *diretório*; few people attended the local meetings and many were frustrated for being unable to get immediate solutions to their problems. In the following years participation increased and local gatherings came to be called Neighborhood Popular Councils (Conselhos Populares de Bairros). Simões argued that the mayor and his immediate staff most often managed to approve a previously prepared budget. According to Gilson, they only made suggestions that were frequently refuted (personal communication, March 17,

2010). An activist from the Canhema neighborhood confirmed Gilson's statement. She described an intensive back and forth between discussions at local council and debates at what she called the Budget Council. The militant reported a strong CEBs presence in her area and admitted that they always succeeded in getting their demands at the Council; it is likely that this was one of the few well-organized communities (Gimenez 1997). Notwithstanding differing views, as the only scholarly account of the process, it is worth reviewing Simões' overall assessment.

> We can say that in practice the Neighborhood Popular Councils of the Gilson Menezes administration show a conception of "popular participation" largely as a consulting and information sharing mechanism aimed at preventing protests and galvanizing a base of massive support for the municipal government. It is worth noting, however, that these initiatives were the solution mayor Gilson Menezes found to deal with conflicts generated by "participation," minimizing its explosive character and this way preserving the participatory ideal as the diacritic mark of his administration. (173)

This incompatible dynamic of political conflicts generated by participation and the participatory ideal are found not only in Diadema. As the next chapter will explore, other PT administrations faced the same problem. The 1980s were marked by attempts to accommodate the participatory ideal to the new political and institutional context of an open representative system with a multitude of conflicting ideologies and interests.

Aside from these three initiatives involving popular councils, the Diadema government spurred participation in other spheres of government. The head of the Health Department, Zé Augusto, brought to the city the decentralized, preventive, and participatory approach to public health that he had helped to implement in the east side of São Paulo. The emphasis of this approach was on educating citizens about health and public policies so that they could actively participate in the health of their communities (Prefeitura do Município de Diadema 1987b). Zé Augusto, however, sided with Gilson and his department was permeated by the party's internal disputes. Augusto was also unwilling to compromise efficiency for "pedagogic participation," and at times bypassed community councils in order to improve the city's calamitous health-care system (Keck

1992). In the long run, public health in Diadema dramatically improved and became recognized as a successful case (Bisilliat 2004, 45–58).

Finally, another noteworthy accomplishment of the Gilson administration involved public transportation. One of the most fruitful fights of the PT government was against the company in charge of municipal buses. The company was notorious for the poor quality of its service, for example, reducing the number of circulating buses at its discretion and regardless of demand. In 1983, the company planned to raise bus fares, which would have had an enormous impact on the family budget of low-income workers. Municipal technical staff with the help of volunteers of the Users' Commission (Comissão de Usuários) conducted a survey of the number of passengers the company carried and showed that there was no basis for the increase. Fares remained the same. Additionally, the city implemented free fares for the unemployed, seniors, and retired citizens—something new at the time but that would later be partially incorporated in the 1988 constitution. Fights with the bus company continued due to the poor quality of service. In 1986, the city bought the company. The Users' Commission became part of the management of the now state-owned bus company (Batista 2004; Prefeitura do Município de Diadema 1986b). As seen in the next chapter, there were attempts to include users' commissions in the 1988 constitution, but the proposed amendment was rejected by majority vote.

THE 1988 ELECTION: NEW AND OLD POLITICS

In 1985, the election of a pro-Gilson *diretório* leadership and the dismissal of the divisive chief of staff eased political tensions. Intrigues resumed when debates started about the selection of a successor for the 1988 elections. Gilson was elected with 31.2 percent of the cast votes in 1982 (Meneguello 1989, 140), and by 1988 a poll showed that 55 percent of the population approved this administration and would reelect him if possible, but reelection was not allowed (Simões 1992, 131). Zé Augusto, head of the Health Department, after years of fighting the Marxists came to an agreement with them: he would be the party's candidate and Marxists could choose a vice mayor. Gilson did not have a say on this deal, and his suggested successor did not stand a chance in the nomination process.

Fights and accusations ensued. The national leadership tried to mediate a compromise but did not directly intervene, probably because they saw the deal as an end to internal disputes. The mayor and his chosen successor quit the PT and launched the latter's candidacy through another party (Batista 2004).

Zé Augusto won the 1988 municipal election with a narrow 32.5 percent of the votes (Bisilliat 2004, 32). In the electoral campaign, Augusto promised to allow popular councils to directly elect department heads. Once elected, he backed down on his promise and after much debate allowed the *diretório* to choose two heads of department. His vice mayor, part of the staff, and party militants became opposition. Augusto kept some participatory initiatives but stopped the participatory budgeting process. The PT once again won the 1992 municipal election. This time the candidate, José de Filippi, had the support of the incumbent mayor, but the victory was still narrow with only 30.5 percent of the votes (Bisilliat 2004, 32). Filippi rekindled the participatory budgeting, which by now was gaining fame because of the Porto Alegre initiative. The PT lost the 1996 election to Gilson, now a candidate of the Brazilian Socialist Party (Partido Socialista Brasileiro, PSB). When interviewed for this study in 2011, Gilson was the vice mayor of a PT-PSB administration elected for 2008–2012. At the time this book was written, the PT-PSB dual was running for re-election, which is now permitted. Diadema still has a low profile participatory budgeting process and occasional participatory initiatives.

The internal struggles of the PT gained more attention than Gilson's attempt to create one of the first participatory administrations in Brazil. "Unlike the MDB administrations that had experience with new forms of popular participation in city government in Lages, Santa Catarina, and Piracicaba, São Paulo, the PT in Diadema did not enjoy a sympathetic national press" (Keck 1992, 199). A study of printed press coverage of Gilson's government showed that emphasis was put on party disputes and the allegedly inefficiency of the administration. The newspaper *Jornal da Tarde* was so disingenuous as to print pictures of historically poor neighborhoods and accuse Gilson of abandoning the city (Alves 2007). The present study, however, showed that the first participatory administration of Diadema had failures and partial successes similar to the better-known experiences of Lages and Boa Esperança, and a precursory PB much like the famous Porto Alegre model. Contrary to Lages, where traditional elites regained power and dismantled participatory programs, and Boa Esperança where citizen participation is dependent on a single politician, the PT made participatory democracy an integral part of Diadema's politics. However, in order to do so, it was necessary to reconsider participatory goals in relation to other important goals of municipal administration. As will be discussed in the next chapter, finding the right way to balance participation and other priorities will take other unsuccessful attempts (Abers 1996) and deliberate efforts to draw lessons from them (Nylen 1997).

THE SOCIOECONOMIC FORMATION of São Paulo was marked by the expansion of coffee farms and the emergence of a relatively homogeneous dominant elite coalition. During the First Republic, this coalition succeeded in making the state of São Paulo defend the interest of coffee growers to the detriment of other economic groups and social classes. In this period, the ABCD region was a rural and underdeveloped periphery of this economic center. The 1930 Revolution weakened the political but not the economic power of the Paulista elite. São Paulo offered the most favorable conditions for industrial investment and grew fast as a consequence of federal policies fomenting encompassing industrialization. The ABCD region was transformed in the 1940–1960 period with the establishment of numerous industries, especially auto factories, the symbol of the Brazilian modernization project. In this period of fast population growth, two forms of political patronage coexisted in the region. Inside the factories, a strict corporatist structure allowed little autonomy in political organization. Within the region, two populist networks competed for the votes of the new urban popular groups. In Diadema, two populist politicians competed for the municipal government, though in practice, their emphasis on the infrastructure development of the downtown core was the same.

The ABCD region was the heart of the new unionism movement that reacted against the corporatist structure, and later evolved into the PT. Gilson Menezes won the municipal election of Diadema and tried to put into practice the participatory ideal of the party. However, the party had two distinct participatory approaches, one that privileged the participation of party members and one that tried to reach the entire population.

The conflicts that ensued between these two groups made participatory initiatives difficult to implement, and pressures for administrative efficiency created additional tension among the various government departments. The PT administration in Diadema was markedly different from the other two case studies in that there was a clear conflict between party goals and the participatory ideal. The most promising participatory initiative of Diadema, the urbanization of shantytowns, was put aside not only because of internal conflicts but also due to pressures for administrative efficiency directly related with electoral goals.

The history of civil society in this case offers an interesting paradox. The participatory ideals that fuelled this administration came mainly from a civil society movement but a type of movement (unions) that did not build the organizational structure necessary for municipal-level initiatives. Though at the geographic heart of the unionism movement, the few organized groups in Diadema seem to have been spurred above all by CEBs. Contrary to Boa Esperança, where the economic activity of the city and the format of participatory initiatives coincided, in Diadema union leaders and militant health practitioners tried to organize shantytowns. As an urban center, Diadema was more heterogeneous than Lages and Boa Esperança, and it was difficult to have a participatory administration solely focused on the needs of a single excluded socioeconomic group. Trying to have multiple socio-groups directly participate in governments would also prove difficult. As the next chapter shows, it would be necessary to adapt the radical approach to citizen participation to a pluralistic method that allowed for the participation of various social groups. Diadema illustrates the clash between the radical participatory ideal that emerged in times of façade representative institutions and the more moderate participatory ideal that became predominant in the 1990s.

CHAPTER SIX

The Tempering of Participatory Ideals and Practices

In Brazil the 1980s is most commonly remembered as a "lost decade" marked by economic stagflation and a sluggish democratization process controlled from above. Those certainly were distinguishing aspects of it. The decade witnessed numerous failed attempts to end high inflation that mostly only worsened economic stagnation. In 1983 and 1984, hundreds of thousands of citizens participated in protests demanding a direct presidential election. Congress denied the popular appeal and instead indirectly elected a military-approved civilian candidate who passed away before his inauguration, leaving the presidency to his conservative vice president—a rather anticlimactic end to twenty years of authoritarian government.

That said, the 1980s were also a fascinating time of social and political experimentation wherein social movements that had organized under the authoritarian regime could finally gain the streets. Countless political parties, social movements, unions, and civil society organizations were created in this period; some of these were ephemeral, but others such as the Workers' Party (PT), the Brazilian Social Democratic Party (PSDB), and the Landless Workers' Movement (MST) remained key political actors to this date. By the end of the decade, the establishment of a multiparty representative democratic system based on a constitution that endorsed citizen participation in public administration and promised universal social service had significantly changed the political-institutional context. It is possible to characterize this period as the beginning of an open access order hitherto unseen in the country, despite the limitations discussed below. This chapter shows how the participatory ideals and practices examined in the previous chapters were adapted to this new social order.

Scholars have examined the explosion of civil society in 1980s Brazil (Avritzer 2000, 2002; Holston 2008), the fragmentation of certain social movements (Alvarez 1990a; Hochstetler and Keck 2007), and changes in the forms in which civil society actors interacted with the state, which began in the 1980s and continued through the 1990s (Doimo 1995; Hochstetler 2000; Dagnino 2004, 2007). The restructuring of old parties and the creation of new ones following the political liberation of the late 1970s have also been studied (Fleischer 1986; Hagopian 1996; Power 2000; Motta 2007), with particular attention paid to the creation of the PT and its gradual adoption of an electoral logic (Meneguello 1989; Keck 1992; Nylen 1996, 1997; César 2002). The drafting of the 1988 constitution was a key moment in this decade and has been the topic of thorough analyses (Michiles et al. 1989; Souza 1997). The focus of this chapter is both more specific and broader than other studies of the period. It is more specific in that it pays exclusive attention to the process of changing participatory ideals and practices—other changes, challenges, and strategies of civil society actors and political parties are not taken into account. It is broader in that it situates these changes in their historical context, that is, as part of the processes examined in previous chapters, and in the broad political-institutional context of the time, that is, as a process cutting through these other already researched processes. In other words, this chapter adds a thread to the weaved rope of social and political processes that constitute a fascinating period in Brazilian history.

This chapter is divided into five sections. The first section presents a broad portrayal of Brazilian civil society in the 1980s. The second section discusses the Catholic Church's decision to refrain from direct political involvement as well as the fate of the CEBs. The two subsequent sections shift the focus to political parties. The third section describes how the PMDB sidelined its most progressive members and how they eventually formed a new party that was programmatically committed to participatory democracy but did not actively promote it. The fourth section focuses on the PT: the successes and failures of Diadema and other participatory administrations in the 1980s and their deliberate efforts to create a pragmatic approach to the inclusion of citizen participation in municipal government. The final, fifth section shows that while the 1988 constitution contains progressive legal devices that encourage partici-pation, numerous proposals of more radical forms of participation were rejected in the drafting of the document. Overall, this chapter describes and explains the trend of the tempering of participatory ideals and practices.

CIVIL SOCIETY EXPLOSION AND FRAGMENTATION

According to Avritzer (2000, 2002), the pattern of civic association dra-matically changed in Brazil during the democratization period. This change was quantitative and qualitative. In São Paulo, 2,553 civil asso-ciations were created in the 1980s, in contrast with 1,871 in the 1970s, and 966 in the 1960s. Rio de Janeiro witnessed the appearance of 2,498 new civic associations in the 1980s, as opposed to 1,233 in the 1970s, and 1,093 in the 1960s. The figures for Belo Horizonte are 1,597, 584, and 459, respectively (Avritzer 2000, 65). The qualitative change concerns the kind of association created, the kinds of demands these organizations made, and the tactics they used to advance their claims. This plethora of new civil associations did not follow the "tradition of clientelist political inter-mediation" (Avritzer 2000, 66). Instead they followed social movements that "contested the privatization of the public arena, the homogeniza-tion of collective action, and the lack of independent associations" (78). What emerged, Avritzer argues, were "participatory publics" demanding the politicization of the public sphere, the recognition of the plurality of demands and identities, and autonomy from the state. These participa-tory publics were found in urban centers to which the military regime forcefully pushed rural people.

Holston (2008) argues that booming urban centers occupied by rural migrants who had left behind their ties to the rural oligarchy were con-ducive to the rise of insurgent citizens. The city was not a democratic heaven, but unlike rural areas dominated by powerful landlords, it gave inhabitants access to property in the form of land and house. However, the rights associated with the acquisition of property were not auto-matically granted to poor inhabitants of urban peripheries; they had to struggle for the recognition of their land titles, the paving of their streets, the extension of bus lines, and the building of sewage systems, among other things. Democratization granted formal political rights to its "citizens," but de facto citizenship was achieved through numerous relatively small, but extremely significant, struggles that took place predominately in urban peripheries in the 1980s.

Democratization also posed challenges to existing social movements that were not used to working in a context with multiple channels for political participation. Environmentalists and women's movements are good illustrative examples. Environmentalists "had to decide on the form that their participation in the democratization process would take, as they moved from protest to active political engagement" (Hochstetler and Keck 2007, 87). In the 1980s, environmentalists had to decide whether and how to participate in the constituent assembly which, contrary to their preference, was a partisan process. At the same time, environmentalists had to choose between backing the newly created Green Party (Partido Verde) and supporting a "green list" of candidates of various parties. Later in the decade and into the 1990s, these predominantly grassroots groups had to decide whether to professionalize; the relatively few that chose to do so had to decide whether to accept state and corporate funding or rely solely on donations from the membership. Environmentalists also had to decide whether and how to bring poverty and environment concerns together. Most groups ended up adopting a social environmentalist approach, at least partially in response to the need to join broader political coalitions; neutrality and isolation seemed impracticable in a period of heightened politicization (Hochstetler and Keck 2007).

Women's movements also underwent marked changes in the 1980s. Alvarez (1990a) explains that in the 1960s and 1970s, the striving developmental state did not see the need to promote family planning; the idea was that Brazil was going to grow in every way. The 1970s' women's movements had clear antistate attitudes and were very wary of state-sponsored family planning programs due to the neo-Malthusian approach dominant at the time, that is, less births equaled less state spending on the poor. Movements focused mostly on access to day care and other urban services. At the beginning of the 1980s, the International Monetary Fund (IMF) imposed family planning as one of the conditions for rescuing the country from its debt crisis. Family planning became part of the state's agenda both at the federal and state levels, and although motivated by a type of neo-Malthusian rationale, government programs adopted the women-centered discourse of feminists. Incapable of opposing their own discourse, some women's groups decided to engage with the state in order to ensure that programs would not become coercive population controls. Women activists closely associated with programmatic left groups continued to refuse to collaborate with government agencies.

The decade also witnessed the escalation of tensions between middle class and popular women's groups who disagreed on the relevance of class dynamics and material demands, with the former arguing that the latter placed exaggerated emphasis on these issues. By the end of the decade, women's movements had dispersed into a myriad of fronts; some became active within political parties, whereas others took feminism into less directly political spheres of life such as arts, media, and education. The fact that government and political parties in Brazil were (and continue to be) male domains made the question of whether and how to participate in formal politics even knottier for women's movements. In response to the claim that social movements had disappeared after democratization, Alvarez states that "dispersion rather than disappearance would be a more accurate way to describe the state of the [women's] movement in the late 1980s" (Alvarez 1990a, 228).

Finally, theses have been put forward regarding the outcome of civil society's changes in the 1980s. Hochstetler (2000) argues that the democratization process changed the "master frame" under which social movements operated from an opposition to the military regime to a struggle for citizenship rights. Like Alvarez, Hochstetler challenges the once widespread idea that social movements of the 1970s had demobilized following the political opening of the country and new movements had emerged in the 1990s. Hochstetler found a marked continuity in the practices and strategies adopted by movements in these two periods, which led her to argue that social movements had adapted to new domestic and international political contexts. What the country witnessed in the 1990s was a new cycle of mobilization. In a similar line of argument, Doimo (1995) states that activists had to "temper a sort of Christian romanticism driven by a consensual-solidaristic logic, start to make use of rational calculation, and [face] social plurality in its fullness" (213). According to Doimo, social movements' confrontational approach to interactions with the state morphed into an intricate set of strategies; the "struggle against the state" gave way to "society's participation in decision-making," and there was an increasing emphasis on "active-propositive" instead of antagonistic engagement with governments.

Dagnino (2004, 2007, 2010) heads a line of critics that sees a split in Brazilian civil society. Dagnino argues that the democratizing and participatory political project that emerged in the early 1980s continued to work for the deepening of democracy, especially "the creation of spaces where the power of the State can be shared with society" (Dagnino 2004, 96). However, this political project eventually had to share space with a different vision of civil society and participation. In the 1990s, neoliberals promoted civil society and participation as part of a strategy to reduce the state's regulatory role. Dagnino (2007) contends this is a "perverse confluence" since both political projects "not only require a vibrant and proactive civil society, but also share several core notions, such as citizenship, participation, and civil society, albeit used with very different meanings" (550). In this perspective, what we witnessed in the 1990s was the coexistence of two types of civil societies, one demanding the state to share its power with society and another willing to provide services hitherto provided by the state (Dagnino 2010; Medeiros 2007).

These changes in forms of political organization and participation typified the beginning of an open access order hitherto unseen in Brazil. Elites had controlled access to social, political, and economic participation from colonial times to the beginning of the twentieth century. Beginning in the 1930s, institutional reforms and industrialization programs spurred the emergence of new political actors, whose partial and controlled inclusion occurred in the 1945–1964 period. During the rule of the military regime, citizens had the choice to participate in the controlled legislature, to join the armed struggle, to enroll in state-controlled unions, and to partake in movements that tried to address local issues. The latter was done by either demanding action from the state in a confrontational manner or by winning municipal elections and implementing forms of direct democracy. In the 1980s, Brazilian citizens finally had "the right to form organizations that can engage in a wide variety of economic, political and social activities" (North, Wallis, and Weingast 2009, 23). As Doimo (1995) noticed, the term "popular movement," widely used in the 1970s to refer basically to any and all citizen groups, became increasingly associated with one category of organization within the broader "organized civil society" (223). There were now numerous ways to participate in political life, and participation itself was no longer the goal as much as the means to achieve other ends.

The advent of an open access order presented new challenges to the social movements of the 1970s. Tensions emerged at the intersection of competing participatory arenas, ideals, logics, and strategies. In some parts of the country, we witnessed the coexistence of the varied forms of participation discussed in this book (clientelism, populism, party politics, multiple channels for direct participation). Political actors had to take sides, pick an arena, choose strategies, and adopt certain logics at the detriment of others. The tensions present in Diadema, and to a lesser extent in Lages, escalated in the 1980s as political actors committed to the participatory ideal of the 1970s adapted to the new, pluralistic political-institutional context. By the end of the decade, participatory democracy began to become an integral part of the representative system, and no longer as an alternative or affront to it. It is in this context that the PB model and the public policy councils became the main instruments of participatory democracy in Brazil.

THE WITHDRAWAL OF THE CHURCH

In 1996, during a trip to Guatemala, Pope John Paul II declared that Liberation Theology had crumbled following the fall of socialism and no longer represented a problem ("Papa diz que teologia da libertação caducou," 1996). The internal conservative reaction to the Church's "preferential option for the poor" began in the 1970s and became dominant in the course of the 1980s when the papacy persecuted militant Latin American clergy. By the early 1990s, the institutional focus of the Brazilian Catholic Church had moved away from support for grassroots movements and back to more traditional moral concerns. Politically active CEBs showed signs of demobilization. Nonetheless, a portion of those who had been politicized under the auspices of Liberation Theology and trained in the CEBs went on to participate in a multiplicity of civic and political organizations. The 1980s' conservative retraction of the Catholic Church has been widely discussed in the specialized literature and will be only briefly reviewed in the first part of this section. The legacy of the grassroots period has received less attention. The second part of this section draws on work on the latter to argue that the participatory ideal the Church promoted in the 1970s spread broadly throughout Brazilian society and helped to build a more democratic society, although the cohesive structure and discourse that initially supported it were no longer present.

As examined in chapter 2, the progressive arm of the Catholic Church gained dominance at the end of the 1960s and became a firm opposition to the military regime in the early 1970s. In this period, the Church denounced cases of torture, advocated for the respect of human rights, and promoted the growth of CEBs. The Church was also involved in the struggle of various segments of society through its pastoral commissions; for example, in 1975 the Land Pastoral Commission (Comissão Pastoral da Terra) was created to assist rural workers and peasants. It was also in the early 1970s that conservative forces started to unite against what was seen as a disruption of the Church's mission. In 1968, the Medellin Conference of the Latin American Episcopal Council (Consejo Episcopal Latinoamericano, CELAM) marked the rise of the progressive clergy in the region. However, CELAM members elected a conservative bishop to head the organization and tried to reverse the progressive trend. Alfonso López Trujillo began by hassling progressive bishops in the region and then formed the Euro-Latin Alliance with the conservative arm of the West German Church, which aimed to push the Catholics back into their traditional roles. Although some advocates of the "Church of the Poor" chose to present the 1979 CELAM Conference in Puebla as an advancement of their cause, Trujillo succeeded in controlling the meeting's agenda. The conference ended in a stalemate in part due to the vocal opposition of progressive Brazilian bishops (Della Cava 1986).

Conservative bishops maintained that exponents of Liberation Theology reduced faith to politics and by doing so threatened the integrity and unity of the Catholic Church. They criticized the latter's emphasis on socioeconomic issues and held that spirituality, not social justice, was the main focus of the Church. Conservative bishops also disagreed with the "preferential option for the poor," which, according to them, isolated the other segments of society. Liberation theologians' use of Marxist concepts and proximity with Marxist movements greatly distressed conservative and even moderate bishops. Moreover, the conservative current advocated for a more hierarchical Church; in its view,

Christ had endowed the pope and the Church with the authority to lead his followers. Finally, although not opposed to the CEBs, conservative bishops saw their main role to be ecumenical, not social or political (Mainwaring 1986).

In Brazil, the leader of the conservative movement was Rio de Janeiro Archbishop Don Eugênio Sales. His views epitomize what would become the dominant approach of the Church in Brazil. In 1983, Don Sales stated that "a new period for the Brazilian Church is beginning. The Church had a very active role in the period when Brazil was becoming a closed society. It was the 'voice of those who had no voice.' Today, the parliament, press, and parties are functioning fully. They should speak, and the Church should take care of its own affairs" (quoted in Mainwaring 1986, 240). Concerning the role of the CEBs, the Rio de Janeiro archbishop declared that, "the CEBs are [part of the] Church and therefore are born from Christ; their mission is not determined by the people" (quoted in Mainwaring 1986, 251). This vision faced strong opposition within Brazil where adepts of Liberation Theology were numerous and influential. Ultimately, Rome sided with the conservative faction and used its prerogative to appoint bishops and rearrange dioceses to make its vision prevail.

In the early 1980s, recently elected Pope John Paul II began a systematic persecution of militant clergy committed to Liberation Theology. The most common reprimands included the relocation of militant priests to conservative dioceses; the division of dioceses headed by militant bishops, which was intended to decrease their zone of influence; calls for consultations in Rome, where clergymen were scolded by the pope in person; and temporary suspensions of clergy from activities such as offering the Eucharist, teaching, and writing (Burdick 2004). In Brazil, the most visible scapegoats were Leonardo Boff, Clovodis Boff, and Dom Pedro Casaldáliga; all three had their writing, teaching, preaching, and travelling privileges suspended for periods at a time between 1985 and 1989 (Hewitt 1991). Leonardo Boff, the most actively persecuted, renounced the Church in 1992. The outspoken archbishop of São Paulo, Don Paulo Arns, was punished with the arbitrary division of his archdiocese into five dioceses in 1989.

The magnitude of the phenomenon of the CEBs has been difficult to measure. The few reliable statistical studies available were done in the 1980s, which makes it impossible to evaluate whether there was a significant nationwide decline of the number of CEBs in this period. Nevertheless, there is a consensus in the literature about the weakening of CEB's activism. Hewitt's (1991) longitudinal studies of the Archdiocese of São Paulo showed a 14 percent increase in the number of official CEBs between 1983 and 1988, which roughly corresponded to the population growth in the area. The author noted that the new political freedoms and the deteriorating economic scenario would have led one to expect a higher increase. Most importantly, his qualitative analysis showed a decrease in political activity in the most militant CEBs (Type VI); the average membership in these groups went from thirty-six to twenty-three members between 1983 and 1988. Overall, there was an increasing focus on devotional activities and less attention paid to discussion groups (*conscientização*) and collective actions (*reinvidicações*).

One explanation for this shift toward devotional activities is the fact that after 1985 conservative bishops encouraged priests to centralize power and control the activities of their parishes. As a result, "more time is spent on religious training of laity, and political and social education has been dropped off the agenda. This has meant the clear separation of politics and religion in communities, with a return to a more spiritual and charitable content with regard to CEB activities" (Levy 2000, 172).

Another factor contributing to this dwindling process was the lack of leadership. Following the reestablishment of political parties, there was an intense debate about the role of the Church in the upcoming elections. In 1981, the Church determined that CEBs could encourage participation in electoral processes without supporting any specific party. Partisan involvement was strongly discouraged (Della Cava 1986). Ultimately, a number of CEB leaders opted for working for the PT; as the party began to win elections, job opportunities opened in government, and migration toward the party grew. Moreover, some of the older lay leaders seemed disillusioned by the conservative turn of the Church and were unwilling to continue to fight with the institution (Levy 2000). According to Burdick (2004), "by the start of the 1990s, laypeople still committed to an explicitly liberationist agenda found they had few ecclesiastical resources left to conduct political struggle" (7).

The Church's withdrawal of institutional support for political involvement did not impede progressive clergy and activists trained at CEBs to support the democratization process of the country. The bishop of São

Mateus, Dom Aldo Gerna, was not removed from his position, but was disciplined by Rome. In spite of Rome's demand that he tune down his political activism, and two death threats from large landowners, Dom Aldo actively supported the MST (personal communication, January 23, 2011). Since its inception, the MST has received unremitting assistance from the Land Pastoral; the genesis and history of the two organizations are intrinsically related (Fernandes 2000). In this sense, it is important to mention that although the heads of the large archdioceses in the south and southeast regions played crucial roles in influencing the Church's progressive political stance in the 1970s, clergymen in rural areas of the country have been extremely active in the defense of their marginalized parishes. Although São Paulo's Dom Paulo Arns was the most visible opponent to the military government, the first bold actions against the repressive regime took place in the north, northeast, and center region, where overt violence against poor segments of the society was more common (Della Cava 1986; Krischke 1979).

Writing in 1986, Mainwaring noted that democratization was not having an even effect across Brazil, and that in rural areas where "forms of domination continued to be unsophisticated and repressive," the Church continued to play an active political role (Mainwaring 1986, 241). In the Amazon region, for example, the Church leadership helped the rubber tappers movement, whose leader Chico Mendes was assassinated in 1988. Marina Silva of the Green Party, the third-place contender in the 2010 presidential elections, was from this region and was trained in the CEBs before joining social movements and later becoming a politician (Hochstetler and Keck 2007). The brutal assassination of activist nun Dorothy Stang in 2005 in the interior of the northern state of Para verifies the continuing validity of Mainwaring's observation.

The Brazilian black movement received strong support from the Catholic Church's Black Pastoral created in the early 1980s, but it is interesting to note that the former inspired the latter. During its progressive period, the Church attracted an unusual number of seminarians from lower social classes; in Brazil, this meant that many of them were nonwhite. The growth of the black movement in the late 1970s and the creation of the United Negro Movement (Movimento Negro Unificado, MNU) called the attention of nonwhite seminarians trained under the doctrine of Liberation Theology to racial divides within the Church structure. Previously self-identified simply as being from lower social classes, nonwhite seminarians and priests started to organize meetings and to attend MNU events, and eventually adopted the title "black pastoral agents." They interpreted the struggle against racial inequality as integral to Liberation Theology's vision and the Church's preferential option for the poor (Burdick 2004).

In the 1980s, the Black Pastoral focused on popular education aimed at disseminating Afro-Brazilian history. Early efforts were only partially successful, and educational campaigns did not attract as many people as black pastoral agents hoped. Later in the decade, the Vatican adopted an "enculturation approach" that aimed at making Catholicism more attuned with local cultures, and in that way secures the Church's international congregation. Many among the progressive clergy found this to be a diversion from underlining socioeconomic issues, but black pastoral agents adopted the approach in order to make their movement more interesting and less strictly educational. In the 1990s, the Black Pastoral turned attention to helping nonwhite students in public secondary schools to prepare for university entrance exams, where their higher-income white counterparts from private schools tended to perform significantly better. Finally, a continuing theme in the work of the Black Pastoral has been the promotion of black self-identity. The argument here is that the widespread idea that the Brazilian people were formed through miscegenation plays down the African element, and that Afro-Brazilians should instead feel comfortable to "assume their negritude" (Burdick 2004). Although it is difficult to draw direct causal links, the work of black pastoral agents seems inexorably related with the recent advances Brazilian society has made on this front.[1]

The relationship between women's movements and the progressive Church has been more convoluted. On the one hand, Liberation theologians gave more emphasis to women than other doctrines, and CEBs helped women to organize and become politically active citizens. Leonardo Boff, for example, recognized that "the Church is basically a church of males, a church of whites, and a church of celibates"; his writings tried to call attention to the unsung women in the Bible (Boff and Tamez 1987, 99–100). Studies have documented the crucial role CEBs and progressive priests had in supporting the political mobilization of women; the Church's "mothers' clubs," for example, served as launching pads for numerous social movements in the early 1980s (Alvarez 1990b; Burdick 2004), including the movement against high living costs (Sader 1988).

On the other hand, the progressive arm of the Church was unwilling to target the family as the key sphere of oppression of women. Alvarez (1990b) has criticized Liberation theologians and clergymen for being unable to support women's struggles beyond traditional gender roles; in her view, the Church helped to make women politically active citizens but has failed to politicize women's issues. Burdick (2004) prefers to emphasize that the progressive Church empowered women who then began to make demands and organize around themes that were beyond the clergy's control. Overall, the relationship with women's movement typifies the Church's general attitude after 1985: Liberation theologians disseminated a progressive but at times evasive discourse, CEBs and pastoral agents supported small communities and specific disfranchised groups, but the Church as a whole refused to take a stand on the most contentious social issues and denied affiliation with any political organization or combative social movement.

To conclude, the conservative turn of the Church's leadership and its withdrawal of direct support to politically active CEBs does not mean that it did not play an important role in the re-democratization of the country. Progressive clergy continued to support and advocate for social movements and disfranchised citizens, and CEB members shored up groups and organizations that carried on the participatory ideals of the 1970s. The community network created in the previous decade was instrumental in the ANC and the creation of the PT, both of which are examined later in this chapter. However, the focus on direct citizen participation was replaced for support to varied forms of political expression and organization. In a political-institutional context that more closely resembled an open access order, progressive Catholics could directly and indirectly participate in social and political life in a variety of forms.

THE PRAGMATIC PMDB

In 1979, the military government passed an electoral reform that ended the two-party system imposed in 1965. The regime's "primary intention was to split the opposition Brazilian Democratic Movement (MDB) into several weaker parties through ruptures on the right and left wings . . . and to create a basically centrist party culture to promote evolutionary change" (Selcher 1986, 55). The tactic worked. The progressive leftist forces split among the PMDB, the PT, and other smaller leftist parties. Whereas Francisco Weffort and José Alvaro Moisés helped to found the PT, Fernando Henrique ran for senate for the PMDB, and Jarbas Vasconcelos, the author of the more radical 1976 mayors' manual, ran for mayor of Recife for a small leftist party.[2] The liberal conservative arm of the PMDB joined the centrist Popular Party (Partido Popular, PP). This party was mainly constituted of representatives of business and finance sectors, and for that reason it was jestingly said that PP stood for partido dos patrões (bosses' party) (Benevides 1986).

Most of ARENA's members joined the Social Democratic Party (PSD); following some desertions to the PP and the entry of some former MDB deputies, the party managed to keep a majority in the legislative chambers. The party reform included a number of gimmicks, often referred to as "electoral engineering," which helped the military to control the transition and avoid dangerous shifts (Fleischer 1986). In the 1982 municipal, gubernatorial, and legislative elections, with 41.5 percent of the total vote, the PSD managed to gain control of two-thirds of the cities in the country, twelve of twenty-two state governments, almost two-thirds of senate seats, and 49 percent of seats in the Chamber of Deputies (Selcher 1986, 61). In 1985, a faction of the PSD broke off and formed the Party of the Liberal Front (Partido da Frente Liberal, PFL), another centrist party; following this split the PMDB became the majority party (Fleischer 1986).

In the context of a competitive party system, the PMDB steadily moved to the center of the political spectrum, forging alliances with the PP and the PFL, and increasingly isolating leftist forces within the party. In 1982, the party declared its commitment to supporting and representing community organizations and social movements without trying to control them (PMDB 1982, 8). In fact, the PMDB became almost solely focused on electoral disputes to the point that it asserted that the only "useful" opposition vote was for its candidates; voting for small opposition parties was wasting opposition votes because the defeat of the PMDB could bring the "death of democracy." This fundamentally undemocratic and arrogant attitude reminded observers of the time of the "enlightened elitism" that had supported the 1964 coup (Benevides 1986).

At lower levels of government there was some continuity with the participatory practices previously espoused by the *autênticos*. One of the best known of these was the Popular Councils created in André Franco Montoro's mandate as governor of São Paulo. Montoro was the author of the chapter on participatory democracy in the MDB's manual for mayor published in 1976 (chapter 2). One of the most experienced of the combative MDB deputies, his pre-1964 affiliation was with the small Christian Democratic Party (Partido Democrata Cristão, PDC). Throughout the dictatorship, Montoro was a serene but defiant voice within the party, and was supported by a substantial portion of Paulista voters. He was elected state senator in 1970 and 1978, and became governor in the first direct gubernatorial elections in 1982 (Kinzo 1988).

In 1979, the appointed PSD mayor of São Paulo, Reynaldo de Barros (the nephew of the populist leader Adhemar de Barros), passed a decree creating popular councils in the city. In the following year, eleven councils with representatives of civil society groups discussed the city's budget. According to Gohn (2001), councils functioned mostly as a space for citizens to make demands that were compiled by public officials and later ignored. In 1984, Mario Covas, Montoro's appointed mayor, created popular councils under the umbrella of the Secretariat of Family and Social Welfare (Secretaria da Família e do Bem-Estar Social, FABES) that were organized by a sector of government, for example, housing and adult education. According to the Secretariat, councils were meant to "guarantee the real and effective presence of the city's social forces in the process of planning, evaluation, control and reorientation of the FABES' operation" (quoted in Gohn 2001, 73). These councils embodied the idea of citizen participation as part of the policy-making process, and not as any form of direct citizen rule.

The PMDB popular councils were criticized by the militant left, who saw the initiative as an attempt to co-opt social movements. For example, Sílvio Caccia Bava, an intellectual and PT militant, argued these councils tried to control participation.

It is very important for [Montoro] to impose on the population and social movements forms of participation that avoid initiatives coming from workers that put the government against the wall. To institutionalize popular participation means to control and channel [citizens'] demands and manifestations of popular protest to a space created from above. . . . This is so important for the Montoro government that he even created a State Secretariat to take care of the popular participation question. (Bava 1983, 89–90)

Bava contrasted this format of citizen participation with the type of popular council advocated by the PT, which was autonomous from both the government and political parties. Bava offered as examples the truly spontaneous, bottom-up popular councils of Osasco, Campinas, and the health councils of São Paulo. The role of the party, in his view, was simply to support these initiatives.

The PT later learned that working with popular councils was more complicated than the party's intellectuals imagined in the early 1980s. Most important at this point is to call attention to the growing complexity of debates about participation. The PMDB's councils and the PT opposition to them raised important questions about how to include popular participation in government and for what purpose. The clear-cut 1970s' state-society dichotomy started to give way to a more complex institutional scenario, which involved political parties and distinct ideas about participation.

At the national level, the progressive faction of the PMDB became increasingly dismayed with the centrist approach of the leadership and urged party members to revive the ideals of the 1970s. In the mid-1980s, politicians in this group formed a faction called the Progressive United Movement (Movimento de Unidade Progressista, MUP). In preparation for the ANC, the MUP issued a document advocating bolder reforms that the party leadership did not seem willing to defend. In his speech at the conference where this document was drafted, Fernando Henrique Cardoso, then party leader at the Senate, insisted that the Assembly was a crucial opportunity to regain the population's trust in the PMDB as a party that could promote change. Covas, now state senator, argued that if the Assembly pitched workers against capital, the party's obligation was to defend the former. The PMDB performance in the ANC was frustrating for this group and led to the split that created the Brazilian Social Democratic Party (Partido da Social Democracia Brasileira, PSDB).

At the moment of the creation of the PSDB, the national leader of the PMDB was the centrist and compromising Ulysses Guimarães, whereas the most populous state of the country, São Paulo, was in the hands of Orestes Quércia and his extended clientelist network (Christiano 2003). The PSDB was the last refuge for *autênticos* like Montoro, Cardoso, and Covas, who had opted for staying in the PMDB instead of joining newer and more progressive parties such as the PT.

In the PSDB founding statement, "modern democracy" was qualified as "participatory and pluralist." In the same document, the party committed itself to struggle for

> the decentralization of political power, the respect for the autonomy of civil society organizations, and the expansion of information, discussion, and consultation channels in decision-making of public interest . . . conditions for the increasing adoption of new forms of direct exercise of citizenship, which enhance and validate the classic mechanisms of representative democracy. (Partido da Social Democracia Brasileira 1992, 11)

In this view, the purpose of direct citizen participation was clearly to improve the quality of the representative system, which by now was valued and worth defending.

The city of Campinas, one of the PSDB's showcase municipal administrations, was run in the late 1980s and early 1990s by one of the party's founders, José Roberto Magalhães Teixeira. This mayor created a decentralized public service infrastructure that increased the efficiency of public service delivery. Teixeira also created the program Renda Minima (Minimum Income), a conditional transfer program that assisted families living in poverty as long as they kept their children in school (Figueiredo and Lamounier 1996). This program was a precursor of today's internationally known Bolsa Família. Notwithstanding progressive programs such as these, as with the aforementioned commitment with direct citizen participation, the party did not promote participatory democracy as actively as the 1970s' *autênticos* or the PT.

In 1994, Fernando Henrique became the first PSDB president. His administration created an agency within the executive branch called Solidary Community (Comunidade Solidária, CS), which was headed by anthropologist and first lady Ruth Correa Cardoso. The main objective of the CS was to help to strengthen civil society organizations, to promote state-civil society partnerships, and to facilitate government consultation with key civil society actors. The CS succeeded in engaging important civil society actors, but received harsh criticisms (Friedman and Hochstetler 2002). Critical scholars saw the CS as part of a political project that displaces the meaning of participation and civil society from the radical participatory project of the 1980s to a neoliberal agenda that tries to off-load state responsibilities and transform civil society groups into mere service providers (Dagnino, Olvera, and Panfichi 2006a). By the mid-1990s, the two distinct normative approaches to citizen participation reviewed in the introductory chapter were already well established, and the PSDB, originally the party of *autênticos*, adopted an approach more in line with what has here been called the conventional view.

This section examined the evolution of one of the forces behind the participatory ideology and experiences of the late 1970s. The *autênticos* who stayed in the PMDB were responsible for some of the first participatory policy councils in the country, which at the time were criticized as being an attempt to co-opt social movements. Eventually, the progressive members of the party found it impossible to remain in a centrist party solely focused on electoral results and allied with some of the most conservative groups in Brazil. The PSDB presented an option between the then-radical approach to participation espoused by the PT and the increasing conservatism of the PMDB. The party was not a champion of local-level participatory initiatives, as was the PT, and later participatory innovations at the federal level have also been criticized. Nevertheless, PSDB deputies played a key role in the ANC; as seen below, their moderate proposals made more headway than amendments pitched on a radical tone. The key is to note the emergence of a more complex political-institutional context and new ideas and forms of organizing participation.

PT'S PARTICIPATORY ADMINISTRATIONS

The PT brought together a number of progressive forces, including CEB members, leftist intellectuals, Marxists, autonomous professionals, and, the most prominent group, workers from the new unionism movement

(Keck 1992; Meneguello 1989). From its inception the PT was devoted to making popular participation a pivotal aspect of the party's political program, but there was a less clear idea about the format participation would take. The absence of consensus on participation was in part due to the internal heterogeneity of the party. The orthodox Marxist factions of the party envisioned an eventual socialist revolution, and participation was seen as an instrumental part of this project. The more democratic factions were concerned with broadening the PT's constituency and making it a competitive political party; in this view participation should include all citizens and not be limited to those committed to the party's socialist program. In Diadema, the first PT administration, these two views collided and led to an administrative stalemate.

Throughout the 1980s the party continued to experiment with participatory democracy. In the process, a pragmatic view of participatory programs emerged and became widely accepted within the party. The first part of this section reviews party documents that illustrate the consolidation of the more democratic and less sectarian vision for the party at the national level. The second part discusses challenges the party faced in trying to implement participatory initiatives in Vitória, São Paulo, Porto Alegre, and some smaller cities; it presents both accounts of these administrations and the analysis of influential party intellectuals directly involved in these first experiments, which helped to shape the party's thinking about the format of popular participation in PT administrations.

The Consolidation of a Democratic Party

In the 1980s, two dominant *tendências* (factions) argued over the PT's political program. On the one hand, a democratic faction saw the party as a mass party and held democracy over socialism. On the other hand, a more statist faction hung on Leninist ideals envisioned the PT as a proletarian party and placed less emphasis on democracy. A general trend marked the party's discourse: the democratic faction was paramount from foundation to the mid-1980s; in 1986, the country's economic and political crisis, allegedly a revolutionary opportunity, backed the rise of the statist faction; the loss of the 1989 presidential elections, the crumbling of socialist role models, and a new analysis of capitalism brought the democratic faction back to the forefront in the early 1990s

(César 2002). The consolidation of the more democratic vision was a necessary condition for the party's support for participatory democracy.

In its founding manifesto of 1980, the PT defined itself as a workers' party that aspires "to be the true political expression of all who are exploited by the capitalist system"; therefore, "an ample party open to all committed to the workers' cause and to the party's programs" (Partido dos Trabalhadores 1998, 66). The first party program, issued in June of 1981, stated that, "the rights of all workers are neglected, from peasants to doctors, from industrial workers to engineers to teachers . . . from menial workers to experts, artists, journalists, tradesmen, rural and urban autonomous workers" (71). The document Points for the Elaboration of the PT's Program noted that "it should be clear an interest identity (and not simply an 'alliance') between urban and rural workers" (quoted in César 2002, 248). This statement marks a significant break with orthodox Marxist doctrines that either disregard peasants or instrumentally conceive alliances with rural sectors (César 2002).

More orthodox statements are found in official documents when the statist faction led the party from the mid- to the late 1980s. The final report of the 1987 annual meeting stated that "the industrial work force is the most important and concentrated [popular] sector and the one capable of leading the revolutionary process. Poor peasants and urban wageworkers are the main allies of the proletariat"; semi-proletariat and marginalized groups should be attracted to help the outburst of the revolutionary process, and progressive and democratic intellectuals and small shop owners are segments that can be attracted to the revolutionary bloc (Partido dos Trabalhadores 1998, 325). The document elaborated extensively on the struggle for socialism and made references to the Russian Revolution, Mao's China, and the Sandinista uprising in Nicaragua. It was the first time that the PT officially presented itself as a socialist party (César 2002).

In 1991 the party held its first national congress, and by then the orthodox Marxist tone was no longer central. The final report started with the following statement:

> The Workers' Party wishes to share the revision of its historical project with workers and all democratic and socialist forces, [a project] which is the fruit of 11 years of struggle for democracy and social equality. We consider our natural interlocutors all those who hope

for the end of misery and the elimination of Brazil's brutal injustices. (Partido dos Trabalhadores 1998, 481)

The same document criticized the Brazilian Left for

> Having an egocentric training wherein the Capital [versus] Work question has always been considered the explanatory base for all the contradictions found in society; this has prevented [the left] from understanding that this contradiction is fundamental, but it does not take into account all forms of oppression that the general working population is subjected to. (523)

Other examples of oppression included racism, police violence, and sterilization of women. Finally, commenting on the crumbling of real socialism, the document stated that

> For decades real socialist regimes deprived entire populations from political participation and democracy. For this reason, the PT welcomes the transformations taking place in these countries; they represent the rebirth of the labor movement, of civil society, and of cultural debates. (Partido dos Trabalhadores 1998, 492)

The document elaborates extensively on the shortcomings of the regimes of the Eastern bloc, focusing especially on their undemocratic character. However, the document cautions that such criticisms should not serve as justification for compliance with the status quo. In a section titled Neither Real Socialism Nor Social Democracy, the document posited that, "For the PT, socialism is synonymous with the radicalization of democracy" (499), which included the "socialization of the means of governing" and initiatives that allow the population to "appropriate functions that today are reserved to state and institutional spheres" (500).

It is safe to argue that had the statist faction gained control over the party, commitment to popular participation would have lessened or participatory initiatives would have been restricted to the party membership, as a faction of the Diadema PT fancied. In fact, Avritzer (2009) has contended that PB is more common in cities where democratic factions within the PT are more prominent than orthodox segments. The triumph of the democratic faction enabled the party's unremitting support for participatory democracy in the 1990s.

PT's Participatory Administrations in the 1980s

Brazil had three municipal elections in the 1980s. The 1982 election followed the rules of the regime and did not include state capitals and cities with hydro and mineral resources. Diadema was the only city the PT governed for the entire 1982–1988 mandate. In 1985, state capitals and resource-rich cities elected mayors for a three-year interim mandate. The PT elected the mayor of Fortaleza, the capital of the northeast state of Ceará.[3] In 1988, a nationwide municipal election put all mayoral seats in the country up for dispute for four-year mandates. The PT elected thirty-one mayors (Keck 1992, 157); of these, twelve left or were expelled from the party before the end of the mandate due to disagreements similar to those examined in the case of Diadema (Abers 1996). The errors and successes of this period strongly influenced the party's approach to participatory democracy in the following decade (Baiocchi 2003; Nylen 1997, 2003).

In 1985, Maria Luíza Fontenele became the first Brazilian woman and PT politician to be elected mayor of a state capital. Active in the progressive arm of the MDB, she remained in the PMDB for a few years and then joined the PT, but her foremost political commitment was with the orthodox Revolutionary Labor Party (Partido Revolucionário Operário, PRO), which at the time functioned as a faction within the PT. In the election campaign, Fontenele reached out to the poor segments of society but was elected largely by the votes of the middle class discontented with the country's economic recession. Once elected, she neglected middle-class interests and focused on the poorest sectors of the city. However, the Communist Party of Brazil (PCdoB) was well organized among these sectors and opposed the PT. Fontenele then gave preferential treatment to groups not associated with the PCdoB, which fuelled discord among social movements. The administration also faced the opposition of conservative parties who held a majority in the municipal legislative assembly, where the PT did not have a single seat. Finally, the state of Ceará was in the hands of *coronéis*, and at this time state governments were still able to financially boycott opposition municipal governments, as in the case of Lages. Lack of resources greatly limited Fontenele's administration (Pinto 1992).

The creation of Popular Councils was a core electoral promise, but Fontenele admitted that "during the campaign we announced as a commitment that the PT was going to govern the city with Popular Councils. But the idea of Popular Council was not clear in our heads, or was in diverse forms. Once we started to discuss the topic, there were at least five different visions of it" (quoted in Pinto 1992, 9). Public policy councils from previous administrations were maintained, and new ones were created, but all had a timid role in the administration. The Popular Council announced in the campaign was never formed.

As in Diadema, the Fortaleza administration was marked by internal conflict. The PRO saw municipal government as a tool in the revolutionary process, while the moderate sector of the PT was largely concerned with administrative efficiency. In 1987, the PRO managed to isolate the moderate sector and govern alone, but moderates managed to appoint the successor candidate, which led Fontenele to leave the party and support another candidate. In the end, both the PT's and Fontenele's candidates lost the 1988 election. Although the PT made modest but significant advances in social areas (Pinto 1992), the PT's first state capital government became known for its administrative incompetence (Bergamaschi 1988).

Icapuí, a small coastal town in Ceará, also experimented with participatory democracy in the 1980s (Nylen 1997). In the beginning of the decade, CEB militants and university students led the movement to emancipate their district from the city of Aracatí. Once successful, residents of the new town elected José Airton, a young politician from PMDB's leftist faction, as their mayor. Much like Dirceu Carneiro, Airton was isolated from the rest of the party and ran the city with the support of a small group of dedicated activists. They implemented a number of progressive programs, especially in the health and education sectors, and invited excluded citizens to take an active role in the administration of the city. As in Lages, there were mixed results, with numbers of participants below the expected levels and growing frustration among city officials and public servants. Unlike Dirceu Carneiro, Airton openly supported PT's Francisco José Teixeira, who had a tight victory in the 1988 elections. Teixeira continued to invest in citizen participation while also focusing on more immediate priorities. Airton had an easy comeback in the 1992 elections and once again put citizen participation at the top of the city's priorities even though the Municipal Councils he created in his first mandate, which were maintained by Teixeira, had not yet delivered the desired outcomes. In the beginning of his second mandate Airton admitted that, "now we understand that [stimulating citizen participation] is a slow process, and a very difficult one" (as quoted in Nylen 1997, 435). The obstinate mayor decided to set up a Secretariat of Community Action to boost the city's civil society.

In 1985, São Paulo elected the veteran populist leader Jânio Quadros as mayor, showing that populism survived the authoritarian period and participatory movements. In 1988, Paulistas elected Luiza Erundina, a social worker connected with social movements and associated with one of the more orthodox factions of the PT. The party leadership did not back her nomination; the city was of important political strategic value and Plínio de Arruda Sampaio seemed a more sensible option. In the 2010 presidential election Sampaio was the extreme-left candidate with a discourse that many found anachronistic. In 1988, Sampaio was a moderate PT politician, a competent lawyer active in the Constituent Assembly, with a strong relationship with the Catholic Church and international experience with the United Nations. The party leadership thought that Sampaio could gain middle-class votes and forge an alliance with the leftist arm of the PMDB, which at this time was splitting to form the PSDB (Couto 1995).

In a public debate in May 1988 the two pre-candidates discussed the topic of popular councils. The newspaper *Folha de São Paulo* summarized the discussion as follows:

> Erundina affirmed that a PT government in the city of São Paulo cannot simply represent the modernization of the "bourgeois state." Thus, she understands that popular councils should help to spur the construction of socialism, without limiting themselves to current rules. Plínio thinks that councils should have a consultative character, and that the type of council proposed by Erundina is only justified in a "phase of popular insurrection." He then criticized [Erundina's] "pseudo-revolutionary rhetoric." ("Petistas divergem sobre 'Conselhos Populares,'" 1988)

The party membership chose Erundina, and she was elected mayor by a five percent margin over the second contender. She did not have the support of the party's leadership or moderate factions during the campaign, and therefore was free to select her cabinet secretaries. Erundina reached out for independent party militants and a group constituted mainly of autonomous professionals, and put together a team that included educator Paulo Freire, jurist Dalmo Dallari, philosopher Marilena Chaui, and economist Paul Singer (Couto 1995).

Erundina's intellectual dream team faced challenges similar to other PT governments. A debate over the public bus fare illustrates well the tensions within the administration. Mayor Quadros was known for allowing bus companies hired by the city to impose high fares. During the campaign Erundina promised to make public transport affordable; it is needless to explain that bus fares have a considerable impact on the income of poor families. In the months preceding the election, Quadros stopped raising the fare in order to regain some popularity. By the beginning of Erundina's mandate the fare had been significantly depreciated by the country's high inflation rate, and the federal government was about to impose a monetary plan that would forbid price increases for a determined period. The finance staff found it necessary to raise the fare, for which it faced voracious reactions from the political staff and party members who had supported Erundina's candidacy. The problem was common to other PT municipalities in the state, and a meeting with mayors and the national leadership was called. The near-unanimity of mayors defended that the increase was crucial, but Lula and other national leaders insisted that it was not a good political strategy. In the end bus fares were raised (Singer 1996).

This administrative pragmatism was found in other PT administrations. In the tiny Ronda Alta, Rio Grande do Sul, PT Mayor Saul Barbosa (1989–1992) could openly declare that "we realized that the city hall is like a company, so we have to be good business people in here" (Ferreira and Ricci 1992, 23). São Paulo was not Ronda Alta. PT militants and social movements that had supported Erundina were extremely frustrated with what they referred to as *administrativismo*—a pejorative term that implies exclusive focus on technical matters and lack of political vision—and at times criticized the PT as harshly as they criticized Quadros (Singer 1996). The national leadership resented Erundina's unwillingness to try to show results right away and instead choosing to spend the first year putting things in order; 1989 was Lula's presidential campaign and the party had hoped to gain more political capital from a São Paulo government (Couto 1995).

Concerning the popular councils, São Paulo went further than Fortaleza and organized assemblies in various districts of the city with the purpose of discussing the municipal budgeting. These public hearings were much more in line with Sampaio's notion of consultation than with any sort of revolutionary project. Paul Singer, the finance secretary and party intellectual, later admitted that "I went to as many assemblies as I could and felt frustrated with the discrepancy between our conception of what participation should be and the reality of it" (Singer 1996, 121). He explained that the team expected people to discuss how to improve the city as a whole, but citizens, especially in poor neighborhoods, were solely concerned with immediate material demands. Erundina would repeatedly plead with people to "transcend the local and sectorial" and focus instead on broad goals. In 1990, she evaluated these assemblies as "still precarious" and affirmed that it was not the government's responsibility to organize popular councils (Freire and Azevedo 1990, 15). Singer admitted that in the end participation was mostly indirect, through the secretariats' staffs that were closely connected with varied segments of civil society, with some predominance of unionized workers; he wrote, "it couldn't be any other way, it is in fact impossible to negotiate the allocation of resources of a large budget in assemblies with hundreds of people" (Singer 1996, 121). Some militants referred to this type of indirect participation as left-wing clientelism (Kowarick and Singer 1993).

According to Lúcio Kowarick and André Singer (1993), scholars at the time associated with the PT, the Erundina government realized that the social movements with which it had direct links represented a small portion of the population. Movements' delegates represented diverse social groups, some much larger than others, and when given the chance to participate they most often defended the private interests of their groups. This realization led Erundina's team to shift the aim of the administration from "putting the government in the hands of the people," as asserted during the campaign, to "governing the city for all," the maxim that guided the government. While the former was based on notions of direct democracy, the latter relied on the active participation of officials in "negotiation councils" that brought together key shareholders to discuss solutions to specific problems. These scholars noted that, "the popular participation exalted in direct democracy processes stopped being the organizing principle of the city's administration" (205). By 1990, Erundina was focusing more attention on public policy councils, which she argued would spur a *conscientização* process that could lead to the emergence of genuine, bottom-up popular councils (Freire and Azevedo 1990). As seen in the introduction, policy councils are to this date an important aspect of Brazil's participatory democracy, but they did not lead to popular councils.

Abers (1996) compared attempts to create participatory budgeting in six other PT municipal administrations in the 1989–1992 period, namely, Santos, Santo André, Piracicaba, Ipatinga, João Monlevarde, and Porto Alegre. The main challenges these governments faced were the fact that budgetary decision-making required technical knowledge that ordinary citizens did not have and the need to balance citizens' focus on their immediate surroundings with administrators' concern with the city as a whole. PT members expected social movements to jump at the opportunity to participate, whereas in many cases citizens were willing to participate only when material benefits were visible. The first rounds of participation usually mounted to an endless number of demands that could not be paid for with the limited budget of the cities; failure to respond to demands meant that governments lost grassroots support and that the mobilization of citizens for the next round of participation was even more difficult. "According to numerous informants, the administrations' attempts to incorporate popular movements into the formulation of the city budget largely failed in the first years" (43).

Cities addressed these challenges differently. Santos desisted from creating large-scale participatory budgets and replaced them with small consultative councils on specific issue areas, for example, councils to monitor health posts. Ipatinga and Piracicaba opted for using individual surveys to gather information about citizens' concerns and demands. In Santo André and Porto Alegre, citizens were asked to negotiate a list of investment priorities; governments promised to implement only the top priorities. These two cities also focused more than the others on educating citizens about public finances. In Porto Alegre, the two-level participatory pyramid (see Introduction) made it possible for participants at the district level to have simply a general understanding of budgetary processes, whereas their representatives at the municipal level became knowledgeable about city finances.

Santo André and Porto Alegre addressed the dilemma of local demands versus general city planning in different ways. Santo André allocated only a portion of the budget available to new investments to the participatory process, and government officials decided on the utilization of the rest; it also required community-level councils to put forward one proposal for a city-level project (Abers 1996). In 1990, Santo André Mayor Celso Daniel, a university professor who participated in the founding of the PT, wrote an article for one of the party's magazines discussing the character of "popular democratic administrations." Daniel distinguished between two existing approaches for the inclusion of popular participation in municipal administrations. "In the first, the government relinquishes a parcel of its political power with the objective of co-governing with the community; in the second, the government transfers all of its power to the community, establishing a type of community of self-government in the municipality" (Daniel 1990, 12). He supported the first approach, arguing that a government is elected based on a political project and a series of public commitments. A party committed to popular participation should transfer a portion of its power to the community, fulfilling its commitment, but retain the rest of the authority in order to play the governing role for which it was elected. According to Daniel, completely renouncing the authority to govern is only justifiable if the party's sole political commitment was community self-government, which was not the case with the PT.

Porto Alegre allowed citizens to decide how to use the entire investment budget. The city's intensive education efforts were an attempt to increase citizens' awareness of broader issues. City officials also devised an equation wherein the population density and the level of infrastructure of each district were taken into account in determining the amount of resources they received; whereas citizens decided the priority investment areas, how much each district received depended on this technical criteria. The need to make participation work for everyone was clearly a concern of the administration. In 1988, the Porto Alegre mayor, Olívio Dutra, at the time in the capacity of the party's national president, commented on the case of Diadema, "the PT needs to learn that when taking on government in a capitalist society it is not possible to govern only for itself without taking into account society as a whole. . . . The party urgently needs to extract lessons from the Diadema episode" ("PT tenta convencer prefeito de Diadema a ficar no partido," 1988). Dutra publicly asked Menezes to stay in the party. He considered Fortaleza a very different case because Fontenele was never concerned with the PT.

Nylen (1997) has argued that these first PT experiences constituted a key process of institutional learning. "A heterodox PT political project emerged rooted in the practice and experience of PT municipal governance throughout Brazil" (439). Overall, according to the author, PT members put aside the "doctrinal purity" of the initial years without "abandoning the basic principles" in which the party had been founded. A key actor in this institutional learning process was PT's National Secretariat of Institutional Affairs (SNAI). Created in 1988, the SNAI represented a deliberate effort to learn from PT experiences and build a coherent and pragmatic political program. This work was done through numerous seminars and workshops that brought party members from all corners of the country. Much of SNAI's work in the late 1980s and early 1990s was compiled in a book titled *O modo petista de governar* (The PT's way of governing). Organized by the SNAI's director, Jorge Bittar (1992), the book contains a chapter restating PT's commitment with popular participation, but also calling attention to its many challenges. The book was published in the first years of the first PT administration in Porto Alegre, which goes to show that by the time of the creation of the PB, the party had accumulated, organized, and disseminated a considerable amount of knowledge on how to organize popular participation in public administration.

Porto Alegre succeeded in creating a practical and lasting model that has inspired similar initiatives around the world. As of 2015, the Porto Alegre PB remains active. Since 2005, it has shared space with another participatory initiative based on distinct participatory ideals (Tranjan 2011). Baierle (2010) argues that "little by little, the 'cacique' (boss/gatekeeper) culture of the presidents of neighborhood associations, which was supposed to have been buried, returned" (Baierle 2010, 57). Junge (2012) found the growing of an individualist ethos common in NGOs that was much to the detriment of the earlier collective mobilization and spirit of action. Whatever its fate may be, the PB model played an unparalleled role in spreading participatory democracy in Brazil and the world. However, despite its merits and accomplishments, the PB is remarkably less ambitious than the participatory initiatives of the 1970s and the PT's attempts to include popular participation in the 1980s. The PB may have an immense potential in terms of forming active citizens (Baiocchi 2005), but it is ultimately a mechanism that allows people to make specific demands for how to spend a small portion of the budget. This is the type of participation that intellectuals associated with the Erundina administration deemed limited, adding that it was meant to co-opt social movements. Simply put, the PB is not the popular council promised by PT candidates in the 1980s.

As seen in this section, what made this moderate model of citizen participation become PT's main participatory initiative was not lack of political commitment. PT mayors and officials went to long lengths, and even risked their careers, trying to promote citizen participation. However, in the political-institutional context of the late 1980s, it was no longer practical to advance more encompassing forms of citizen participation. The PB was a feasible and ingenious compromise. As Nylen (2003) has put it, "while fundamentally reformist in nature, the [PB] could easily fit into the Left's traditional discourse of radical, even revolutionary, change" (50). If the PB model was less ambitious than the popular councils advocated in the 1980s, it was also more realistic and sustainable, as proven by more than 20 years of the Porto Alegre PB and the adoption of the model in various parts of the world.

THE TEMPERATE CITIZEN CONSTITUTION

The 1988 constitution has an ambiguous legacy. On the one hand, it grants fiscal and political autonomy to municipal governments, includes numerous devices endorsing citizen participation in public administration, and is often referred to as the Citizen Constitution in allusion to the active civil society participation in its drafting. Nearly every study of PB mentions at least in brief the constitution as one of the factors favoring participatory democracy in Brazil. On the other hand, during the National Constituent Assembly (ANC) the aforementioned centrist alliance of self-serving politicians became dominant in the legislative chambers. The *centrão* (broad center) succeeded in controlling the ANC and stalling progressive legislation in matters such as land reform. Although it counted on the input of civil society organizations, in most issue areas the final text expressed the interests and compromises of the pragmatic arm of the PMDB, which at this time forced the last *autênticos* out of the party.

The participation of civil society organizations in the Constituent Assembly and the formation of the *centrão* have already been documented (Michiles et al. 1989; Souza 1997; Spitzcovsky and Tura 1993). The purpose of this section is to examine the lesser-known proposals for the creation of channels of direct citizen participation intended to bypass the representative system. Consistent with the other processes analyzed in this chapter, these challenging proposals were supplanted by more moderate solutions compatible with the new political-institutional context. As the next pages show, the predominant view in the ANC was that participation should enhance and not replace representation. The first part of this section describes the participation of civil society in the drafting of the constitution. Aside from being an interesting process, the participation of civil society groups is significant because they were the proponents of most of the amendments for participatory devices, which are examined in the second part of the section.

Participating for the Right to Participate

Following the defeat of the campaign for direct presidential elections, civil society groups, progressive clergy, and militant intellectuals began to mobilize to influence the drafting of the new constitution. Two umbrella organizations were created in the first months of 1985: the National Movement for the Constituent (Movimento Nacional pela Constituinte), in Rio de Janeiro, and the Assembly Pro Popular Participation in the Constituent (Plenário Pró-Participação Popular na Constituinte), in São Paulo. Numerous similar organizations were then formed across the country with the same purpose of influencing the drafting of the country's Magna Carta. In June 1985, President José Sarney (the indirectly elected vice-president) sent a bill to congress proposing the creation of a constituent assembly. A multi-party committee was created to discuss and further develop the bill and submit it for voting. The president's bill suggested an assembly formed with regular deputies taking place concomitantly and within the same structure of other legislative processes. Civil society organizations lobbied and protested to have an assembly separated from the current institutional apparatus, with representatives elected solely for this purpose; they feared that a constitution written under the auspices of institutions still largely controlled by conservative forces would not echo Brazilians' democratic aspirations. In December congress approved a proposal akin to what the president had suggested (Michiles et al. 1989).

The legislative elections scheduled for 1986 were going to elect the deputies from whom the members of the ANC were to be drawn. Citizen groups concerned with the constituent process tried to make the election about the constitution. They queried parties and candidates about their platforms for the constituent process and launched a number of education campaigns that attempted to teach the population about the importance of the constitution and the special weight of the upcoming legislative election. Despite these efforts, electoral results were unfavorable to participatory movements. According to two estimates of the ideological makeup of the Assembly, 9 percent of deputies were leftists, 23 percent were center-left, and the rest was center, center-right, or right (Rodrigues 1987, 98). [4]

While civil society organizations and militants lost these two important battles, in the process they forged an extensive nationwide network of pro-popular participation that would prove effective in the next phases of the process. A central actor in this network was the National Conference of Brazilian Bishops (CNBB), which still had many progressive elements despite undergoing the internal struggles discussed above. In 1986, the CNBB reignited the idea that had first inspired some of the groups of this network but which had been put aside during previous campaigns: popular participation in the Constituent Assembly. Organizations throughout the country focused their efforts on drafting, promoting, and lobbying for a mechanism that would permit citizens to submit proposed legislation to the Constituent Assembly. They succeeded in collecting the signatures of fourteen senators and seventy-six federal deputies and scheduling a hearing at the commission in charge of determining the procedures of the ANC. Following their official proposal, three members of the commission volunteered to give the popular request an official format: the PMDB's Mavio Covas (Montoro's former appointed mayor of São Paulo, then senator, later founder of the PSDB and governor of the state of São Paulo), the PT's Plínio Arruda de Sampaio, and deputy Brandão Monteiro of the Democratic Labor Party. The chair of the commission was Fernando Henrique Cardoso. The project passed. Citizen amendment proposals required the signature of thirty thousand eligible voters and the sponsorship of three civil society organizations that were responsible for the authenticity of signatures. Proposals that followed these criteria were to be treated as equal to those put forward by legislative representatives (Michiles et al. 1989).

Citizen Amendment Proposals

A total of 122 citizen amendment proposals sponsored by 288 civil society organizations collected more than twelve million signatures; eighty-six of these met the procedural requirements and were presented to the ANC (Michiles et al. 1989, 106–7). Three proposed amendments explicitly focused on citizen participation in government: amendment 021 was sponsored by organizations in Rio de Janeiro and São Paulo and gathered 367,047 signatures; amendment 022 was drafted by organizations in Rio Grande do Sul and collected 31,219 signatures; amendment 056 was put forward by organizations in Minas Gerais and had the support of 35,000 voters. Whereas most of the citizen proposals were sponsored by organizations directly associated with the subject matter of amendments (e.g., the public education amendment was sponsored by teachers' and students' associations), umbrella civil society organizations drafted these three proposals, and numerous different organizations participated in the campaigns for the collection of signatures. Catholic groups were active in all three campaigns. It is noteworthy that the Diocese of São Mateus managed to have close to 20 percent of the citizens in towns under its jurisdiction sign amendment 021, which was the highest inhabitants-signatures ratio for this proposal. Signatures for amendment 021 were collected in all but two states of the country, and although drafted in the southernmost state of Rio Grande do Sul, 30 percent of signatures for amendment 022 were gathered in the northeast state of Bahia (Michiles et al. 1989). The impressive number of signatures supporting these three amendments, the fact that sponsors and signatories were spread through a large portion of the country, and the diverse character of organizations supporting these campaigns corroborate the argument that participatory democracy was a widespread aspiration in 1980s Brazil.

Notably, none of these proposals concerned direct participation in public administration, nor did they employ the defiant tone found in participatory experiences of the late 1970s. The three proposed amendments concerned the creation of mechanisms allowing citizens to propose legislative bills and the procedure through which elected officials and civil society groups could call referendums. As with the project that allowed citizen participation in the ANC, these proposals specified the procedure for submitting popular proposals for the consideration of legislators. The public presentations of these amendments at the ANC exemplify their moderate tone (Assembléia Nacional Constituinte 1988, hereafter ANC). Jurist Dalmo Dallari, the exponent of amendment 021, emphasized the compatibility of mechanisms for direct participation and the representative system. "It is in no way possible to say that popular initiatives or the referendum diminish the Parliament. On the contrary, the Parliament preserves in full its power to decide and will have the last word concerning norms proposed and incorporated in the Constitution or in the legislative system of the Brazilian judiciary order" (ANC 1988, 9A, 429). The exponent of amendment 022 was José Paulo Bisol, a PMDB senator who in the 1970s actively participated in Porto Alegre's Institute for Political, Economic and Social Studies (IEPES). Although Bisol's speech had a more provocative tone than Dallari's, his defense of the importance of popular participation was grounded on notions of government transparency and accountability, for which he drew on liberal theorist Norberto Bobbio. José Gomes Pimenta, a construction worker and political militant, presented amendment 053; his statement ended with the following clarification:

> The purpose of our demand for popular initiative [in legislative matters] is to strengthen Brazilian institutions, to help the National Congress as well as state-level legislative bodies to regain their prerogatives. In participating, the people do not want to interfere in greater matters that concern legislators. . . . We do not want to undertake political leadership, we want to contribute with our work,

intelligence, and organization to the strengthening of democratic institutions. (ANC 1988, 9A, 431)

Thus, the three citizen-proposed amendments for increased popular participation in government advocated for mechanisms that improved the functioning of legislative institutions, and not any sort of self-governing mechanism as the ones tried in the late 1970s. These proposals were included in the final text, which allows for referendums but restricts the right to request one to elected legislators and permits citizens to propose legislation following a procedure similar to the one used in the ANC.[5]

Citizen-proposed amendments on health care (ns. 118 and 71) and urban reform (n. 65) also called for increased citizen participation in the planning and execution of public policies as a way of improving government transparency and the quality of services. Citizen participation was one element of long lists of demands for public sector reforms and was not treated as a separate issue. In the case of the health-care sector, participation was included in the draft of the constitution before the presentation of citizen amendments. Civil society groups lobbied members of the ANC's sub-commission in charge of discussing the health-care system to push for their demands. The center-left MDB deputies in charge of the commission agreed to include most of these demands in their final reports. The redactor of the two first drafts of the Constitution did not edit out the section on citizen participation on the health-care system, and the systematization commission did not raise issues with it (Michiles et al. 1989; ANC 1988).

As reviewed in the introduction, policy councils became the most widely implemented participatory mechanism in the country. However, the format of the approved policy councils was akin to Montoro's purportedly clientelist councils and the informal consultation Erundina's staff had with social movements with which it had links; these links included tripartite councils with representatives of the state, civil society, and public workers, whose mission is to discuss policy and priorities for the sector. These councils are not designed to transfer decision-making power to citizens but instead to include the concern of interested groups in the policy-making process. One of the hurdles of the literature on participatory councils is the assumption that they are meant to mobilize broad participation. In fact, policy councils were created after there was a general disillusionment with the popular councils that failed in Diadema, Fortaleza, São Paulo, and other smaller cities. As the next section shows, proposals for large-scale popular councils with authority over public administration were rejected at the ANC.

The Last Round of Votes

Whereas most of the constitution was decided through deliberations, bargains, and the controversial summarizing of commission secretaries, the last contentious points were decided through voting. The Systematization Commission voted on 535 proposals of revisions to the second draft of the constitution. The majority of these proposals regarded alterations on existing articles, adding new paragraphs, excluding certain sections, or changing the wording. In most cases exponents avidly defended the importance of the proposed change; in fewer instances proposals were presented as mere improvements in the consistency and readability of the text. Likewise, deputies who intervened against a proposal either openly refuted the content of the change or argued it was incompatible with the remaining of the text. Out of 535 proposals, 18 referred exclusively to citizen participation in local government, legislative bodies, unions, and universities.[6] Six were accepted and twelve were rejected by majority vote. The accepted changes were noticeably more moderate and vague than the rejected ones (ANC 1988).

The Systematization Commission unanimously accepted PT Deputy José Genoíno's proposal to insert the sentence "mechanisms of direct popular participation" in the opening paragraph of the constitution, which defined the country's political system (vote n. 7). However, a subsequent proposal suggested the rewording of this paragraph (vote n. 14), altering the text to its final form: "all power belongs to the people, who exert it through its representatives or directly, in the cases prescribed in the Constitution" (ANC 1988, 9B, 75). While Genoíno's exposition exalted the intrinsic value of popular participation and mentioned the possibility of creating a mixed type of democracy wherein representation would be complemented by various forms of direct participation, the proponent of the latter modification noted that "direct" referred to citizens' right to propose legislation and demand referendums, hence the explicatory clause "in the cases described in this Constitution" (ANC 1988, 9B, 81). Although notable that people's direct exercise of power is mentioned in the first paragraph of constitution, it is important to note that it does not refer to direct citizen participation in public administration, as is usually assumed when the 1988 constitution is exalted as an enabling condition of the PB.

Deputy Nelton Friedrich (PMDB/PSDB) suggested the inclusion of two sentences in an existing article on political organization that would have unambiguously asserted the country's commitment with participation democracy (vote n. 28). "The State will stimulate popular participation in all levels of public administration," and in all services offered by the state or by state-commissioned agencies, "there should mandatorily be a commission comprised of representatives of the state or commissioned agency, of its workers, and of its clients," which will inspect the agency's work and participate in planning (ANC 1988, 9B, 142). Deputy Gerson Perez (PSD) accused the exponent and deputies who intervened in favor of the proposal of pushing for a socialist, interventionist state. Ninety-two of the ninety-three members of the systematization commission were present, of these, thirty-two voted in favor and sixty against the proposal. All deputies of the left-leaning parties such as the PT and PCB voted in favor of the proposal. The traditional conservative PSD and the center alliance PL rejected it. The PMDB vote was split in half. This was only two days after eighty-nine deputies had accepted Genoíno's broad statement about participatory democracy.

The moderate tone also prevailed in votes regarding workers' participation in labor unions and associations. Deputy Lula da Silva (PT) presented a proposal that extended to floor workers the right to organize representative labor commissions, which was reserved only to labor union (vote n. 154). This proposal was grounded on the experience of the floor commission that had marked the new unionism movement (chapter 2). A deputy intervened against the proposal and insinuated that Lula was trying to incite a revolution. Thirty-one deputies voted in favor of the proposal, many of the same that supported Friedrich's, and forty-two voted against it. On the following day, a proposal for the creation of tripartite commissions (state, workers, employers) to oversee social assistance organizations was also rejected (vote n. 155). Deputy Nelson Carneiro (PMDB) suggested a revision that secured workers' and employers' participation in public and welfare institutions oversee-ing matters of their interest. Carneiro emphasized in his defense that the proposal did not call for equal participation for workers or employ-ers or any type of co-management arrangement. The proposal passed almost unanimously; only three of the most active leftist deputies voted against it.

Two proposals of popular councils akin to the ones tried in PT administrations earlier in the decade were rejected, while a more mod-est bid of involving civil society organizations in municipal planning passed. Deputy Vivaldo Barbosa (PSB) proposed the insertion of the following paragraph (vote n. 248), "municipalities will be divided in Districts and District Community Councils will be established. Councils will be comprised of non-paid citizens elected in the districts through facultative vote and will exercise the role determined by law" (ANC 1988, 9B, 774). The exponent emphasized the need to foster people's self-government, especially in isolated areas removed from city cores. He was vague about councils' relationship with representative institu-tions: the former was not supposed to replace the latter unless the latter was absent. Four deputies intervened against the proposal, an unusu-ally high number of interventions. The first argued that controlling the form of civil society organization meant returning to the corporatism of the Vargas era. The second found grammatical inconsistencies in the text. The third, Deputy Gastone Righi (PTB), argued that citizen par-ticipation takes place through elected officials and not through "infor-mal representatives of informal community organizations" (ANC 1988, 9B, 773). Righi also added, "accepting this proposal implies negating all the system here sustained of political representation through elections," and then ironically suggested they might as well close all representative institutions. The fourth opponent, Deputy Bernardo Cabral, the redac-tor of the constitution, posited, "*how is it possible to think about a par-ticipatory democracy that does not clash with representative democracy?* It is obvious that in this conflict of competences we will witness the demoralization and weakening of the representative system, and that is not a small thing" (ANC 1988, 9B, 774, emphasis added). Cabral then urged the exponent to withdraw the proposal, which Barbosa did not do. There were twenty-one votes in favor, sixty-four against, and one abstention.

The second popular council proposal was defended on the following day (vote n. 250). It was authored by the PT's Sister Passoni and presented by Plínio de Arruda Sampaio (who in the mayoral campaign of São Paulo admitted to being skeptical of councils). Sampaio posited that in modern cities citizens are too far removed from decision-making and in order to follow and participate in them, "the classic mechanisms of representative democracy are not sufficient. . . . It is necessary to create intermediary bodies closer to the people that will allow for participatory activities that do not challenge the competence of elected representatives" (785). Sampaio tried to emphasize that councils would have a complementary role to representative institutions. Deputy Gerson Perez did not repeat the attacks on the previous proposals but simply jestingly reminded deputies that a similar proposal had already been rejected. The result was twenty-six votes in favor, sixty against, and one abstention.

Finally, a proposal authored by Deputy Octávio Elísio (PMDB/ PSDB) suggested a small but meaningful change in the Organic Municipal Law, the article allowing municipalities to draft their own local statutes within the limitations imposed by the national and state constitutions. Elísio proposed that the list of conditions for the drafting of organic laws included the sentence, "the participation of community organizations in municipal planning" (vote n. 244). The proposal initially circulated to deputies was more ambitious; it read, "the institutionalization of mechanisms that secure the participation of community organizations in municipal planning and decision-making," but it was changed at the last minute (758). The exponent's taming down of the proposal is likely to have helped its close win: forty-eight votes in favor, forty-one against, and one abstention. The swing voters were center-left PMDB politicians; for example, João Hermann Netto (former mayor of Piracicaba) and Artur da Távola (one of the founders of the PSDB) voted against the two popular councils proposals but supported Elísio's amendment. The final text, altered by the redactors, was still slightly more moderate; it substituted the word participation for cooperation, and "community organizations" for "representative associations." Thus, Organic Laws were to include "the cooperation of representative associations in municipal planning."

Though markedly less ambitious than other proposals, Elísio's amendment has succeeded in securing the constitutionality of participatory mechanisms such as the PB. The 1988 constitution has helped to make Brazilian participatory initiatives possible by including articles that, in some cases vaguely, endorse citizens' direct participation in public administration and demand the creation of tripartite commissions. It is not incorrect to present this constitution as an enabler of participatory democracy in Brazil, as most studies of PB and policy councils do. However, it is an oversimplification to state that "during the constituent assembly civil society activists made several proposals that amplified citizen participation in municipal government" (Wampler and Avritzer 2004, 298), and it is inaccurate to say that "the new federal constitution defined Brazil as a representative and participatory democracy" (Gret and Sintomer 2005, 13). A more precise interpretation is that the constitution embodied an attenuated version of the 1970s' participatory ideals, and molded them to fit in the political-institutional context of the country, which had at its core the emerging representative system.

CHAPTER SEVEN

The Making of Participatory Democracy in Brazil

The vast literature on participatory democracy in Brazil has not sufficiently drawn on the rich existing knowledge of socioeconomic,
political, and institutional processes helping to advance and shape participatory ideals and practices in the country. It is widely known that
the rapid industrialization and urbanization of the 1940–1980 period,
the sprouting of an active civil society in the 1970s, the creation of a
political party closely linked with popular sectors, and the passing of
the 1988 constitution were the main catalysts behind the explosion of
participatory initiatives in the 1990s. When studied individually, each
of these processes have particularities and discontinuities common to
the nature of the process, namely, the building of a political party in
a country with a traditionally weak political system, the writing of a
constitution in the context of a negotiated transition to democracy, the
rise of an active civil society in a nation marked by patrimonialism, and
the industrialization of a country in the periphery of the international
economic system. Studies focused on the implementation, functioning,
and results of participatory initiatives in the post-1988 context present
the outcomes of these processes as enabling current practices. This is an
abridged but not incorrect interpretation. In turn, analysis of specific
actors and processes emphasize the objective at hand (e.g., the writing
of a constitution), and not its secondary effects, such as the programs
the current constitution enabled. Against this background, this book
examined these broad processes paying specific attention to the thinking and practicing of citizen participation and contrasted precursory

participatory initiatives with the models widely adopted in the 1990s. In doing so, it shined light on the individual trajectory of participatory democracy in Brazil.

LOCAL-LEVEL DEMOCRATIZATION

The historical account presented here places the world famous participatory budgeting of Porto Alegre at the end of a series of incremental steps toward broader political participation taking place throughout the twentieth century, setbacks restricting direct citizen participation in the 1980s, and short-lived and only partially successful attempts to promote citizen participation in municipal administration. These steps forward and setbacks were the consequences of social, economic, and political changes affecting distinct parts of the country differently. To capture the various dimensions of this trajectory, this study adopted a conceptual framework that allowed us to examine the impact of socioeconomic processes and national-level institutional changes in the power and cohesion of elite coalitions at the local level. Where fragmentation ensued, it was possible to distinguish between clientelist parties promoting the partial and negotiated inclusion of certain social groups and mass radical parties pushing for full democratization, which in these cases meant participatory innovation.

The liberal representative system of the First Republic meant little to local-level politics, which continued to be tightly controlled by *coronéis*. The impact of the 1930 Revolution varied from region to region. In Santa Catarina, the Vargas government helped to augment the political power of the Ramos family while introducing economic changes that eventually undermined its hegemony. In Espírito Santo, the *tenentista* governor made investments in education and agriculture that took into account family farming, but these policies were interrupted by the re-establishment of elections and the government's need to forge alliances with *vendeiros* and *coronéis*. The Revolution managed to break the political hegemony of the Paulista elite, but this did not have an impact on the rural peripheries of the state's capital. What did have a significant impact in the Paulista capital was the accelerated industrialization that started in this period and the subsequent controlled inclusion of urban workers through the Vargas corporatist state apparatus.

The 1945–1964 period witnessed the establishment of a national-level democratic system and the continuation of industrialization. The already-incorporated urban working class tried to gain autonomy from the state and found in the Communist Party a vehicle to increase its political participation. As seen in chapter 5, Santo André had the necessary conditions to implement a participatory administration as early as 1947, but the elite coalition was still sufficiently strong to demand the arrest of the elected mayor and the dismantling of citizen committees that could have served as basis for a participatory structure. During this period, populist leaders also tried to rally excluded and emerging social groups in order to break the monopoly of dominant elites. In São Paulo, eccentric schoolteacher Jânio Quadros promised the emerging middle classes that he was going to moralize politics; in Espírito Santo, intellectual "Chiquinho" presented himself as the father of family farmers; a few years later, Furtado managed to put an end to nearly a century of uninterrupted Ramos governments in Lages. Clientelist networks backed populist leaders and votes were exchanged for favors through the intermediation of community leaders. These populist and clientelist practices and the selective inclusion of some groups to the detriment of others may not be fully commendable from a democratic standpoint, but these were laudable steps toward the consolidation of an open access order wherein access to economic and political participation would no longer be controlled by small elite coalitions.

The 1964–1985 period witnessed a paradoxical phenomenon: the emergence and growth of participatory movements under an authoritarian government. Too often these movements have been described simply as a reaction to the regime. As shown in chapter 2, they were much more than that. The Catholic Church's reform was essentially an internal institutional process with a dialectical relationship to the social and political changes taking place in the country. The new unionism movement was the outcome of a long-initiated reaction against the corporatist apparatus assembled during Vargas's regime, and the industrial growth of the 1960s and 1970s was a key variable in its strengthening. MDB *autênticos* were a direct reaction against the façade representative system of the time.

However, as the analysis of the group's discourse and educational material showed, they were also opposed to the political practices that had become dominant in the previous democratic period, especially populism and clientelism.

These movements gained force in a time when the political system offered few options for citizen participation. This context conferred a radical tone onto such movements. They were not simply in favor of citizen participation but against all forms of partial, controlled, or negotiated political inclusion, which at the time included the representative system. Participatory initiatives inspired in these movements were thought of as alternatives to existing political institutions; their goal was to implement forms of direct democracy and self-government that empowered previously excluded social groups and fundamentally transformed statecivil society relations. The three case studies show how these movements ascended to power in different parts of Brazil, describe the participatory administrations they implemented, and call attention to how local economic contexts influenced the format of participatory initiatives.

Lages was the clearest case of class struggle. Beginning in 1930, industrialization policies profoundly altered the socioeconomic landscape of the city and weakened the dominant elite's ability to control access to economic activities and political participation. It was during this time that two new political groups entered the dispute for the control of the city. The first was a populist leader who tried to build a broad class alliance based on the exchange of favors through a clientelist network. The second was a more progressive group that tried to rally excluded subaltern classes against the dominant elite coalition that had governed the city for almost a century. Participatory democracy was the political project of the latter, and its prospect depended on the group's ability to gain and retain control of the city.

The Lages urban middle class was pleased with Furtado's investments in the downtown core, and *coronéis* had the support of the state government, which provided material benefits for poor citizens that were way beyond the means of the municipal government. In 1982, traditional politicians regained control of the city. Most members of the team in charge of the participatory administration were not an integral part of local social groups and soon disbanded. A study of social movements in the city and my interview with a local community leader suggest that there were only a few timid developments in political organization in the city in the 1980s and 1990s (Silva 2009; Geraldo Löcks, personal communication, December 16, 2010). A research group at the Universidade Federal de Santa Catarina is currently doing a study of participatory city master plans in eight cities in the state, including Lages. Elson Pereira, the principal investigator and a native of the state, admitted that he initially expected to find high levels of participation in Lages given the attention the city received in the 1980s. Preliminary results show low levels compared to other cities (personal communication, August 12, 2013). The traditional political and economic elite effectively removed participatory democracy from the Lages political agenda.

It is also impossible to fully comprehend the participatory experience of Boa Esperança without taking into account the city's socioeconomic context. The initiative was a clear reaction to decades of neglect of the needs of small farmers. The target of the participatory administration was not a local political group but state and federal policies favoring industrialization and large-scale agriculture. The participatory administration brought small-scale farmers together to make such farms a viable economic alternative, independent from *vendeiros*, less vulnerable to coffee prices, and capable of resisting the encroachment of cattle and eucalyptus farms. The economic results of the initiative were very palpable. The efficient Mayor Covre made participation more likely, but high coffee prices made small-scale farmers autonomous and cooperation less necessary. In the 1970s, the Diocese of São Mateus actively promoted the participatory ideals and practices that allowed Mayor Covre to turn the economic condition into an opportunity for participatory democracy. As seen in chapter 6, the Church stopped playing this role in the mid- to late 1980s. As a result, in Boa Esperança, participation is strictly associated with material benefits.

The Diadema participatory administration was also clearly rooted in the city's economic context. The ABCD region is a by-product of the industrialization policies introduced in the 1930s. In the 1970s, the region became the heart and mind of the new unionism movement that emerged against the state's corporatist apparatus. A key demand of the movement was a union structure that allowed the organization and participation of workers at the factory-floor level. In the early 1980s, this movement coalesced with other participatory movements and formed a

political party committed to citizen participation, which won the municipal elections of Diadema in 1982 by a very narrow margin.

Although residents of the region largely supported the PT, not all
residents were directly involved with the new unionism since the partial industrialization and fast urbanization of Brazil was incapable of
adequately accommodating rural exodus. In the ABCD region this was
true especially for Diadema, the poorest city of the region. The Menezes
administration had to deal not only with the lack of organizational
structure of poor, recently settled inhabitants, but also with a group of
PT Marxists that found his approach to city government overly moderate and typical of the well-paid bourgeois workers of São Bernardo. The
participatory administration of Diadema was convoluted and marked by
internal struggles, just as other PT administrations in the 1980s examined in chapter 6. Nevertheless, the party has succeeded in imposing itself
and securing consecutive elections in this overcrowded industrial town.
The weight and scope of participatory initiatives have varied, but have
remained on the city's political agenda since 1982.

Scholars studying participatory democracy in Brazil have devoted
great attention to the challenges of implementing participatory mechanisms and to the necessary conditions for their successful institutionalization. Theoretical analyses focus on the interplay between civil society
strength (density and experience), political willingness (ideological or
strategic), and institutional design (Wampler 2007; Borba and Lüchmann
2007; Avritzer 2009). These frameworks are very useful in explaining
variations in the outcome of initiatives in the post-1988 Brazilian context.
However, if, as Avritzer (2009, 3) posited, the main challenge of theory
building in the field is to discover whether "the successful experiences in
Brazilian cities [can] be reproduced in places where the conditions may
be very different," then the analysis will need to move beyond this specific context. One important step would be to have a more comprehensive understanding of the Brazilian experience with various participatory
models. To contribute to this effort, this book examined the trajectory
participatory democracy up to 1988, using a conceptual framework that
bridges the gap between studies of local-level participation and established democratization theories. In doing so, it hopes to contribute to the
advancement of the still incipient literature on comparative democratic
deepening and participatory democracy.

Goldfrank (2011) compared participatory budgetings in Brazil (Porto Alegre), Venezuela (Caracas), and Uruguay (Montevideo). His study corroborated previous arguments that the open format of the Porto Alegre initiative and Brazil's high level of decentralization are key factors in the success of PB. Most interesting, Goldfrank argued that the level of institutionalization of parties opposing participatory innovation had a significant impact on the success of initiatives implemented by newly elected leftist parties. In Porto Alegre, opposition was fragmented and unable to put up a fight. In Venezuela, the deeply institutionalized opposition party launched a "three-year war" against the participatory administration, managed to regain the city, and then completely dismantled the participatory program. In Montevideo, the two historically dominant parties jointly launched a defamatory campaign against the mass radical party that had dared to displace them from the country's most important subnational government. The leftist party had enough electoral support to remain in power, but the dominant elite parties successfully forced it to tame the design of participatory institutions. What the book does not explore in detail is the basis of the institutional strength of opposition parties, though it points out some important links, like the Caracas opposition party's connection with the municipal workers' union, and Montevideo traditional parties' strong ties with the federal government. As the case studies above showed, socioeconomic processes have a direct impact on the fragmentation of dominant elites, which increases the chances of mass radical parties to push participatory innovation. In Lages, the only partial weakening of the landed class allowed it to halt participatory reforms, whereas Diadema's fast growth dramatically changed the city's demographics to one more organically close with the PT. It would be interesting to examine the socioeconomic basis of the coalitions responsible for the meager outcome of participatory reforms in Caracas and Montevideo. Is it possible that no socioeconomic process has sufficiently fragmented dominant elite coalitions that are still able to block innovation from outside contenders?

Canel's (2011) study of decentralization and participatory reforms in Montevideo pays more attention to socioeconomic variables, but from the civil society perspective. Canel compared three districts of Montevideo, taking into account how associative cultures helped or hindered adaptation to participatory channels. In the absence of political actors like the Catholic Church and political values such as Paulo Freire's teach-ings in Brazil, the associative cultures of the three districts were almost exclusively rooted in the local economic contexts, with the exception of an artistic group in one of the districts. As a result, associative culture varied sharply from one district to another, while in Brazil the praxis of *conscientização* was a uniting thread in distinct participatory move-ments. Interestingly, the district with a strong union tradition was the least successful in using the new channels for political participation. In an in-depth analysis of the district that most successfully adapted to the reforms, Canel (2012) argues that experience in earlier clientelist prac-tices helped to prepare citizens for the new participatory forums. These findings are in sharp contrast to the present study, in which Diadema stands out as the long-lasting participatory initiative and Lages as a suc-cessfully halted democratization.

The conceptual framework used in this book presented clientelist and mass radical parties as alternatives at the same conjuncture and argued that the latter would bring about participatory innovation. In light of Canel's findings in Uruguay, and the fact that clientelist parties controlled Diadema for decades before the ascension of the PT, and only five years before the Dirceu Carneiro Team came into power in Lages, it is possible that the sequencing of these two types of parties favors long-lasting participatory initiatives. While only mass radical parties will push for increased citizen participation, experience in dealing with clientelist parties may have some consistent positive impact on the outcome of par-ticipatory innovations. This is one of the many questions that could be examined in comparative studies on local-level democratization leading to participatory innovation.

LOCAL-LEVEL PARTICIPATION IN A DEMOCRACY

In the 1980s, participatory ideals and practices adapted to the context of an open access order, which included the establishment of a legitimate representative system and the recognition of the diversity of needs, goals, and strategies within what was no longer referred to as popular move-ments, but instead called civil society. Chapter 6 presented four con-comitant processes that together indicate a marked trend in the 1980s:

the tempering of radical participatory ideals and practices. The dominant interpretation of the emergence of participatory democracy in Brazil describes the late 1980s as the period in which progressive forces coalesced to create defiant initiatives that would profoundly challenge the patterns of civil society and state interaction. The story presented in this book tells otherwise.

In the 1980s, MDB *autênticos* became isolated in a party willing to make alliances with the most conservative political groups in the country. A sizable portion of militants and elected officials, such as José Airton in Icapuí (Nylen 1997), soon realized the PT was a better match (Meneguello 1989). Franco Montoro, Mario Covas, and other *autênticos* opted for staying in the PMDB and trying to create participatory initiatives in São Paulo, which at the time were criticized as inadequate and meant to co-op social movements (Bava 1983), but in retrospect were not too different from models adopted in the 1990s. The model of municipal administration espoused by PMDB "pragmatics," such as Orestes Quércia and Juarez Furtado, became more characteristic of the party itself than the Lages experience. The remaining *autênticos* eventually founded a social democratic party that, notwithstanding its commitment with social justice, did not make citizen participation one of its priorities.

The PT persistently attempted to create channels for citizen participation in municipal administration. The party paid a high political price for this, including the Fortaleza fiasco and the convoluted administrations of Diadema and São Paulo. Some PT mayors opted for devoting less attention to participation and focus instead on administrative efficiency, as in the city of Santos (Abers 1996). In Santo André and Porto Alegre, PT officials tried to find a balance between utopian Popular Councils and abandoning the party's commitment to citizen participation. The ingenious solution was the PB, a mechanism that allows for broad citizen participation on a specific part of government and helps to address the basic needs of marginalized sectors without antagonizing middle- and upper-class groups.

It is important to understand the PT's adaption of the radical participatory ideal as more than a realistic turn akin to that of MDB's pragmatics. The meaning of the PT's commitment to participatory democracy cannot be understated. Latin American history has plenty of examples of leftist parties that mobilize popular sectors around ultimately undemocratic political projects. As seen in chapter 1, the Brazilian Communist Party of the late 1950s was more concerned with the revolution than with the immediate emancipation of social groups or the strengthening of democracy. A faction of the Diadema PT found it more important to secure the party's control over the city's administration than to promote the political inclusion of marginalized sectors. The Dirceu Carneiro Team was indifferent to party politics and unconcerned with the creation of a long-lasting organization capable of advancing the participatory ideals it actively promoted. In Boa Esperança, after the departure of religious lay leaders, popular participation became a one-man endeavor and as such was unsustainable. The PT, in contrast, created a national organization in charge of sharing experiences and lessons that could help to build a strong party without abandoning the participatory ideals in which it had been built (Nylen 1997). In this case, the tempering of participatory ideals and the adaptation of participatory initiatives was not a regression to traditional practices of partial, controlled, or negotiated inclusion but a compromise with the logic and institutions of the representative system, which, at this time, was one worth preserving.

The decade also witnessed the conservative turn of the Catholic Church. As examined in chapter 2, the Catholic Church, under the influence of the Conciliar Vatican II and Liberation Theology, was one of the forces fuelling the participatory ideals and practices of the 1970s. In the 1980s, the Church gradually abandoned its focus on social justice and political participation (Levy 2000; Burdick 2004). Progressive clergy and activists trained in CEBs participated in the democratization of the country by supporting and partaking in varied social movements, civil society groups, and political parties. In the countryside, progressive clergyman continued to aid oppressed populations to whom the effects of democratization were not yet palpable (Mainwaring 1986). Overall, as an institution of unmatched national scope and legitimacy, the Church stopped employing its resources toward the mobilization and *conscientização* of unorganized populations and the training of civil society leaders.

While this was a setback of national proportions, the withdrawal of the progressive Church was a particularly significant loss for rural people. The "participatory publics" (Avritzer 2002) and "insurgent citizens" (Holston 2008) of urban contexts strived with the political liberalization and against the economic debacle that accompanied it. Industrialization and urbanization also created objective conditions for mobilization in the countryside. Rural populations were not left in the past and at the total mercy of *coronéis*. The fragmentation of local elites presented new political opportunities, and the impacts of industrial policies and rural exodus offered material incentives for political mobilization. Nevertheless, as the cases of Boa Esperança and Lages demonstrate, participatory initiatives in rural areas relied heavily on top-down mobilization and the existence of communities and leaders with at least some "consciousness raising" experience. The PT often assumed the role of mobilizer in cities (Nylen 2003; Avritzer 2009) and neighborhoods (Abers 2000, chapter 9) where the organization of civil society was weak. However, as both the case studies and recent analysis suggest, participatory initiatives are more likely to flourish when there is a good synergy between a committed political party and an already organized and autonomous civil society (Wampler 2007; Borba and Lüchmann 2007; Avritzer 2009). The Church played an unmatched role in the organizing of communities in rural Brazil, and no other institution of similar magnitude stepped up to the plate after its withdrawal.

The 1988 constitution epitomized the trend toward more temperate participatory ideals and practices. While members of the ANC were willing to sanction vague clauses endorsing citizen participation, amendments that defied the representative system were outright rejected, even by center-left MDB deputies. The mention of direct participation in the preamble of the constitution, and the paragraph that endorses "the cooperation of representative associations in municipal planning" (ANC 1988, 9B, vote 224), both frequently cited in the PB literature, were moderate versions of bolder commitments to participatory democracy. Just as with the case of the PT, the tempering of more radical amendments was an unprecedented yet moderate step toward increased citizen participation. In the context of a negotiated transition to democracy, the constituent assembly bent to conservative forces on various issues (Souza 1997), which partially explains the rejection of certain amendments for increased citizen participation. Another important factor was the concern with preserving representative institutions that in the past had succumbed to assaults and manipulations. "How is it possible to think about a participatory democracy that does not clash with representative democracy?" (ANC 1988, 9B, 774), prodded the redactor of the constitution. Similarly to the case of the participatory administrations of the 1980s, persistence and flexibility were in order. Deputies pushing pro-participation legislation submitted proposals in the form of similar amendments more than once, changed the wordings of proposals, and pitched speeches in strategic ways so as to avoid outright opposition. In the end, the constitution endorsed citizen participation in public administration in various forms, but also imposed limits to it.

In a recent study, Heller (2012) compares decentralized participatory governance in Brazil, India, and South Africa, "three cases of participatory politics that have similar origins but different outcomes" (648). While participatory reforms in Brazil and India (Kerala) had lasting effects and became an integral aspect of political life, participatory institutions in South Africa were dismantled or hollowed "in the name of efficiency and more rapid delivery" (655). Heller argues that the party in power in South Africa enjoyed a political hegemony and as such had little incentive to bring civil society in instead of simply subsuming it. In the other two countries, progressive parties created participatory mechanisms that by bringing civil society in helped them to displace local oligarchies and challenge patronage politics. Heller concludes by calling attention to the need to pay attention to the balance between political power and civil society.

While one of the most interesting of the kind, Heller's analysis is weakened by the fact that he takes the Porto Alegre case to represent the Brazilian trajectory in participatory reform. As a result, he overlooks the limits and constraints the political system imposed on the type of participation demanded by civil society groups in the 1970s and 1980s. Heller draws on findings from cities with less ideal conditions than Porto Alegre to enrich his comparison. However, in the cities he discusses, initiatives had been put in place in the late 1990s (Baiocchi, Heller, and Silva, 2011), that is, after participatory ideals and practices had been tempered. Heller argues that the three countries had similar, appropriate institutional designs, but political power imbalances affected their fates differently. Taking into consideration the account presented in this book, it is possible to argue that the Brazilian institutional design was "right" because it had already been adjusted to power balances.

LOCAL-LEVEL DEMOCRATIZATION LEADING TO PARTICIPATORY DEMOCRACY

The comparisons and contrasts between this book's findings and the works by Goldfrank, Canel, and Heller point to a promising and still largely unexplored comparative research agenda. Together this research calls attention to the fact that local-level participatory innovation cannot be adequately examined without considering national-level political and institutional variables, nationwide economic policies, and local-level economic conditions, all of which are more fully understood within their historical contexts. Goldfrank and Heller use the language of "deepening democracy," but I favor "local-level democratization," in order to emphasize the usefulness of existing knowledge on democratization. Regardless of the adopted terms, much can be learned about the creation of channels for direct citizen participation through comparative research that examines the broad political, institutional, and socioeconomic processes in which local-level initiatives are embedded.

Scholars of participatory democracy in Brazil now seek to draw comparative lessons from the country's experience and build theories applicable elsewhere. This study demonstrated that it is possible to learn about participatory democracy in Brazil from existing work on the country's democratization processes and employ concepts and theoretical insights from the comparative literature on democratization processes. This book does this by treating participatory innovation as the outcome of local-level democratization processes, which were entangled with national-level processes but responded to them distinctively, depending on local histories and conditions. While this approach may or may not prove useful for future studies, the account presented here offers a more comprehensive understanding of the making of participatory democracy in Brazil. It is hoped that this account will contribute to knowledge in the field and the creation of more democratic and participatory societies.

NOTES

Introduction

1. I was also told this when interviewing one of these officials (interview with Tarso Nuñez, former member of the first PT administration in Porto Alegre, July 2008).

2. Noteworthy attempts to broaden this geographic focus are found in Nylen (1997) and Avritzer (2007).

3. The archives of the Instituto Brasileiro de Administração Municipal (Arquivo IBAM) contain short descriptions of participatory initiatives between 1978 and 1985 in the following cities: Americana (São Paulo), Caeté (Minas Gerais), Camaçari (Bahia), Colinas (Maranhão), Matão (São Paulo), Nilópolis (Rio de Janeiro), Santa Cruz do Capibaribe (Pernambuco), Toledo (Paraná), and Vila Velha (Espírito Santo). In the same archives, references to various small participatory programs are also found. The archives of the newspaper *Folha de São Paulo* contain references to experiences in Pindamonhangaba (São Paulo) and Feira de Santana (Bahia) in the late 1970s ("Governo com as bases em Feira de Santana," 1976; "Pindamonhangaba," 1976). A smaller newspaper published an article about participatory budgeting in São José dos Campos (São Paulo) between 1978 and 1980 (Costa 2001). Public officials in Porto Alegre often refer to Pelotas (Rio Grande do Sul) as the first experience; see Gugliano, Loeck, Orsato, and Pereira 2008. Relatively better-known cases in the second half of the 1980s include São Paulo (Couto 1995), Fortaleza (Pinto 1992), Recife (Soares and Lostao 1992), and Salvador (Fernandes 2004).

4. See DelPicchia (1982) for a journalist's book on Piracicaba's experience, and Herrmann Neto (1984) for a testimony of the mayor responsible for the initiative.

5. A volume edited by Tina Hilgers (2012) offers an interesting discussion about the coexistence of democratic and clientelist practices in Latin America.

6. With exception to its support to the Movimento Sem Terra (Landless Workers' Movement), see Burdick 2004, chapters 5 and 6.

7. Basic sanitation, housing policies, street paving, education, social assistance, health, accessibility and urban mobility, youth, transport, leisure areas, sport and leisure, public illumination, economic development, tourism, culture, and environment sanitation (Orçamento Participativo 2008, 19).

8. Transport; culture; economic development and tourism; education, sports, and leisure; city organization, urban and environmental development; and health and social assistance (Orçamento Participativo 2008, 27–29).

9. In the first five years of OP technical discussions were absent; the population demanded whatever they deemed necessary. The result was upset engineers, unfinished projects, and wasted resources. In 1995 the administration began to ask city agencies to discuss with councillors the technical limitations of public works (Abers 2000, 8).

10. In total figures, Wampler (2007, 106) estimated that in Porto Alegre between 1996 and 2003 close to US$400 million was channeled through participatory budgeting.

11. Numerous studies can be found in the journals *Cadernos Cedec, Boletim Participação e Saúde, Saúde e Sociedade, Sáude em Debate*, and *São Paulo em Perspectiva*.

12. This study compared forty-eight cities with participatory budgets with a control group of cities without the program. Researchers managed to isolate the impact of PT administrations, which are known for having progressive pro-poor policies and are the most likely to implement PB. The percentage of votes for the PT was included as a permanent control variable, which helped to isolate long-run political processes from the impact of the PB.

13. The remaining are the rule of law, competition, vertical and horizontal accountability, respect for civil and political freedoms, and the progressive implementation of political equality.

Chapter One

1. The term *coronel* (pl. *coronéis*) is explained in Leal (1949/2009), "For nearly a century [starting in 1831], a body of the National Guard existed in each of our municipalities. The rank of colonel was generally accorded to the political boss of the community. . . . It was usually the wealthiest landowners or the richest members of the commercial and industrial community, who exercised, in each municipality, the high command of the National Guard, and at the same time the patriarchal—all but dictatorial—political control invested in them by the provincial government. This state of affairs existed under the Republic as well as under the monarchy. . . . But the system was so engrained in the mentality of the rural population that even today the style of the *coronel* is still accorded to those who hold in their hands the political staff of office, or the leaders of the parties which have the greatest influence in the community, that is to say the despots of village conventicles" (xvi).

2. His suicide is a convoluted episode in Brazilian history. Power struggles and intrigue led a faction of the military to demand that he renounce the

presidency; instead of fighting or stepping down, the now old and fatigued Vargas opted to defy his opponents with his suicide. See D'Araujo (1999) and Skidmore (1967).

3. Quadros was the UDN candidate in the 1960 presidential election, but he stressed that his nomination did not entail a commitment to the party. Therefore, his election is hardly described as a UDN victory.

Chapter Two

1. For analyses of the different movements in this period see Kadt (1970) and Mainwaring (1986).

2. See Moisés (1979) for a detailed analysis or Keck (1992, 61–67) for a short summary.

Chapter Three

An earlier version of this chapter was first published as "The Political Economy of Participatory Democracy in Brazil: A Case Study of Lages, 1977–1982," in *Studies in Political Economy* 90 (2012): 137–64.

1. "Brazilians" is used in juxtaposition to *gringos*, the name given to Italian migrants in the region.

2. Both thought to deserve it for different reasons. In the 1930 military campaign, Aristiliano headed the Lages front that joined the troops from Rio Grande do Sul and together seized the capital. Nereu was the leader of the opposition in the late 1920s and together with his father founded the Liberal Alliance.

3. This fact was confirmed in interviews with the mayors of Boa Esperança and Diadema; fully aware of the Lages initiative, they reported having thought about sending people to Lages to learn about specific programs.

4. State-level financing of networks of traditional politicians as a way to prevent the growth of democratic forces was a widespread practice in the last years of the military regime (Hagopian 1996, chapter 5).

5. See Gay (1994) for a discussion of factors contributing to communities' willingness to exchange votes for favors in roughly the same period.

Chapter Four

1. These included Companhia de Ferro e Aço Vitória, Realcafé Solúvel do Brasil, Indústria de Chocolates Garoto, Fábrica de Cimento Nassau, Usina Paineiras, and Aracruz Celulose (Bittencourt 1987b).

2. The remaining four people directly involved in the administration were not available for interviews. Luiz Cardoso, responsible for the administration's finances; Eroisa da Rocha, in charge of human resources; Laura Alzilia Covre, a religious woman who sporadically helped with community mobilization; and an out-of-town educator known as Rita, who led workshops on family economy, health, and nutrition.

3. Souza's (1981, 119) chapter reports that Boa Esperança went from last to twenty-third place. This may have been a typing mistake, since the other two sources explained that the city moved up twenty-two positions, reaching thirty-third place.

Chapter Five

1. Defined by Weber (1958/2003, 21) as "predominantly of an irrational and speculative character, or directed to acquisition by force, above all, the acquisition of booty, whether directly in war or in the forms of continuous fiscal booty by exploitation of subjects."

2. As seen in the case of Lages, the separation of the certain districts could also be a political maneuver by the state government to weaken an opposition municipal government.

3. In Portuguese, *professor* is the only word for professor and teacher.

4. This was yet another of the regime's gimmicks to try to control the democratization process. The rationale behind this regulation was grounded on the logic of the "governor's politics" (chapter 1); in rural areas where municipal elections were controlled by *coronéis*, votes for mayors picked by local elites would boost the gubernatorial candidates closest to the regime, who would help the military to control the democratization process at the federal level. In some cases, as in Diadema, the regulation backfired on the military.

5. Document reprinted in Gadotti and Pereira 1989.

6. His department was close with Gilson, but his secretary was the president of the *diretório*.

Chapter Six

1. The 2010 census showed for the first time in the country's history that black and mixed citizens constitute more than half of the population (50.74 percent). According to statistical analysis, the large growth observed in these two categories in comparison to the 2000 census is mathematically unsound. The only explanation is that in the recent survey more people chose to self-identify as mixed or black than had been the case in 2000 (Caniello 2011).

2. A group of intellectuals tried to create a Socialist Party that would bring together MDB *autênticos*, leftist thinkers, and the new unionism movement, but the project did not flourish, largely because the latter preferred to have its own independent Workers' Party (Christiano 2003).

3. A leftist coalition led by the small Socialist Party succeeded in electing Jarbas Vasconcelos mayor of Recife, the capital of the state of Pernambuco, where a participatory experience took place in the 1986–1988 mandate. As with other experiences in the period, this administration had various shortcomings and some successes; the succeeding mayor dismantled participatory programs (Soares and Soler 1992).

4. The Departamento de Pesquisa da Folha de São Paulo and scholar David Fleischer separately reached the exact same estimates.

5. An exemplary use of the latter was the Lei da Ficha Limpa (Clean Record Law). According to Law n. 135/2010, public officials who had their mandates revoked due to corruption charges or who resigned a position in order to avoid the revocation of their mandate are not eligible to compete in elections at any level for eight years. The bill was put forward by civil society organizations after the collection of the due amount of citizen signatures.

6. There were also proposals with numerous items that included citizen participation as one of them, but these will not be considered here because it is not possible to determine why they were accepted or rejected.

WORKS CITED

"76 votos dão vitória ao MDB em Piracicaba" 1976. *Folha de São Paulo*, November 18, Nacional: 7.

"A tese de Campinas no Congresso de Itanhaem." 1973. *Folha de São Paulo*, May 3: 22.

Abers, Rebecca Neaera. 1996. "From Ideas to Practice: The Partido dos Trabalhadores and Participatory Governance in Brazil." *Latin American Perspectives* 23(4): 35–53.

———. 2000. *Inventing Local Democracy: Grassroots Politics in Brazil.* Boulder: Lynne Rienner.

Acharya, Arnab, Adrián Gurvan Lavalle, and Peter Houtzager. 2004. "Civil Society Representation in the Participatory Budget and Deliberative Councils of São Paulo, Brazil." *IDS Bulletin* 34(1): 40–48.

Achiamé, Fernando. 2010. *O Espírito Santo na Era Vargas (1930–1937).* Rio de Janeiro: Editora FVG.

Almeida, Carla, and Luciana Tatagiba. 2012. "Os conselhos gestores sob o crivo da política: Balanços e perspectivas." *Serviço Social & Sociedade* 109: 68–92.

Almeida, Maria Herminia Tavares de. 1983. "O sindicalismo brasileiro entre a conservação e a mudança." In *Sociedade e polítca no Brasil pós-64*, edited by Bernardo Sorj and Maria Hermínia Tavares de Almedia, 191–214. São Paulo: Editora Brasiliense.

Almeida, Maria Hermínia Tavares de. 1975. "O sindicato no Brasil: Novos problemas, velhas estruturas." *Debate e Crítica* 6: 49–74.

Alvarez, Sonia E. 1990a. *Engendering Democracy in Brazil: Women's Movements in Transition Politics.* Princeton: Princeton University Press.

———. 1990b. "Women's Participation in the Brazilian 'People's Church': A Critical Appraisal." *Feminist Studies* 16 (Summer): 381–408.

Alves, Alexandre. 2001. "Os imigrantes do Núcleo Colonial de São Bernardo e a constituição do subúrbio paulistano (1877–1902)." In *Diadema nasceu no Grande ABC: História retrospectiva da Cidade Vermelha*, edited by Zilda Márcia Grícoli Iokoi. São Paulo: Humanitas/ FFLCH/ USP.

Alves, Alice da Conceição. 2007. *A impressa e a primeira administração do Partido dos Trabalhadores: Diadema 1983–1988.* São Paulo: História, Pontifíca Universidade Católica de São Paulo.

Alves, Márcio Moreira. 1973. *A Grain of Mustard Seed: The Awakening of the Brazilian Revolution*. New York: Anchor.

———. 1980a. "Em Lages o povo toma conta de seus assuntos." *Isto É*, August 20: 28–30.

———. 1980b. *A força do povo: Democracia participativa em Lajes*. São Paulo: Editora Brasiliense.

———. 1983. "Lajes, experiência pioneira." *Folha de São Paulo*, March 30.

Alves, Maria Helena Moreiva. 2005. *Estado e oposição no Brasil: 1964–1984*. Bauru: EDUSC.

Andrade, Edinara Terezinha de. 1996a. "Democracia participativa no município de Lages-SC e a cultura política da esquerda brasileira nos anos 70." *Revista Katálysis* 96: 74–81.

———. 1996b. *A força do povo: Do clientelismo didático ao clientelismo de massas*. Blumenau: Letra Viva.

Araujo, Braz José de. 1976. "O significado das eleições municipais." *Opinião*, August 6: 3.

Assembéia Nacional Constituinte (ANC). 1988. Atas de Comissões. Comissão de Sistemação (9A, 9B, 9C). Anais do Senado Federal. http://www.senado.gov .br/publicacoes/anais/asp/CT_Abertura.asp.

Avritzer, Leonardo. 2000. "Democratization and Changes in the Pattern of Association in Brazil." *Journal of Interamerican Studies and World Affairs* 42(3): 59–76.

———. 2002. *Democracy and the Public Space in Latin America*. Princeton: Princeton University Press.

———, ed. 2004. *A participação em São Paulo*. São Paulo: Editora da UNESP.

———. 2006. "New Public Spheres in Brazil: Local Democracy and Deliberative Politics." *International Journal of Urban and Regional Research* 30(3): 623–37.

———, ed. 2007. *A participação social no Nordeste*. Belo Horizonte: Editora UFMG.

———. 2009. *Participatory Institutions in Democratic Brazil*. Baltimore: Johns Hopkins University Press.

Azevedo, Marcello de C. 1987. *Basic Ecclesial Communities in Brazil: The Challenge of a New Way of Being Church*. Washington, DC: Georgetown University Press.

Azevedo, Eliusson Antônio de, and Rafael Kohlz. n.d. *Família Livramento marca início da povoação do município*. Câmara Municipal de Boa Esperança. http://www.cmbe.es.gov.br/frames/frame-historia.html.

Baer, Werner. 1972. "Import Substitution and Industrialization in Latin America: Experiences and Interpretations." *Latin American Research Review* 7(1): 95–122.

———. 1977. "O crescimento brasileiro e a experiência desenvolvimentista: 1964–1974." *Estudos CEBRAP* 20: 7–26.

Baierle, Sérgio Gregorio. 2010. "Porto Alegre: Popular Sovereignty or Dependent Citizens." In *Participation and Democracy in the Twenty-first Century City*, edited by Jenny Pearce, 51–75. New York: Palgrave Macmillan.

Baiocchi, Gianpaolo. 2003. "Radicals in Power." In *Radicals in Power: The Workers' Party (PT) and Experiences in Urban Democracy in Brazil*, edited by Gianpaolo Baiocchi, 1–26. New York: Zed.

——. 2005. *Militants and Citizens: The Politics of Participatory Democracy in Porto Alegre.* Stanford: Stanford University Press.

Baiocchi, Gianpaolo, Patrick Heller, and Marcelo K. Silva. 2011. *Bootstrapping Democracy: Transforming Local Governance and Civil Society in Brazil.* Stanford: Stanford University Press.

Batista, Pedro César. 2004. *Gilson Menezes—O operário prefeito, experiências e desafios.* Brasília: Brasilgrafia.

Bava, Sílvio Caccia. 1983. "Os conselhos populares: As propostas do PMDB e do PT." *Desvios* 2: 88–96.

Benevides, Maria Victória. 1986. "Ai que saudade do MDB!" *Lua Nova, Cultura Política* 3(1): 27–34.

Beras, César. 2008. *Orçamento participativo de Porto Alegre e a democratização do estado—A configuração específica do caso de Porto Alegre: 1989-2004.* PhD diss., Universidade Federal do Rio Grande do Sul.

Bergamaschi, Mara. 1988. "Guerra de facções determina fracasso do PT em Fortaleza." *Folha de São Paulo*, November 27: A11.

Betto, Frei. 1981. *O que é comunidade eclesial de base?* São Paulo: Editora Brasiliense.

Bisilliat, Jeanne. 2004. *Lá onde os rios refluen: Diadema 20 anos de democracia e poder local.* São Paulo: Editora Fundação Perseu Abramo.

Bispo Júnior, J. P., and J. J. C. Sampaio. 2008. "Participação social em saúde em áreas rurais do nordeste do Brasil." *Revista Panamericana de Salud Publica* 23(6): 403–9.

Bispos do Centro Oeste. 1973, May 6. Marginalização de um Povo. (1. IGR. CEBS, N. 20.01.83) Centro de Documentação e Pesquisa Vergueiro, São Paulo.

Bittar, Jorge. 1992. *O modo petista de governar.* São Paulo: Teoria & Debate.

Bittencourt, Gabriel. 1987a. *Café e modernização (O Espírito Santo no século XIX).* Vitória: Livraria Editora Cátedra.

——. 1987b. *A formação econômica do Espírito Santo (O roteiro da industrialização).* Vitória: Editora Cátedra.

Boff, Leonardo. 1980. "Theological Characteristics of a Grassroots Church." In *The Challenge of Basic Christian Communities: Papers from the International Ecumenical Congress of Theology, February 20–March 2, 1980, São Paulo, Brazil*, edited by Sergio Torres and John Eagleson, 124–43. Maryknoll: Orbis.

Boff, Leonardo, and Elsa Tamez. 1987. "Leonardo Boff." In *Against Machismo: Interviews by Elsa Tamez*, edited by Elsa Tamez, 96–105. Oak Park: Meyer Stone.

Borba, Julian, and Lígia Helena H. Lüchmann. 2007. "Orçamento participativo: Análise das experiências desenvolvidas em Santa Catarina." In *Orçamento participativo: Análise das experiências desenvolvidas em Santa Catarina*, edited by Julian Borba and Lígia Helena H. Lüchmann, 21–59. Florianópolis: Editora Insular.

Borgo, Ivan, Léa Brígida Rocha de Alvarenga Rosa, and Renato Pacheco. 1996. *Norte do Espírito Santo: Ciclo madereiro e povoamento*. Vitória: Edufes.

Braga, Teodorimo. 1976. "As duas cartilhas do MDB." *Movimento*, October 11: 6.

Bresser-Pereira, Luiz. 1984. *Development and Crisis in Brazil, 1930–1983*. Translated by Marcia Van Dyke. Boulder: Westview.

Bresser-Pereira, Luiz Carlos. 2009. "From the Patrimonial to the Managerial State." In *Brazil: A Century of Change*, edited by Ignacy Sachs, Jorge Wilheim, and Paulo Sérgio Pinheiro, 141–73. Chapel Hill: University of North Carolina Press.

Bruneau, Thomas C. 1974. *The Political Transformation of the Brazilian Catholic Church*. New York: Cambridge University Press.

Buarque de Holanda, Sérgio. 1936/2002. *Raízes do Brasil*. São Paulo: Companhia das Letras.

Burdick, John. 2004. *Legacies of Liberation: The Progressive Catholic Church in Brazil and the Start of a New Millennium*. Aldershot: Ashgate.

Burgos, Raúl. 2002. "The Gramscian Intervention in the Theoretical and Political Production of the Latin American Left." *Latin American Perspectives* 29(1): 9–37.

Cabannes, Yves. 2006. "Les budgets participatifs en Amérique latine." *Mouvements* 47–48: 128–38.

"Campinas cidade planejada para o ano 2000." 1972. *Folha de São Paulo*, February 1, Caderno 1: 11.

Camurça, Marcelo Ayres. 2007. "A limitância de esquerda (cristã) de Leonardo Boff e Frei Betto: Da Teologia da Libertação à mística ecológica." In *Revolução e Democracia (1964– . . .)*, edited by Jorge Ferreira and Daniel Aarão Reis, 389–408. Rio de Janeiro: Civilização Brasileira.

Canel, Eduardo. 2011. *Barrio Democracy in Latin America: Participatory Decentralization and Community Activism in Montevideo*. University Park, PA: Pennsylvania State University Press.

———. 2012. "Fragmented Clientelism in Montevideo: Training Ground for Community Engagement with Participatory Decentralization." In *Clientelism in Everyday Latin American Politics*, edited by Tina Hilgers. New York: Palgrave Macmillan.

Caniello, Márcio. 2011. "O Brasil mostra sua cor." Centro de Desenvolvimento Sustentável do Semiárido. http://www.cdsa.ufcg.edu.br/portal/index.php?option=com_content&view=article&id=836:o-brasil-mostra-a-sua-cor&catid=92:artigos&Itemid=460.

Caponi, Helô. 1981. "A cidada da democracia: Boa Esperança prova que poder e povo podem andar juntos." *Folha de São Paulo*, June 27.

Cardoso, Fernando Henrique, and Enzo Faletto. 1979. *Dependency and Development in Latin America*. Berkeley: University of California Press.

Carvalho, José Murilo de. 2001. *Cidadania no Brasil: O longo caminho*. Rio de Janeiro: Civilização Brasileira.

CEAG/SC. 1980. *Evolução histórico-econômica de Santa Catarina*. Florianópolis: CEAG.

Central Única dos Trabalhadores. 1984. *I Congresso Nacional da Classe Trabalhadora*. Rio de Janeiro: Editora Limitada.

César, Benedito Tadeu. 2002. *PT: A contemporaneidade possível—perfil social e projeto político (1980/1991)*. Porto Alegre: Editora da UFRGS.

Cherem, Rosângela Miranda. 2001. "Do sonho ao despertar: Expectativas sociais e paixões políticas no início republicano na capital de Santa Catarina." In *História de Santa Catarina no século XIX*, edited by Ana Brancher and Silvia Maria Fávero Arend, 297–344. Florianópolis: Edição da UFSC.

Christiano, Raul. 2003. *De volta ao começo! Raízes de um PSDB militante, que nasceu na oposição*. São Paulo: Geração Editorial.

Christo, Alberto Libano. 1977. "O canto do galo (Relatório pastoral de uma visita à prelazia do Acre e Purus)." *Revista Eclesiástica Brasileira* 37 (July): 146 (separata).

CIDADE. 2008. "Um fantasma assombra o governo municipal." *Boletim Cidade* 7(43).

CNBB. 1981. Reflexão cristã sobre a conjuntura política. (IGR. POL., 3a. Reunião Ordinária do Conselho Permanente). São Paulo: Centro de Documentação e Pesquisa Vergueiro, São Paulo.

———. 1982. As comunidades de base na Igreja do Brasil. (IGR.POL., N. 02.03.83, 7a. Reunião Ordinária do Conselho Permanente). São Paulo: Centro de Documentação e Pesquisa Vergueiro, São Paulo.

CNBB Regional Extremo Oeste. 1982. O cristão e a política: Subsidios para reflexão. (IGR. POL. ELE.). São Paulo: Centro de Documentação e Pesquisa Vergueiro, São Paulo.

CNBB Regional Sul 4. 1981. A Igreja em Santa Catarina e a conjuntura sóciopolítica. (IGR. POL., N. 16.08.82). São Paulo: Centro de Documentação e Pesquisa Vergueiro, São Paulo.

Codato, Adriano Nervo. 2010. "A elite destituída: A classe política paulista nos anos 30." In *História do Estado de São Paulo: A formação da unidade paulista*, edited by Nilo Odalia and João Ricardo de Castro Caldeira, 275–304. São Paulo: Editora UNESP.

Coelho, Vera Schattan P. 2004. "Brazil's Health Councils: The Challenge of Building Participatory Political Institutions." *IDS Bulletin* 35(2): 33–39.

Coelho, Vera Schattan P., and José Veríssimo. 2004. "Considerações sobre o processo de escolha dos representantes da sociedade civil nos conselhos de saúde em São Paulo." In *A participação em São Paulo*, edited by Leonardo Avritzer, 105–22. São Paulo: Editora da UNESP.

Cohen, Jean L., and Andrew Arato. 1992. *Civil Society and Political Theory*. Cambrigde, MA: MIT Press.

Cohn, Amélia. 1987. "O sistema unificado e descentralizado de saúde: Descentralização ou desconcentração?" *São Paulo em Perspectiva* 1(3): 55–58.

———. 1992. "Descentralização, cidadania e saúde." *São Paulo em Perspectiva* 6(4): 70–76.

Collier, Ruth Berins, and David Collier. 1991. *Shaping the Political Arena: Critical Junctures, the Labor Movement, and Regime Dynamics in Latin America*. Princeton: Princeton University Press.

"Conselho vai fiscalizar o novo prefeito." 1983. *Folha de São Paulo*, January 24.

Cornwall, Andrea, Jorge Romano, and Alex Shankland. 2008. "Brazilian Experiences of Participation and Citizenship: A Critical Look." *IDS Discussion Paper* 389.

Cortes, Soraya Vargas. 2011. "As diferentes instituicoes participativas existentes nos municipios brasileiros." In *Efetividade das instituições participativas no Brasil: Estratégias de avaliação*, edited by Roberto Rocha C. Pires, 137–50. Brasília: Instituto de Pesquisa Ecônomica Aplicada.

Costa, Licurgo. 1982. *O Continente das Lagens: Sua história e influência no sertão da terra firme*. Vols. 1–4. Florianópolis: FCC Edições.

Costa, Luiz Paulo. 2001. "Orçamento participativo." *Vale Paraibano*, December 18.

Couto, Cláudio Gonçalves. 1995. *O desafio de ser governo: O PT na prefeitura de São Paulo (1989–1995)*. São Paulo: Editora Paz e Terra.

Covre, Amaro. 1980. *Remédio para o municipalismo: A comunidade no poder; Experiências dos Munícipio de Boa Esperança-ES 1977–1980*.

Cunha, Idaulo José. 1982. *Evolução econômico-industrial de Santa Catarina*. Florianópolis: FCC Edições.

D'Araujo, Maria Celina. 1999. "Nos braços do povo: A segunda presidência de Vargas." In *As instituições brasileiras na Era Vargas*, edited by Maria Celina D'Araujo, 97–118. Rio de Janeiro: Editora FVG.

Dadalto, Maria Cristina. 2003. "Imigração italiana e memória do trabalho." In *Trajetória: Trabalho solidário do imigrante italiano no Espírito Santo*, edited by Adilson Vilaça and Maria Cristina Dadalto, 51–68. Vitória: Textus Editora.

Dagnino, Evelina. 2002. *Sociedad civil, esfera publica y democratización en América Latina: Brasil.* Campinas: Editora Unicamp.

———. 2003. "Citizenship in Latin America: An Introduction." *Latin American Perspectives,* 30(2): 3–17.

———. 2004. "¿Sociedade civil, participação e cidadania: De que estamos falando?" In *Políticas de ciudadanía y sociedad civil en tiempos de globalización,* edited by Daniel Mato, 95–110. Caracas: FACES, Universidad Central de Venezuela.

———. 2007. "Citizenship: A Perverse Confluence." *Development in Practice* 17(4 & 5): 549–56.

———. 2010. "Civil Society in Latin America: Participatory Citizens or Service Providers?" In *Power to the People? (Con-) Tested Civil Society in Search of Democracy,* edited by Heidi Moksnes and Mia Melin, 23–41. Uppsala: Uppsala Centre for Sustainable Development.

Dagnino, Evelina, Alberto J. Olvera, and Aldo Panfichi, eds. 2006a. *A disputa pela construção democrática na América Latina.* São Paulo: Editora Paz e Terra.

———. 2006b. "Para uma outra leitura da disputa pela construção democrática na América Latina." In *A disputa pela construção democrática na América Latina,* edited by Evelina Dagnino, Alberto J. Olvera, and Aldo Panfichi, 13–91. São Paulo: Editora Paz e Terra.

Dagnino, Evelina, and Luciana Tatagiba. 2007. *Democracia, sociedade civil e participação.* Yarralumla, Australia: Argos Press.

———. 2010. "Mouvements sociaux et participation institutionnelle: Répertoires d'action collective et dynamiques culturelles dans la difficile construction de la démocratie brésilienne." *Revue Internationale de Politique Comparée* 17: 167–85.

Daniel, Celso. 1990. "As administrações democráticas e populares em questão." *Espaço & Debates* 10(30): 11–27.

Dawson, Andrew. 2002. "A Very Brazilian Experiement: The Base Education Movement." *History of Education* 31(2): 185–94.

Della Cava, Ralph. 1986. "A Igreja e a abertura, 1974–1985." In *A Igreja nas bases em tempo de transição,* edited by Paulo J. Krischke and Scott Mainwaring, 13–45. Porto Alegre: L&PM and CEDEC.

DelPicchia, Pedro. 1982. *A batalha da colina (A democracia chega a Piracicaba).* Piracicaba: MPGD.

Demo, Pedro, and Elizeu F. Calsing. 1977. "Relatório de pesquisa sobre CEBs." In *Comunidades: Igreja na base,* edited by CNBB, 13–64. São Paulo: Edições Paulinas.

Diacon, Todd A. 1990. "Peasants, Prophets, and the Power of a Millennarian Vision in Twentieth-Century Brazil." *Comparative Studies in Society and History* 32(3): 488–514.

Diamond, Larry, and Leonardo Morlino. 2005. "Introduction." In *Assessing the Quality of Democracy*, edited by Larry Diamond and Leonardo Molino, ix–xliii. Baltimore: Johns Hopkins University Press.

Diocese de Juazeiro. 1981. Politica: A luta de um povo. (IGR. POL.). São Paulo: Centro de Documentação e Pesquisa Vergueiro, São Paulo.

Diocese de São Mateus. 1977. Exigências cristãs de uma ordem política: Versão Popular. (IGR.POL., N. 2722). São Paulo: Centro de Documentação e Pesquisa Vergueiro, São Paulo.

———. 1979. Pela estrada: Informativo das comunidades. Vol. 1. (IGR. CEBS). São Paulo: Centro de Documentação e Pesquisa Vergueiro, São Paulo.

Doimo, Ana Maria. 1995. *A vez e a voz do popular: Movimentos sociais e partição política no Brasil do pós-70*. Rio de Janeiro: Relume Dumará, ANPOCS.

Draghichevich, Perla. 2001. "Da vocação industrial e ausência de políticas sociais: Os movimentos populares pela moradia." In *Diadema nasceu no grande ABC: História retrospectiva da Cidade Vermelha*, edited by Zilda Márcia Grícoli Iokoi, 177–98. São Paulo: Humanitas/ FFLCH/ USP.

Egler, Walter Alberto. 1962. "A zona pioneira ao Norte do Rio Doce." *Boletim Geográfico* 20(167): 147–80.

"Em defesa dos interesses populares." 1976. *Movimento*, September 27.

"Em Diadema, conselhos populares." 1982. *O Estado de São Paulo*, December 12: 43.

Equipe Caderno Debate. 1982. Cadernos Debate. Série: As eleições. Vol. 5. (IGR. POL., N. 30.11.82, Apoio da Igreja Metodista e UNIMEP). São Paulo: Centro de Documentação e Pesquisa Vergueiro, São Paulo.

Faria, Claudia Feres, and Uriella Coelho Ribeiro. 2011. "Desenho institucional: Variáveis relevantes e seus efeitos sobre o processo participativo." In *Efetividade das instituições participativas no Brasil: Estratégias de avaliação*, edited by Roberto Rocha C. Pires, 125–36. Brasília: Instituto de Pesquisa Econômica Aplicada.

Faria, Vilmar. 1989. "Changes in the Composition of Employment and the Structure of Occupations." In *Social Change in Brazil, 1945–1985: The Incomplete Transition*, edited by Ednar L. Bacha and Herbert S. Klein, 141–70. Albuquerque: University of New Mexico Press.

Fausto, Boris. 1972. "Pequenos ensaios de história da República: 1889–1945." São Paulo: Centro Brasileiro de Análise e Planejamento.

———. 1999. *A Concise History of Brazil*. Cambridge: Cambridge University Press.

Fedozzi, Luciano. 1999. *Orçamento participativo: Reflexões sobre a experiência de Porto Alegre*. Porto Alegre: Tomo Editorial.

———. 2007. *Observando o orçamento participativo de Porto Alegre: Análise histórica de dados; Perfil social e associativo, avaliação e expectativas*. Porto Alegre: Tomo Editorial.

Fernandes, Antônio Sérgio Araújo. 2004. *Gestão municipal e participação social no Brasil: A trajetória de Recife e Salvador (1986–2000)*. São Paulo: Annablume Editora.

Fernandes, Bernardo Mançano. 2000. *A formação do MST no Brasil*. Petrópolis: Editora Vozes.

Ferreira, Ana Luiza S. Souto. 1991. "Lages: Um jeito de governar." *PÓLIS* 5: 3–31.

Ferreira, Ana Luiza Souto, and Rudá Ricci. 1992. "Estudos de gestão: Ronda Alta e São João do Triunfo." *PÓLIS* 8.

Figueiredo, Rubens, and Bolivar Lamounier. 1996. *As cidades que dão certo*. Brasília: MH Comunicações.

Fine, Ben. 1999. "The Developmental State is Dead—Long Live Social Capital?" *Development and Change* 30: 1–19.

Fleischer, David. 1986. "The Brazilian Congress: From *Abertura* to New Republic." In *Political Liberalization in Brazil: Dynamics, Dilemmas, and Future Prospects*, edited by Wayne A. Selcher, 97–133. Boulder: Westview.

Fonseca, Silmara Cristiane. 2001. "Diadema e o Grande ABC: Expansão industrial a economia de São Paulo." In *Diadema nasceu no Grande ABC: História retrospectiva da cidade vermelha*, edited by Zilda Márcia Grícoli Iokoi, 107–41. São Paulo: Humanitas/ FFLCH/ USP.

Font, Mauricio A. 2010. *Coffee and Transformation in São Paulo, Brazil*. Lanham: Lexington.

Freire, Alípio, and Ricardo Azevedo. 1990. "Entrevista: Luiza Erundina: Sem medo de ser governo." *Teoria & Debate*, August 11: 10–15.

French, John D. 1988. "Workers and the Rise of Adhemarista Populism in *São Paulo*, Brazil 1945–47." *The Hispanic American Historical Review* 68(1): 1–43.

———. 1992. *The Brazilian Workers' ABC: Class Conflict and Alliances in Modern São Paulo*. Chapel Hill: University of North Carolina Press.

Friedman, E. J., and K. Hochstetler. 2002. "Assessing the Third Transition in Latin American Democratization: Representational Regimes and Civil Society in Argentina and Brazil." *Comparative Politics* 35(1): 21–42, 125.

Fung, Archon, and Erik Olin Wright, eds. 2003. *Deepening Democracy: Institutional Innovations in Empowered Participatory Governance*. London: Verso.

Gadotti, M., and Pereira, O. 1989. *Pra que PT? Origem, projeto e consolidação do Partido dos Trabalhadores*. São Paulo: Cortez Editora, 231–39.

Garcia, Francisco José Teixeira. 2002. *A distribuição de ICMS aos municípios do Espírto Santo: Concentração ou desconcentração?* Rio de Janeiro: Escola Brasileira de Administração Pública, Fundação Getúlio Vargas.

Garcia, Marco Aurélio. 1986. "Contribuições para uma história da esquerda brasileira." In *Inteligência brasileira*, edited by Reginaldo Moraes, Ricardo Antunes, and Vera B. Ferrante, 193–223. São Paulo: Editora Brasiliense.

———. 1996. "Esquerdas: Rupturas e continuidades." In *Os anos 90: Política e sociedade no Brasil*, edited by Evelina Dagnino, 119–36. São Paulo: Editora Brasiliense.

Garcia, Mauri, and Timothy Harding. 1979. "Interview with Luis Inácio da Silva ('Lula'), President of the Sindicato dos Metalúrgicos de São Bernando do Campo." *Latin American Perspectives* 6(4): 90–100.

Gay, Robert. 1994. *Popular Organization's and Democracy in Rio de Janeiro: A Tale of Two Favelas*. Philadelphia: Temple University Press.

George, Alexandre L., and Andrew Bennett. 2005. *Case Studies and Theory Development in the Social Sciences*. Cambridge, MA: MIT Press.

Gret, Marion, and Yves Sintomer. 2005. The Porto Alegre Experiment: Learning Lessons for Better Democracy. London: Zed Books.

"Gilson já começa a delinear seu trabalho." 1982. *Jornal do Planalto*, December 8: 3.

Gimenez, Alaídes dos Santos. 1997, July 1. Interview by Maria de Lourdes Ferreira. [tape recording]. Centro de Memória de Diadema, Diadema.

Gohn, Maria da Glória. 2001. *Conselhos gestores e participação sociopolítica*. São Paulo: Cortez Editora.

Goldfrank, Benjamin. 2011. *Deepening Local Democracy in Latin America: Participation, Decentralization, and the Left*. University Park, PA: Pennsylvania State University.

———. 2012. "The World Bank and the Globalization of Participatory Budgeting." *Journal of Public Deliberation* 8(2): Article 7.

"Governo com as bases em Feira de Santana." 1976. *Movimento*, November 22: 6.

Graham, Richard. 1990. *Patronage and Politics in Nineteenth-Century Brazil*. Stanford: Stanford University Press.

Gugliano, Alfredo Alejandro, Robson Becker Loeck, Andréia Orsato, and André Luis Pereira. 2008. "Processos participativos e estratégias de redistribuição: Resgatando o orçamento participativo em Pelotas (1984–1985)." In *Democracia participativa e redistribuição: Análise de experiências de orçamento participativo*, edited by Adalmir A. Marquetti, Geraldo Ariano de Campos, and Roberto Pires. São Paulo: Xamã.

Hagopian, Frances. 1996. *Traditional Politics and Regime Change in Brazil*. Cambridge: Cambridge University Press.

Hees, Regina Rodrigues, and Sebastião Pimentel Franco. 2003. *República no Espírito Santo*. Vitória: Multiplicidade.

Heller, Patrick. 2009. "Democratic Deepening in India and South Africa." *Journal of Asian and African Studies* 41(4): 123–49.

———. 2012. "Democracy, Participatory Politics and Development: Some Comparative Lessons from Brazil, India and South Africa." *Polity* 44(4): 643–65.

Herrmann Neto, João. 1984. "Administração municipal de Piracicaba: A Serviço de quem?" In *Democracia feita em casa*, edited by João Herrmann Neto, 87–92. Brasília: Câmara dos Deputados.

Hewitt, W. E. 1986. "Strategies for Social Change Employed by Comunidades Eclesiais de Base (CEBs) in the Archdiocese of São Paulo." *Journal for the Scientific Study of Religion* 25(1): 16–30.

———. 1991. *Base Christian Communities and Social Change in Brazil.* Lincoln: University of Nebraska Press.

Hewitt, W. E., and John Burdick, eds. 2000. *The Church at the Grassroots in Latin America: Perspectives on Thirty Years of Activism.* Westport: Praeger.

Hilgers, Tina, ed. 2012. *Clientelism in Everyday Latin American Politics.* New York: Palgrave Macmillan.

Hoare, Quintin, and Geoffrey Nowell-Smith. 1971. *Selection of Prison Notebooks.* New York: International Publishers.

Hochstetler, Kathryn. (2000). Democratizing Pressures from Below? Social Movements in the New Brazilian Democracy. In *Democratic Brazil: Actors, Institutions, and Processes.* Edited by P. R. Kingstone & T. J. Power, 162–182. Pittsburgh: University of Pittsburgh Press.

Hochstetler, Kathryn, and Margaret E. Keck. 2007. *Greening Brazil: Environmental Activism in State and Society.* Durham, NC: Duke University Press.

Holston, James. 2008. *Insurgent Citizenship: Disjunctions of Democracy and Modernity in Brazil.* Princeton: Princeton University Press.

Houtzager, Peter P., and Adrián Gurvan Lavalle. 2010. "Civil Society's Claims to Political Representation in Brazil." *Studies in Comparative International Development* 45(1): 1–29.

Howell, Jude, and Jenny Pearce. 2001. *Civil Society and Development: A Critical Explanation.* Boulder: Lynne Rienner.

Huntington, Samuel P. 1991. *The Third Wave: Democratization in the Late 20th Century.* Norman: Oklahoma University Press.

Instituto Brasileiro de Administração Municipal. 1984. Estudo de caso: Boa Espernaça. Volta Redonda: Seminário Sobre Diretrizes de Governor.

Instituto Brasileiro de Geografia e Estatística (IBGE). 1960. Censo demográfico de 1960. São Paulo. Rio de Janeiro: IBGE.

———. 1970a. Atualidade estatística do Brasil 1970. Rio de Janeiro: IBGE.

———. 1970b. Censo agropecuário do Espírito Santo. Rio de Janeiro: IBGE.

———. 1970c. Sinopse estatística do Espírito Santo 1970. Rio de Janeiro: IBGE.

———. 1979. Censo agropecuário Espírito Santo. Rio de Janeiro: IBGE.

———. 1982. Censo demográfico. Dados gerais - Migração - Instrução - Fecundidade - Mortalidade. São Paulo. Rio de Janeiro: IBGE.

———. 1983. Censo agropecuário do Espírito Santo. Rio de Janeiro: IBGE.

———. 1983a. Censo demográfico. Famílias e domicílios. São Paulo. Rio de Janeiro: IBGE.

———. 1983b. Censo demográfico. Mão-de-obra. São Paulo. Rio de Janeiro: IBGE.

———. 1985. Censo agropecuário do Espírito Santo. Rio de Janeiro: IBGE.

———. 1987. Estatísticas históricas do Brasil. Vol. 3. Rio de Janeiro: IBGE.

———. 1996. Anuário estatístico do Brasil. Vol. 56. Rio de Janeiro: IBGE.

———. 1997. Contagem da população 1996. Vol. 1. Rio de Janeiro: IBGE.

Instituto de Estudos Políticos, Econômicos e Sociais. 1976. Curso de Formação para Prefeitos e Vereadores.

Ji-Paraná, Prelazia de. 1982. "Fé e empenho politico: Pra grupos de famílias." (1. IGR. POL., N.20.12.82). São Paulo: Centro de Documentação e Pesquisa Vergueiro, São Paulo.

Junge, Benjamin. 2012. "NGOs as Shadow Pseudopublics: Grassroots Community Leaders' Perceptions of Change and Continuity in Porto Alegre, Brazil." *American Ethnologist* 3: 407–24.

Justino, Antonio. 1997, November 11. Interview by Absolon de Oliveira [tape recording]. Centro de Memória de Diadema, Diadema.

Kadt, Emmanuel de. 1970. *Catholic Radicals in Brazil.* London: Trinity Press.

Keck, Margaret. 1984. "Update on the Brazilian Labor Movement." *Latin American Perspectives* 11(1): 27–34.

———. 1992. *The Workers' Party and Democratization in Brazil.* New Haven: Yale University Press.

Kenez, Kátia Cristina. 2001. "A transição do trabalho escravo ao trabalho livre no Grande ABC e os fluxos populacionais: 1880/1920." In *Diadema nasceu no Grande ABC: História reprospectiva da cidade vermelha,* edited by Zilda Márcia Grícoli Iokoi, 77–106. São Paulo: Humanitas/ FFLCH/ USP.

Kinzo, Maria D'Alva G. 1980. *Representação política e o sistema eleitoral no Brasil.* São Paulo: Edições Símbolo.

———. 1988. *Legal Opposition Politics under Authoritarian Rule in Brazil: The Case of the MDB, 1966–79.* London: Macmillan Press.

Kowarick, Lúcio, and André Singer. 1993. "A experiência do Partido dos Trabalhadores na Prefeitura de São Paulo." *Novos Estudos CEBRAP* 35: 195–216.

Krischke, Paulo José. 1979. *A Igreja e as crises políticas no Brasil.* Petrópolis: Editora Vozes.

———. 2010. *Populism and the Catholic Chruch: Political Crisis in Brazil, 1964.* New York: Nova Science.

Krischke, Paulo, and Scott Mainwaring, eds. 1986. *A Igreja nas bases em tempo de transição* (1974–1985). Porto Alegre: L&PM and CEDEC.

Lago, Paulo Fernando. 1968. *Santa Catarina: A terra, o homem e a economia.* Florianópolis: Edição da UFSC.

Lavalle, Adrián Gurza. 2011. "Após a participação: Nota introdutória." *Lua Nova* 84: 13–24.

Lavalle, Adrián Gurza, Arnab Acharya, and Peter Houtzager. 2005. "Beyond Comparative Anecdotalism: Lesson on Civil Society and Participation from São Paulo, Brazil." *World Development Journal* 33(6): 951–64.

Leal, Victor Nunes. 1949/2009. *Coronelismo: The Municipality and Representative Government in Brazil*. Cambridge: Cambridge University Press.

Leftwich, Adrian. 1993. "Governance, Democracy and Development in the Third World." *Third World Quarterly* 14(3): 605–24.

Lenzi, Carlos Alberto Silveira. 1977. *Poder político e mudança social (estudo sobre poder político oligárquico no município de Lages—SC)*. MA thesis, Universidade Federal de Santa Catarina.

———. 1983. *Partido e políticos de Santa Catarina*. Florianópolis: Editora da UFSC.

Lerner, Josh. 2011. "Participatory Budgeting: Building Community Agreement around Tough Budget Decisions." *National Civic Review* 100(2): 30–35.

Lesbaupin, Yvo. 1997. "Communautés de base et politique au Brésil." *Arch. de Sc. soc. des Rel.* 97: 33–45.

Levy, Charmain. 2000. "CEBs in Crisis: Leadership Structures in the São Paulo Area." In *The Church at the Grassroots in Latin America: Perspectives on Thirty Years of Activism*, edited by John Burdick and W. E. Hewitt, 167–210. Westport: Praeger.

———. "Influência e contribuição: Aigreja católica progressista brasileira e o fórum social mundial." *Religião & Sociedade* 29(2): 177–197.

Lobo, Maria Thereza Larque de Souza, Isabel Cristina Eiras de Oliveira, Alberto Costa Lopes, Nilton Almeida Rocha, and Rogério Vieira Cortez. 1984. *Perspectivas de desenvolvimento: Teorias x praticas*. Rio de Janeiro: Centro de Estudos e Pequisas Urbanas do Instituto Brasileiro de Administração Municipal.

Love, Joseph L. 1980. *São Paulo in the Brazilian Federation 1889–1937*. Stanford: Stanford University Press.

Löwy, Michael. 1999. "Pontos de referência para uma história do marxismo na América Latina." In *O marxismo na América Latina: Uma antologia de 1909 aos dias atuais*, edited by Michael Löwy, 9–64. São Paulo: Editora Fundação Perseu Abramo.

Lüchmann, Lígia Helena Hahn. 2010. "Participação e o aprendizado político no orçamento participativo: Estudo de caso em um municipio catarinense." *Educação & Sociedade* 33 (119): 513–32.

———. 2011. "Associações, participação e representação: Combinações e tensões." *Lua Nova: Revista de Cultura e Política* 84: 141–74.

Maclean, Iain S. 1999. *Option for Democracy: Liberation Theology and the Struggle for Democracy in Brazil*. New York: Peter Lang.

Mainwaring, Scott. 1986. *The Catholic Church and Politics in Brazil, 1916–1985*. Stanford: Stanford University Press.

Marquetti, Adalmir A. 2008. "Orçamento participativo, redistribuição e finanças municipais: A experiência de Porto Alegre entre 1989 e 2004." In *Democracia participativa e redistribuição: Análise de experiências de orçamento participativo*, edited by Adalmir A. Marquetti, Geraldo Ariano de Campos, and Roberto Pires. São Paulo: Xamã.

Marshall, T. H. 1950. *Citizenship and Social Class: And Other Essays*. Cambridge: University Press.

Martendal, José Ari Celso. 1982. "Propostas alternatives de educação no meio rural." In *Seminário Educação no Meio Rural, Ijui (RS) 1 a 4 de junho de 1982*, edited by INEP.

Martendal, José Ari Celso, Maria Julieta Costa Calazans, Hélio Raymundo Santos Silva, and Sérgio Sartori. 1982. Relatório do projeto de educação e cultura popular: A experiência de Lages 1977/1982. Florianópolis: FAPEU, Universidade Federal de Santa Catarina.

"MDB projeto e campanha." 1976. *Opinião*, November 12: 3.

"MDB quer assembléia constituinte." 1971. *Folha de São Paulo*, July 5, Caderno 1: 7.

"MDB quer reforma através do município." 1974. *Folha de São Paulo*, July 6, Nacional: 3.

"MDB: O que fazer nas prefeituras?"1976. *Movimento*, June 26.

Medeiros, Rogério de Souza. 2007. "Crítica e resignação nas atuais relações entre as ONGs e o Estado no Brasil." In *Democracia, sociedade civil e participação*, edited by Evelina Dagnino and Luciana Tatagiba, 167–202. Chapecó: Argos Editora Universitária.

Meirinho, Jali. 2009. *1893–1894—História e historiografia da revolução em Santa Catarina*. Florianópolis: IHGSC and Editora Insular.

Melhem, Célia Soibelmann. 1998. *Política de botinas amarelas: O MDB-PMDB paulista de 1965 a 1988*. São Paulo: Editora HUCITEC.

Melo, Marcus André. 2011. "Democratizing Budgetary Decisions and Execution in Brazil: More Participation or Redesign of Formal Institutions." In *Participatory Innovation and Representative Democracy in Latin America*, edited by Andrew Selee and Enrique Peruzzotti, 17–39. Baltimore: Johns Hopkins University Press.

Meneguello, Rachel. 1989. *PT: A formação de um partido, 1979–1982*. São Paulo: Editora Paz e Terra.

Mericle, Kenneth S. 1977. "Corporatist Control of the Working Class: Authoritarian Brazil since 1964." In *Authoritarianism and Corporatism in Latin America*, edited by James M. Malloy, 303–38. Pittsburgh: University of Pittsburgh Press.

Mesquita, Erle Cavalcante. 2007. "Participação, atores políticos e transformação institucional no Ceará." In *A participação social no Nordeste*, edited by Leonardo Avritzer and Aurea Mota, 65–84. Belo Horizonte: Editora UFMG.

"Metodo de Boa Esperança válido para o Estado." 1980. *A Tribuna*, June 19.

Michels, Ido Luiz. 1998. *Crítica ao modelo catarinense de desenvolvimento: Do planejamento econômico, 1956, aos precatórios, 1997*. Campo Grande: Editora UFMS.

Michiles, Carlos, Francisco Whitaker, João Gilberto Lucas Coelho, Emmanuel Gonçalves Vieira Filho, Maria da Glória Moura da Veiga, and Regina de Paula Santos Prado. 1989. *Cidadão constituinte: A saga das emendas populares*. Rio de Janeiro: Paz e Terra.

Moisés, José Álvaro. 1976. "A questão do poder local." *Opinião*, July 9: 8.

———. 1978. *Classes populares e protesto urbano*. PhD diss., Universidade de São Paulo.

———. 1979. "Current Issues in the Labor Movement in Brazil." *Latin American Perspectives* 6(4): 51–70.

———. 1982. "Qual é a estratégia do novo sindicalismo?" In *Alternatives populares da semocracia*, edited by CEDEC, 11–39. Petrópolis: Editora Vozes.

Moore, Barrington. 1966. *Social Origins of Dictatorship and Democracy: Lord and Peasant in the Making of the Modern World*. Boston: Beacon.

Moraes, Tetê. 1983. *Lages, a força do povo*. Brazil: Empresa Brasileira de Filmes SA. Documentary.

Morais, Clodomir Santos de. 2002. "História das Ligas Camponesas do Brasil." In *História e natureza das Ligas Camponesas*, edited by João Pedro Stedile, 11–69. São Paulo: Expressão Popular.

Motta, Rodrigo Patto Sá. 2007. "O MDB e as esquerdas." In *Revolução e democracia (1964–. . .): As esquerdas no Brasil*, edited by Jorge Ferreira and Daniel Aarão Reis, 285–302. Rio de Janeiro: Editora Civilização Brasileira.

Movimento Democrático Brasileiro. 1976a. Programa do Movimento Democrático Brasileiro. São Paulo: Diretório Regional de São Paulo.

———. 1976b. Uma prefeitura de oposição. Recife: Diretório Regional de Pernambuco.

Munarim, Antonio. 1990. *A práxis dos movimentos sociais na região de Lages*. MA thesis, Universidade Federal de Santa Catarina, Florianópolis.

Nardoto, Eliezer, and Herinéa Lima. 2001. *História de São Mateus*. São Mateus: Editora Atlântica.

Neckel, Roselane. 2003. *A república em Santa Catarina: Modernidade e exclusão (1889–1920)*. Florianópolis: Editora da UFSC.

North, Douglass C., John Joseph Wallis, and Barry R. Weingast. 2009. *Violence and Social Orders: A Conceptual Framework for Interpreting Recorded Human History*. Cambridge: Cambridge University Press.

Nylen, William. 1996. "Popular Participation in Brazil's Workers' Party: 'Democratizing Democracy' in Municipal Politics." *Political Chronicle, Journal of the Florida Political Science Association* 8: 1–9.

———. 1997. "Reconstructing the Workers' Party (PT): Lessons from North-Eastern Brazil." In *The New Politics of Inequality in Latin America: Rethinking Participation and Representation*, edited by Douglas A. Chalmers, Carlos M. Vilas, Katherine Hite, Scott B. Martin, Kerianne Piester, and Monique Segarra, 441–46. New York: Oxford University Press.

———. 2003. *Participatory Democracy versus Elitist Democracy: Lessons from Brazil*. New York: Palgrave Macmillan.

———. 2011. Review: "Participatory Institutions in Latin America: The Next Generation of Scholarship." *Comparative Politics* 43(4): 479–97.

"O MDB e a questão Local." 1976. *Opinião*, September 24: 3–4.

"O MDB e as prefeituras." 1976. *Movimento*, September 20: 4–5.

"O município da oligarquia a nosso dias." 1976. *Opinião*, November 5.

"O poder do MDB. 1976." *Movimento*, May 5: 5.

O'Donnell, Guillermo. 1973. *Modernization and Bureaucratic-Authoritarianism: Studies in South American Politics*. Berkeley: Institute of International Studies.

Oliveira, José Teixeira de. 1975. *História do Estado do Espírito Santo*. Vitória: Author.

Oposição Sindical Metalúrgica. 1981. *Comissão de fábrica: Uma forma de organização operária*. Petrópolis: Editora Vozes.

Orçamento Participativo. 2008. "Regimento interno—Critérios gerais, técnicos e regionais—2008/2009." Porto Alegre: Prefeitura Municipal de Porto Alegre.

Osório, Carla, Adriana Bravin, and Leonor de Araujo Santanna. 1999. *Negros do Espírito Santo*. São Paulo: Escrituras Editora.

Oxhorn, Philip. 2006. "Conceptualizing Civil Society from the Bottom Up: A Political Economy Perspective." In *Civil Society and Democracy in Latin America*, edited by Richard Feinberg, Carlos H. Waisman, and Leon Zamosc, 59–84. New York: Palgrave Macmillan.

———. 2011. *Sustaining Civil Society: Economic Change, Democracy, and the Social Construction of Citizenship in Latin America*. University Park, PA: Pennsylvania State University Press.

Page, Joseph A. 2002. "Ou, finalmente, o que aconteceu com o nordeste Brasileiro." In *História das Ligas Camponesas no Brasil*, edited by João Pedro Stedile, 127–51. São Paulo: Editora Expressão Popular.

"Papa diz que teologia da libertação caducou." 1996. *Jornal do Brasil*, February 6.

"A participação popular e a autonomia dos municípios." 1976. *Movimento*, November 15.

Partido da Social Democracia Brasileira. 1992. *Manifesto, programa, estatuto*. Brasília: Diretório Nacional Partido da Social Democracia Brasileira.

Partido dos Trabalhadores. 1979. *Carta de princípios*. http://www.pt.org.br/arquivos/cartadeprincipios.pdf.

———. 1980. *Manifesto*. http://www.pt.org.br/arquivos/manifesto.pdf.

———. 1998. *Partido dos Trabalhadores: Resoluções de encontros e congressos*. São Paulo: Editora Fundacão Perseu Abramo.

Pateman, Carole. 1970. *Participation and Democratic Theory*. Cambridge: Cambridge University Press.

———. 2012. "Participatory Democracy Revisited." *Perspectives on Politics* 10(1): 7–19.

Pearce, Jenny. 2010. "Introduction." In *Participation and Democracy in the Twenty-First Century City*, edited by Jenny Pearce, 1–33. New York: Palgrave Macmillan.

Peixer, Zilma Isabel. 2002. *A cidade e seus Tempos: O processo de constituição urbano em Lages*. Lages: Editora UNIPLAC.

Peluso Júnior, Victor Antônio. 1949. "Fazendo do Cedro: Planalto de São Joaquim." *Boletim Geográfico* 6 (71): 1379–91.

———. 1991. *Aspectos geográficos de Santa Catarina*. Edited by Victor Antônio Peluso Júnior. Florianópolis: FCC Edições.

Pereira, Adriana Freire. 2007. "A gestão democrática do Conselho Municipal do Orçamento Participativo de Campina Grande: Impasses, desafios e avanços." In *Mobilização, participação e direitos*, edited by Evelina Dagnino and Regina Pahim Pinto, 29–46. São Paulo: Editora Contexto.

Peruzzotti, Enrique, and Andrew Selee. 2009. "Participatory Innovation and Representative Democracy in Latin America." In *Participatory Innovation and Representative Democracy in Latin America*, edited by Andrew Selee and Enrique Peruzzotti, 1–16. Baltimore: Johns Hopkins University Press.

"Petistas divergem sobre 'Conselhos Populares.'" 1988. *Folha de São Paulo*, May 31: A–4.

Pierucci, Antônio Flávio, and Reginaldo Prandy. 1996. "Religiões e voto: A eleição presidencial de 1994." In *A realidade social das religões no Brasil: Religião, sociedade e política*, edited by Antônio Flávio Pierucci and Reginaldo Prandy, 211–38. São Paulo: Editora HUCITEC.

"Pindamonhangaba." 1976. *Folha de São Paulo*, December 12, Caderno 1: 25.

Pinnington, Elizabeth, Josh Lerner, and Daniel Schugurensky. 2009. "Participatory Budgeting in North America: The Case of Guelph, Canada." *Journal of Public Budgeting, Accouting & Financial Management* 21(3): 455–84.

Pinto, Valeska Peres. 1985. "Os desafios do PT em Diadema." *Desvios* 4: 109–23.

———. 1992. "Prefeitura de Fortaleza: Administração popular—1986/88." *PÓLIS* 6: 3–52.

Pires, Roberto Rocha C. 2011. *Efetividade das instituições participativas no Brasil: Estratégias de avaliação*. Brasília: Instituto de Pesquisa Econômica Aplicada.

PMDB. 1981a. "O PMDB e a ação municipalista: Prefeitura alternativa." *Revista do PMDB* 1(2): 89–102.

———. 1981b. "Prefeitura de Lajes: O povo no poder." *Revista do PMDB* 1(2): 103–11.

———. 1982. "O PMDB e a transformação democrática." *Revista do PMDB* 2(4): 7–16.

Pogrebinschi, Thamy, and Fabiano Santos. 2010. "Entre representação e participação: As conferências nacionais e o experimentalismo bemocrático brasileiro." Brasília: Instituto Universitário de Pesquisas do Rio de Janeiro and Programa das Nações Unidas para o Desenvolvimento.

"População discute o orçamento de Diadema." 1984. *Diário do Grande ABC*, April 14.

Power, Timothy J. 2000. *The Political Right in Postauthoritarian Brazil: Elites, Institutions, and Democratization*. University Park, PA: Pennsylvania State University Press.

Prado Júnior, Caio. 1975. "O fator geográfico na formação e desenvolvimento da cidade de São Paulo." In *Evolução política do Brasil e outros estudos*, edited by Caio Prado Júnior, 93–110. São Paulo: Editora Brasiliense.

Prefeitura de Belo Horizonte. 2012. *Orçamento participativo 2013/2014, metodologia e diretrizes*. Belo Horizonte: Secretaria Municipal Adjunta de Planejamento e Gestão. Gerência do Orçamento Participativo.

Prefeitura de Boa Esperança. 2008. *Boa Esperança: A terra do ouro verde.*

Prefeitura do Município de Diadema. 1984. *População discute o orçamento municipal. Informativo Municipal*, May.

———. 1985. Representantes discutem orçamento. *Informativo Municipal*, February.

———. 1986a. "Discussão do orçamento já está nos bairros." *Informativo Municipal*, July: 4.

———. 1986b. Empresa municipal de transporte com participação popular. *Informativo Municipal*, July.

———. 1987a. Conselho popular: Uma experiencia pioneira. *Informativo Municipal*, Fevereiro-Março.

———. 1987b. "Participação ativa do povo na saude municipal." *Informativo Municipal*, February–March.

"PT tenta convencer prefeito de Diadema a ficar no partido." 1988. *Folha de São Paulo*, May 29: A9.

Putnam, Robert. 1993. *Making Democracy Work: Civil Traditions in Modern Italy*. Princeton: Princeton University Press.

———. 1995. "Bowling Alone: America's Declining Social Capital." *The Journal of Democracy* 6 (1): 65–78.

Quinteiro, Juricema. 1991. *A "força do povo" em Lages: Mas o que foi mesmo, esta experiência?* MA thesis, Pontifíca Universidade Católica de São Paulo.

Ricci, Rudá. 1992. "Estudos de gestão: São José do Triunfo." *PÓLIS* 8: 57–97.

"Resoluções." 1978. Congresso dos trabalhadores nas indústrias metalúrgicas, mecânicas e de material elétrico de São Bernardo Campo e Diadema. http://www.abcdeluta.org.br/textos.asp?id_CON=469.

Rennó, Lucio. 2003. "Estruturas de oportunidade política e engajamento em organizações da sociedade civil: Um estudo comparado sobre a América Latina." *Revista de Sociologia e Política* 21: 71–82.

Rocha, Haroldo Correa, and Ângela Maria Morandi. 1991. *Cafeicultura e grande indústria: A transição no Espírito Santo 1955-1985*. Vitória: Fundação Ceciliano Abel de Almeida.

Rodrigues, Leôncio Martins. 1987. *Quem é quem na constituinte: Uma análise sócio-política dos partidos e deputados*. São Paulo: Oesp-Maltese.

Roussopoulos, Dimitrios, and C. George Benello, eds. 2003. *Participatory Democracy: Prospects for Democratizing Democracy*. Montreal: Black Rose.

Rueschemeyer, Dietrich, Evelyne Huber Stephens, and John D. Stephens. 1992. *Capitalist Development and Democracy*. Chicago: University of Chicago Press.

Sader, Eder. 1988. *Quando novos personagens entram em cena: Esperiências, falas e lutas dos trabalhadores da Grande São Paulo*. Rio de Janeiro: Paz e Terra.

Saletto, Nara. 1996. *Transição para o trabalho livre e pequena propriedade no Espírito Santo (1888-1930)*. Vitória: Edufes.

Sangha, Soni. 2012. "Putting In Their 2 Cents." *New York Times*, April 1: MB1.

Santos, Boaventura de Souza, ed. 2002. *Democratizar a democracia : os caminhos da democracia participativa*. Rio de Janeiro: Civilização Brasileira.

Santos, Boaventura de Souza, and Leonardo Avritzer. 2002. "Para ampliar o cânome democrático." In *Democratizar a democracia: Os caminhos da democracia participativa*, edited by Boaventura de Souza Santos, 39-82. Rio de Janeiro: Civilização Brasileira.

Santos, Joana Darc Virgínia. 2009. "Democracia participativa e lutas por moradia em Diadema (1983-1996)." *História em Revista* 15: 117-39.

Santos, Wanderley Guilherme dos. 1994. *Razões da desordem*. Rio de Janeiro: Rocco.

Schmitter, Philippe C. 1971. *Interest Conflict and Political Change in Brazil*. Stanford: Stanford University Press.

Selcher, Wayne A. 1986. "Contradictions, Dilemmas, and Actors in Brazil's *Abertura*, 1975-1985." In *Political Liberalization in Brazil: Dynamics, Dilemmas, and Future Prospects*, edited by Waymer A. Selcher, 55-95. Boulder: Westview.

Sell, Carlos Eduardo, and Roberto Wöhlke. 2007. "O orçamento participativo no berço das oligarquias: O caso de Itajaí/SC." In *Orçamento participativo: Análise das experiências desenvolvidas em Santa Catarina*, edited by Julian Borba and Lígia Helena H. Lüchmann, 145-65. Florianópolis: Editora Insular.

Seminário Central do Ipiranga. 1969. "Conclusão do encontro de dormação de comunidade eclesial de base—Região Sul de São Paulo." (1. IGR.CEBS). Centro de Documentação e Pesquisa Vergueiro, São Paulo. April 30.

Shah, Anwar. 2007. "Overview." In *Participatory Budgeting*, edited by Anwar Shah, 1-20. Washington, DC: World Bank.

Silva, Elizabeth Farias. 1994. *O fracasso da oposição no poder. Lajes: 1972-1982*. Santa Catarina: Letras Contemporâneas.

Silva, Ilson Chaves. 1981. "Prefeitura de Lajes: O povo no poder." *Revista do PMDB* 1 (2): 104–10.

Silva, Marta Zorzal. 1995. *Espírio Santo: Estado, interesses e poder.* Vitória: FCAA/SDC.

Silva Neto, Manuel Nunes da. 1995. "Memórias para a história da Escola Santa Helena—em Lages—Estado de Santa Catarina." Curitiba.

Silva, Rony Petterson da. 2009. *Movimentos, organizações sociais e educação popular: Uma educação para além da sala de aula.* MA thesis, Universidade do Planalto Catarinense.

Silva, Salomão L. Quadros da. 1999. "A Era Vargas e a economia." In *As instituições brasileiras na Era Vargas,* edited by Maria Celina D'Araujo, 137–54. Rio de Janeiro: Editora FVG.

Silveira, Lori Terezinha da. 2004. *Mostras de campo de Lages: Educação e cultura na democracia participativa (1977–1983).* MA thesis, Universidade Federal de Santa Catarina.

Silveira, Rosa Maria Godoy. 1978. *Republicanismo e federalismo: Um estudo da implementação da república brasileira.* Brasília: Editora Universitária.

Simões, Júlio Assis. 1992. *O dilema da participação social: A etnogradia de um caso.* São Paulo: Marco Zero.

Singer, Paul. 1968. *Desenvolvimento econômico e evolução urbana (análise da evolução econômica de São Paulo, Blumenau, Porto Alegre, Belo Horizonte e Recife).* São Paulo: Editora Nacional e Editora USP.

———. 1976. "Evolução da economia brasileira: 1955–1975." *Estudos CEBRAP* 17 (July, August, September): 61–83.

———. 1996. *Um governo de esquerda para todos: Luiza Erundina na prefeitura de São Paulo (1989–1992).* São Paulo: Editora Brasiliense.

———. 2009. "Economic Evolution and the International Connection." In *Brazil: A Century of Change,* edited by Ignacy Sachs, Jorge Wilheim, and Paulo Sérgio Pinheiro, 55–100. Chapel Hill: University of North Carolina Press.

Sintomer, Yves, Carsten Herzberg, Giovanni Allegretti, and Anja Röcke. 2010. "Learning from the South: Participatory Budgeting Worldwide—an Invitation to Global Cooperation." *Dialog Global* 25.

Sintomer, Yves, Carsten Herzberg, and Anja Röcke. 2008. "Participatory Budgeting in Europe: Potentials and Challenges." *International Journal of Urban and Regional Research* 32(1): 164–78.

Skidmore, Thomas E. 1967. *Politics in Brazil, 1930–1964: An Experiment in Democracy.* New York: Oxford University Press.

Soares, José Arlindo, and Salvador Soler Lostao. 1992. *Pode local e participação popular.* Rio de Janeiro: Rio Fundo Editora.

Souza, Celina. 1997. *Constitutional Engineering in Brazil: The Politics of Federalism and Decentralization.* London: Macmillan Press.

Souza, Herbert José de. 1982. "Município de Boa Esperança: Participação popular e poder local." In *Alternativas populares da democracia: Brasil, anos 80*, edited by José Álvaro Moisés, Luiz Gonzaga de Souza Lima, Tilman Evers, Herbert José de Souza, and Ximena Barraza, 99–120. Petrópolis: Editora Vozes.

Souza, Maria do Carmo Campello de. 1976. *Estado e partidos políticos no Brazil (1930 a 1964)*. São Paulo: Editora Alfa-Omega.

Spitzcovsky, Celso, and Marco Antonio Ribeiro Tura. 1993. "As reinvidicações populares e a constituição." *PÓLIS* 13.

Teixeira, Ana Claudia Chavez, Clóvis Henrique Leite de Souza, and Paula Pompeu Fiuza Lima. 2012. "Arquitetura da participação no Brasil: uma leitura das representações políticas em espaços participativos nacionais." *Polis* 52: 49–76.

Thery, Hervé. 2009. "A Cartographic and Statistical Portrait of Twentieth-Century Brazil." In *Brazil: A Century of Change*, edited by Ignacy Sachs, Jorge Wilheim, and Paulo Sérgio Pinheiro, 1–19. Chapel Hill: University of North Carolina Press.

Tragtenberg, Maurício. 1981. "Administração comunitária ressuscitou Boa Esperança." *Folha de São Paulo*, April 1.

Tranjan, J. Ricardo. 2011. "Civil Society Discourses and Practices in Porto Alegre." In *The Brazilian State: Debate and Agenda*, edited by Mauricio A. Font and Laura Randall, 145–67. Lanham: Lexington.

Touchton, Michael, and Brian Wampler. 2014. "Improving Social Well-Being through New Democratic Institutions." *Comparative Political Studies* 46(10): 1442–69.

Valle, Rogério, and Marcello Pitta. 1994. *Comunidades eclesiais católicas: Resultados estatísticos no Brasil*. Petrópolis: Vozes.

Vasconcellos, João Gualberto M. 1995. *A invenção do coronel*. Vitória: SPDC.

Vásquez, Manuel A. 1998. *The Brazilian Popular Church and the Crisis of Modernity*. Cambridge: Cambridge University Press.

Vilaça, Adilson, and Maria Cristina Dadalto. 2003. "A construção da cidadania: De Santa Teresa a Nova Venécia." In *Trajetória: Trabalho solidário do imigrante italiano no Espírito Santo*, edited by Adilson Vilaça and Maria Cristina Dadalto, 69–94. Vitória: Textus Editora.

Wampler, Brian. 2007. *Participatory Budgeting in Brazil: Contestation, Cooperation, and Accountability*. University Park, PA: Pennsylvania State University Press.

———. 2008. "When Does Participatory Democracy Deepen the Quality of Democracy? Lessons from Brazil." *Comparative Politics* 41(1): 61–81.

Wampler, Brian, and Leonardo Avritzer. 2004. "Participatory Publics: Civil Society and New Institutions in Democratic Brazil." *Comparative Politics* 36(3): 291–312.

Weber, Marx. 1958/2003. *The Protestant Ethic and the Spirit of Capitalism*. Translated by Talcott Parsons. New York: Dover.

Weffort, Frascisco C. 1980. *O Populismo na política brasileira*. Rio de Janeiro: Editora Paz e Terra.

World Bank. 2008. "Brazil: Toward a More Inclusive and Effective Participatory Budget in Porto Alegre." Vol. 1: Main Report. Washington, DC: World Bank.

INDEX

North, Douglass C., 34, 36–37
Nova Venécia (Espírito Santo),
    141–43
Nylen, William, 9–10, 19, 203, 204

October Eighth Revolutionary
    Movement, 59
O'Donnell, Guillermo, 46
open access orders, 36–39
    in Espírito Santo, 124–30
    during the 1980s, 175–76, 180–81
    populism's role in, 49–50
    in Santa Catarina, 98–103
    in São Paulo, 154–62
    transitions toward, 46–47
Opinião (magazine), 68–69
Organic Municipal Law, 213
Oxhorn, Philip, 34–35

Palmares Revolutionary Armed
    Vanguard, 60
participatory administrations
    in Diadema, 149–50, 165–71
    in Fortaleza, 196–97
    in Icapuí, 197–98
    in São Paulo, 198–201
participatory budgeting
    benefits of, 17–18, 29–31
    in Diadema, 169–70, 172–73
    in Lages, 109–11
    limitations of, 18
    in Porto Alegre, 1, 17–19, 66, 75,
        201–4, 221, 230n9–10
    in PT administrations, 201–4
    variables impacting, 10–11,
        19–21, 221
    widespread impact of, 18–19,
        230n12
Participatory Budgeting (Shah), 29
participatory democracy
    in the citizen amendment
        proposals, 207–10
    historical origin of, 1–3, 56

incremental steps toward, 216–22
    1988 constitution's impact on,
        210–14
    during the 1980s, 180–81, 222–26
    normative debates on, 27–31
    processes impacting, 215–16
    PT's vision of, 164, 193–96
    role of autênticos in forming of,
        61–70
    role of CEBs in forming of, 70–81
    role of Marxism in forming of,
        58–61
    role of new unionism in forming
        of, 46–47, 81–87
    socioeconomic impacts on, 5–8
    tempering of, 8–16
    theoretical approaches to, 3–5
    variables for success of, 19–21
"Participatory Democracy Revisited"
    (Pateman), 29
participatory governance, 28
participatory initiatives
    archival records of, 229n3
    in Boa Esperança, 130–32, 138–43
    case study comparisons, 14, 131,
        164, 174, 218–20
    challenges faced by, 143–46
    civil society organizations and,
        134–36
    in Diadema, 149–50, 165–72, 172–73
    in Lages, 104–11, 113–15
    of the PMDB, 189–91
    processes impacting, 1–2, 19–21,
        215–16
    widespread impacts of, 146–47
    See also participatory budgeting
Participatory Innovation and Rep-
    resentative Democracy in Latin
    America (Peruzzotti and Selee),
    30–31
participatory movements
    of the autênticos, 61–70
    of the CEBs, 70–81

J. RICARDO TRANJAN

is a public policy consultant and independent scholar.